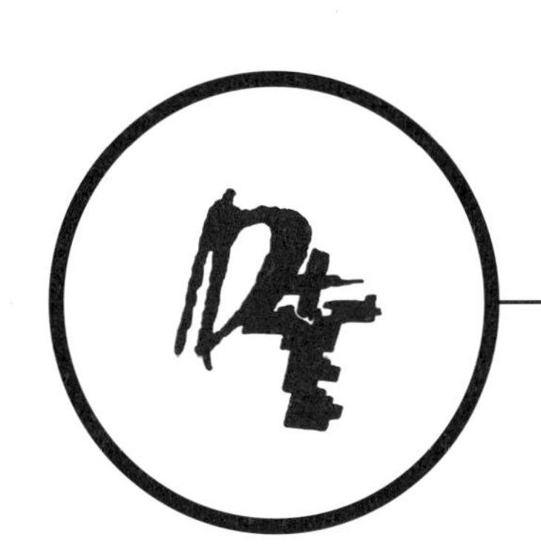

Graphics

Addison Wesley Longman Limited
Edinburgh Gate, Harlow, Essex, CM20 2JE, England, and Associated Companies throughout the World

First published 1996
Second impression 1997
ISBN 0582 23468 9

Set in ITCKabel and Times
Designed and produced by Tracy Hawkett, Pentacor, High Wycombe, Bucks HP12 3DJ
Illustrations and other materials by Nathan Barlex, Tracy Hawkett, Oxford Illustrators, Sally Taylor and Emma Taylor.
Picture researcher Louise Edgeworth
Copy editor Monica Kendall
Indexer Richard Raper/Indexing Specialists
Produced by Longman Asia Limited, Hong Kong. GCC/02

The publisher's policy is to use paper manufactured from sustainable forests.

Project Directors
Executive Director Dr David Barlex
Co-directors Prof. Paul Black and Prof. Geoffrey Harrison
Deputy Director Dissemination David Wise
Contributors
David Barlex, Thomas Barlex, Sheela Hammond, India Hart
Brenda Hellier, Debbie Howard, Marilyn Kenny, Paul Lowry
Judith Powling, Peter Reeves, Ann Riggs, Anne Roberts
Ruth Wright

We are grateful to the following for permission to reproduce photographs and other copyright material:

BBC Copyright ©, page 27; Gareth Boden, pages 72 above (Explosive Pop-Up greetings card. Published by Second Nature Ltd. Paper engineering by Paper Power and 3rd Dimension Paper Engineering Ltd), 124, 125, 126–7, 134, 135, 137, 144 above left, 167, 170, 176 below, 177, 178, 179, 180, 199 above; BT Archive, page 51; BT Corporate Picture Library, page 52; British Telecommunications plc, page 53; Canon (UK) Ltd, pages 175 above, 176 above; J.Allan Cash, page 143; Trevor Clifford Photography, pages 7, 44, 45, 46, 67, 68, 70–71, 72 below, 91, 92, 97, 100, 110, 112, 116, 117, 119, 120, 121, 122, 128, 129, 136 above, 136 below, 138, 139, 145, 172, 195, 196, 198, 201; Crown copyright is reproduced with the permission of the Controller of HMSO, pages 47, 48, 49; Designing, pages 64, 65, 66, 69 below; Mary Evans Picture Library, pages 26, 30, 34 above; Format/Michael Ann Mullen, page 55 below; © 1996 Games Workshop Ltd. Warhammer is a registered trade mark of Games Workshop Ltd. All rights reserved, page 140; Intermediate Technology, pages 55 above, 56; David King Collection, page 136 centre; Kodak Ltd, page 200; London Transport Museum, pages 34 below, 35, 36; Paul Mulcahy, page 176 centre; PA News/Martin Keene, page 29 above; Pictor International, page 144 above right; Pindar plc, page 69 above; John Plater, page 189; Polaroid/Pankhurst Design and Developments Ltd, pages 74, 75, 76, 77; Popperfoto, page 28; Powergen plc, page 41; David Redfern, page 57; Rex Features/Ian Spratt, page 142 below; Roland Digital Group, page 175 below; The Royal Aeronautical Society/Boeing, page 33; Sanyo, page 133; Spectrum Colour Library, page 197 left; Tony Stone Images, pages 8 & 9 (Ian Shaw); TRIP/H.Rogers, pages 142 above, 144 centre, 197 right; Telegraph Colour Library, pages 19 and 20 (Benelux Press), 144 below (S.Benbow), 199 (J.P Masclet); Top Shop, pages 60, 61; Unipath Ltd, page 31; Montgomery Watson, Consulting Engineers, page 161.

We have been unable to trace the copyright holders of the following and would be grateful for any information that would enable us to do so: page 136, page 156 bottom.

Contents

FANTASIA

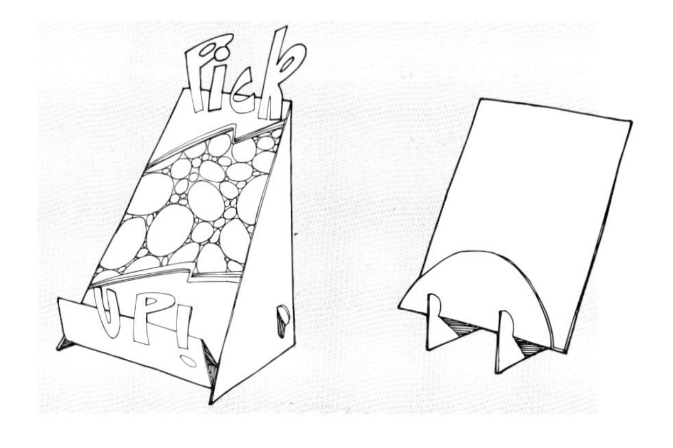

Pick
UP!

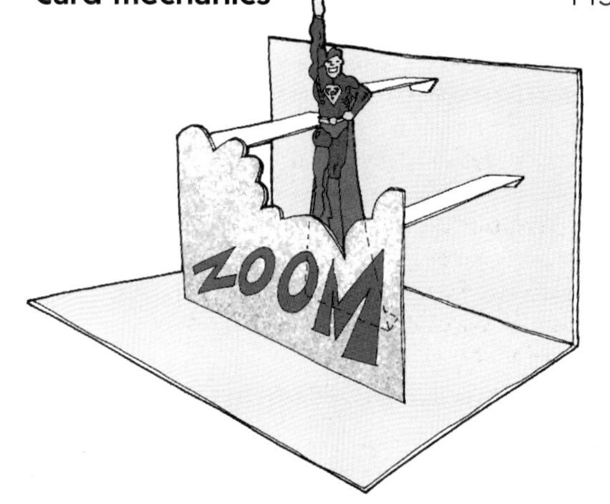

ZOOM

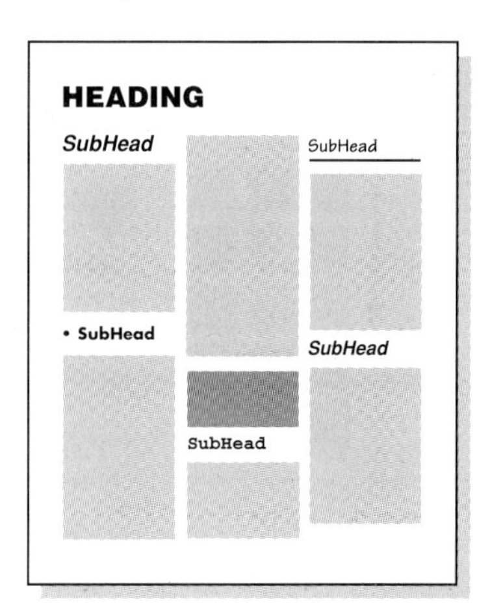

HEADING
SubHead
SubHead
• SubHead
SubHead
SubHead

Part 1 Learning D&T at 14–16

What will I design and make?

During key stage 3 you used a wide range of different materials for designing and making – textiles, food, wood, metal and plastic. At key stage 4 you are allowed to specialize in a materials area. You have chosen to specialize in designing and making with **graphic media**. This means that you will be using drawing and illustrating equipment on paper, card and board; modelling tools and equipment on more resistant materials such as card, modelling foam, thermoplastic sheet and medium density fibreboard (MDF) and, perhaps, electrical components for lighting and sound effects, and mechanical components for movement.

The reason for specialization is that at key stage 4 you are expected to work to a higher standard in both designing and making; the quality of your products should be better than at key stage 3. The key stage 4 course lasts only two years and you simply don't have enough time to gain the extra skills, knowledge and understanding needed to improve your work in more than one material area. The sort of things that you will be designing and making are shown below. This area of designing and making is usually called graphic design.

Designing and making at key stage 4 is a real challenge. Your products should be good enough for the shops

Of course there is more to design and technology than designing and making, and in your key stage 4 course you will also learn about the way design and technology works in the world outside school. In particular, you will study how industry uses graphic and modelling techniques and processes in its products.

How will I learn?

If you do design and technology the Nuffield way then your teacher will use three different teaching methods. These are described below.

Resource Tasks

These are short practical activities. They make you think and help you learn the knowledge and skills you need to design and make really well.

Case Studies

These describe real examples of design and technology in the world outside school. By reading them you find out far more than you can through designing and making alone. Case Studies help you to learn about the way firms and businesses design and manufacture goods and how those goods are marketed and sold. You will also learn about the impact that products have on the people who use them and the places where they are made.

Capability Tasks

These involve designing and making a product that works. When you tackle a Capability Task, you use what you have learned through doing Resource Tasks and Case Studies. Capability Tasks take a lot longer than either Resource Tasks or Case Studies. Your teacher will organize your lessons so that you do the Resource Tasks and Case Studies you need for a Capability Task as part of the Capability Task. In this way your teacher makes sure that you can be successful in your designing and making.

The way these methods work together is shown here.

Resource Tasks for gaining knowledge, skills and understanding

You will be given a Resource Task as an instruction sheet like the one below. All Resource Tasks are laid out in the same way. You will see that they are different from the ones you used at key stage 3.

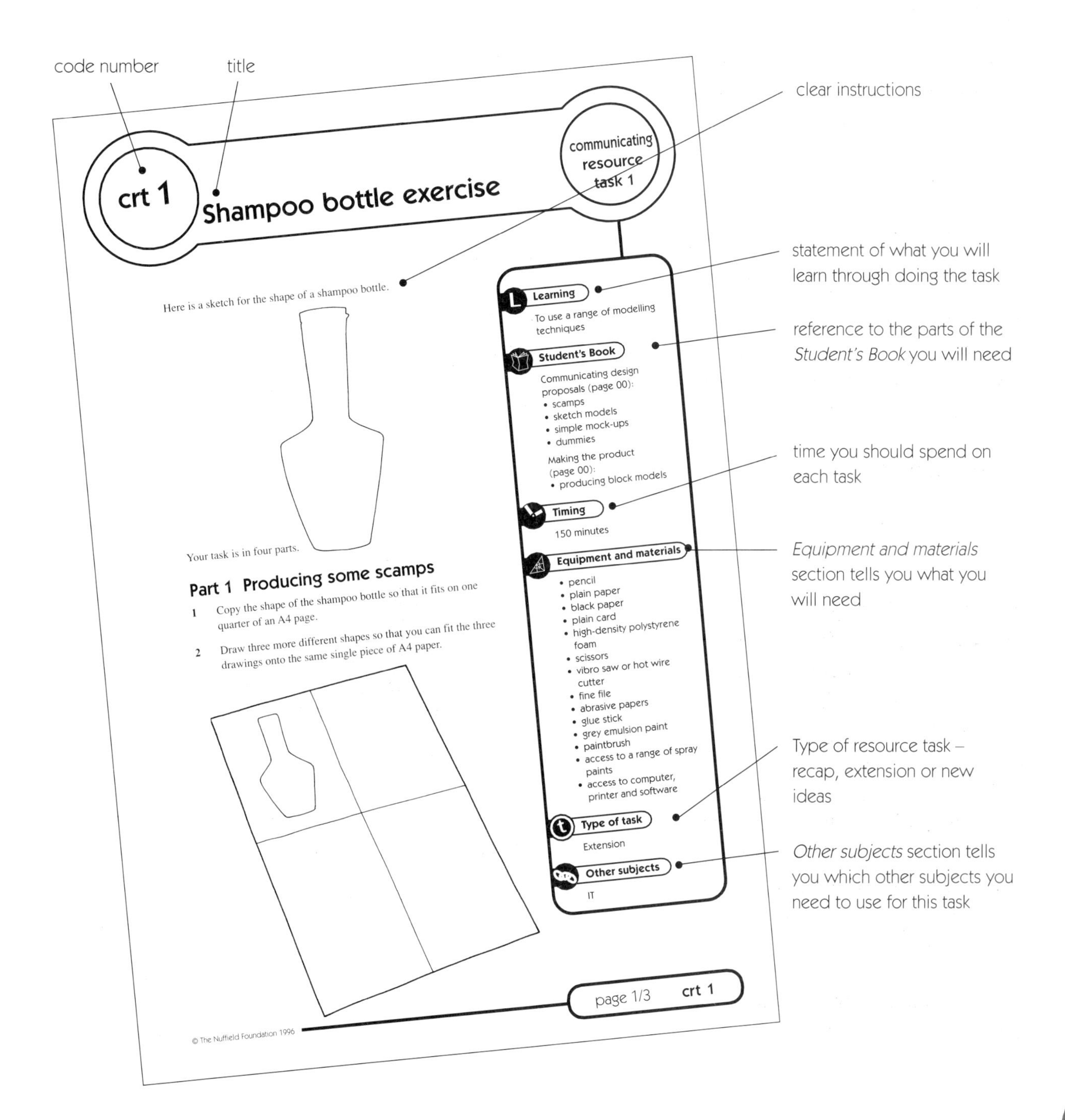

More about Resource Tasks

There are three types of Resource Task.

Recapitulation Resource Tasks

These are tasks that go over things that you probably did during key stage 3. They are very useful for reminding you of things you may have forgotten about or for catching up on things you have missed.

Extension Resource Tasks

These are tasks that take an idea that you were probably taught at key stage 3 and develop it further. They are useful for both revising key stage 3 ideas and helping you to use them in a more advanced way.

New ideas Resource Tasks

These are tasks that deal with knowledge and understanding that are new at key stage 4. It is unlikely that you will have done this sort of work at key stage 3. They are important for helping you to progress.

Your teacher may:

- organize the lesson so that everyone is doing the same Resource Task;
- set different students different tasks;
- allow you to choose from a range of Resource Tasks.

Sometimes you will work on your own and sometimes as part of a team.

Your teacher may introduce a sequence of Resource Tasks by talking to the whole class

Case Studies for awareness and insight

There are two types of Case Studies at key stage 4.

The first type are those that deal with 'large' technologies. These are the technologies which significantly affect the way people live. Often they are associated with a particular period in history. It is important that you read these Case Studies because they will help you to understand the way that technology affects our lives.

The second type are those that deal with products that are similar to those that you will be designing and making yourself. They describe:

- how the designs were developed, manufactured, marketed and sold;
- how the products work;
- how the products affect the people who make them, those who use them and others.

A particular Case Study may deal with just one of these or with all of them. It is important that you read these Case Studies because they will help you to design like a professional designer.

It is easy to lose concentration when you are reading a Case Study so they contain Pauses for thought and Questions which you should try and answer while you are reading them. It is often useful to discuss your answers with a friend. This will help you both to think about and make sense of the study.

The Case Studies also contain Research activities. You will often be set these for homework as they involve finding out information that is not in the Case Study. This is important as it will help you to learn how to get new information as well as understand more about design and technology.

A student presents his Case Study research findings to a group of fellow students

Capability Tasks for designing and making

Each of the products you design and make at key stage 4 will be from a group of product types. These groups of product types are called **lines of interest**. So, for example, you might design and make a product that was from the line of interest 'information'. Your product could range from a community broadsheet dealing with a sensitive local issue to a fanzine giving information about a local pop group. There will be certain sorts of knowledge, skills and understanding that are useful for designing products which involve both images and words. An understanding of typography and layout, print technology, manufacturing techniques and sheet structures will all be needed to design and make products in this area.

We have suggested seven lines of interest for Capability Tasks in the area of graphics. Some possible products from each line of interest are shown here, together with their representative icons.

During your key stage 4 course you will have the opportunity to work in at least three different lines of interest. If you were to work in only one line of interest, you would end up knowing a lot about that particular part of design and technology, but there would be other parts you would know nothing about at all. If you were to work in many more than three lines of interest you wouldn't have the time to study anything in depth, so you would end up knowing very little about any part of design and technology. So working in three lines of interest will enable you to gain a reasonable level and range of knowledge, understanding and skill in design and technology.

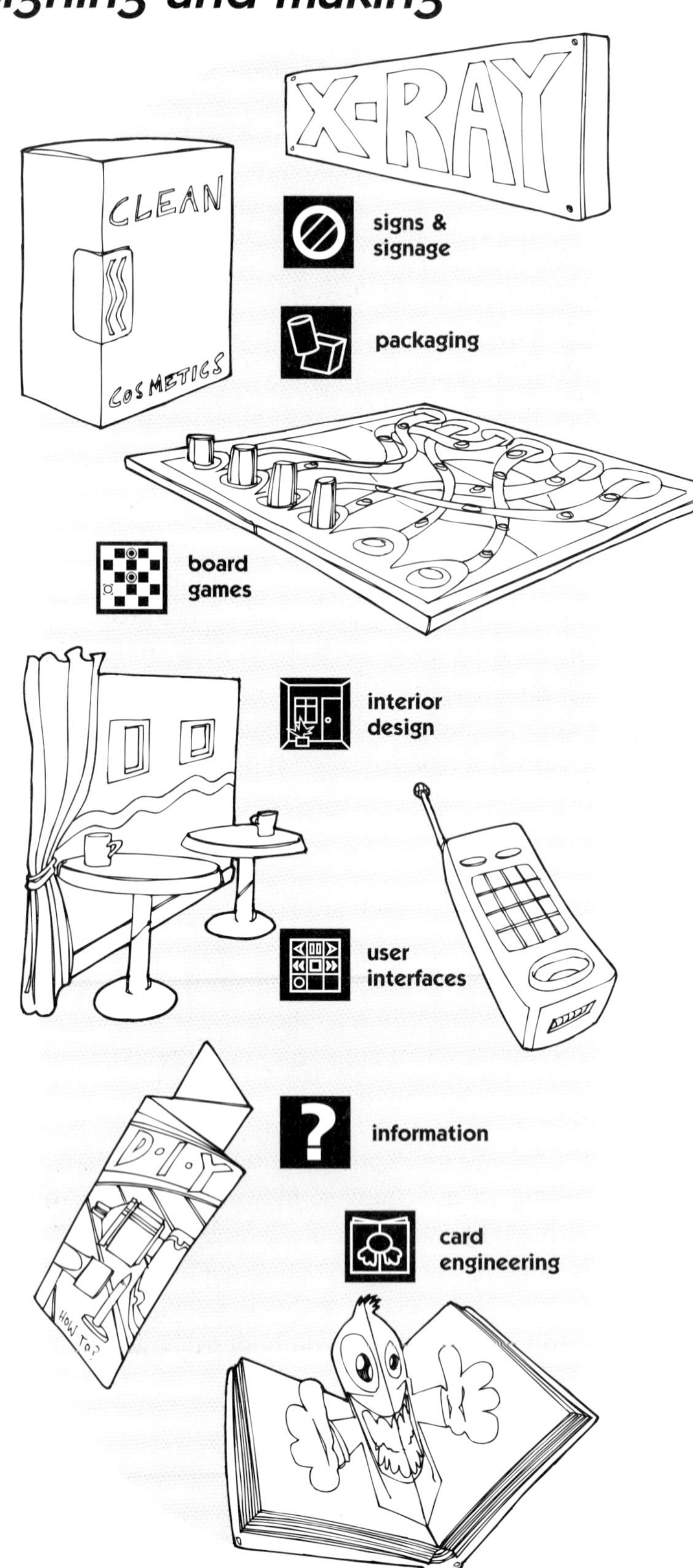

Managing three Capability Tasks

If you are following a full GCSE course, it is likely that you will tackle three Capability Tasks during year 10, each one from a different line of interest. Your teacher will work out with you which ones your class will tackle. In year 11 you can either revisit a line of interest or tackle a new one. The one in year 11 will probably be used for your GCSE coursework. This makes sense because you should be better at designing and making in year 11 than you are in year 10.

It will be quite a struggle to fit three complete Capability Tasks into year 10 so your teacher may organize the lessons so that you only do part of some of these tasks. You will certainly need to do one complete Capability Task where you design, make and test a well-finished product. In another Capability Task you might only produce a working model or collection of models of the product. This means you don't have to spend a lot of time making the finished article.

In another Capability Task you might only produce a series of design proposals as detailed annotated sketches. This cuts down the time you spend on the Capability Task even further.

Your teacher may give the class a design brief plus a specification and ask you to design and make a product that meets those requirements. Your teacher might even give you the brief, the specification and the working drawings and ask you to make the product so that you can learn about the manufacturing process. Of course it is important that you carry out the Resource Tasks and Case Studies needed for each of these Capability Tasks. In this way you acquire a lot of design and technology knowledge, understanding and skills and still keep in touch with designing and making. This will put you in a strong position to tackle a full Capability Task in year 11.

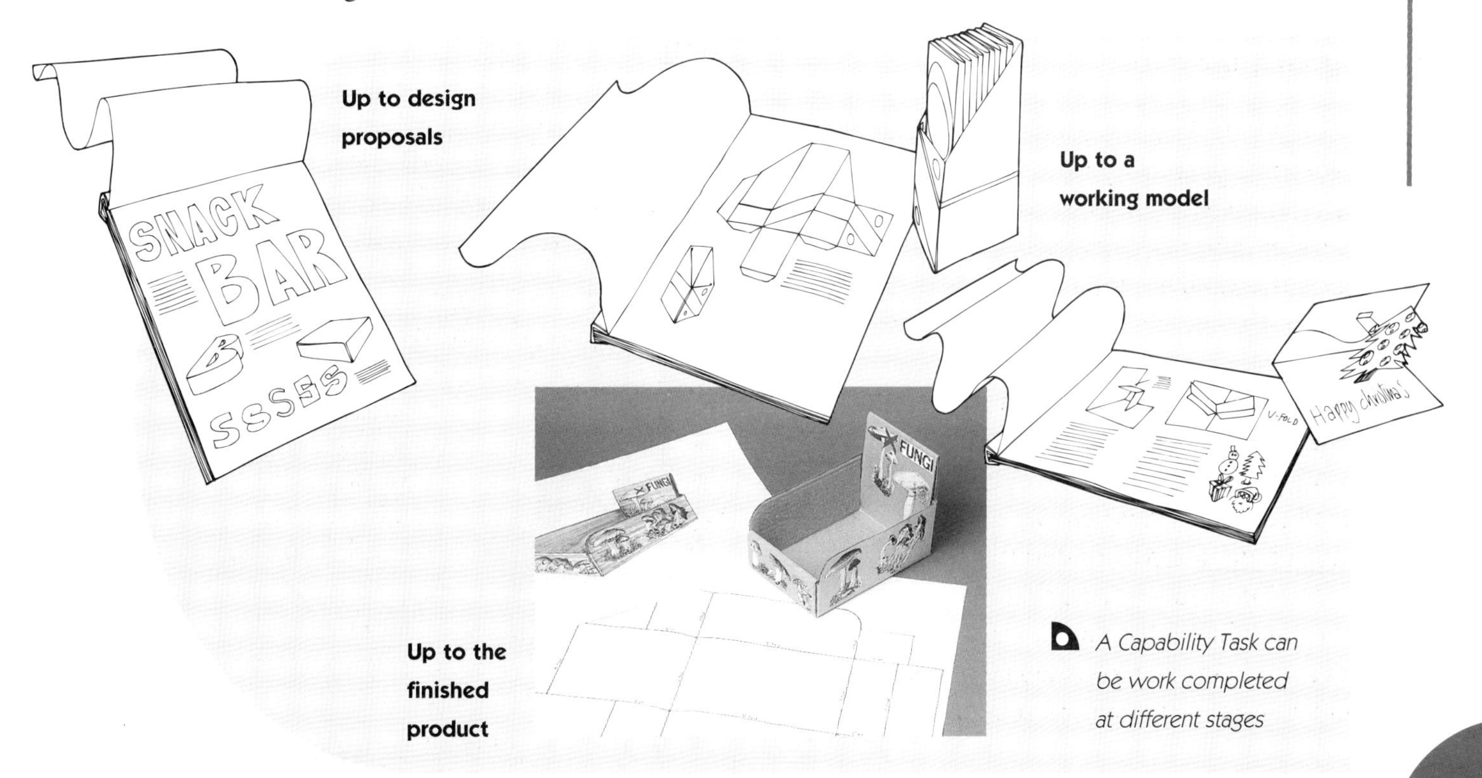

A Capability Task can be work completed at different stages

Ensuring your designing makes sense

You will be working to a brief which summarizes the following information about your product:

- what it will be used for;
- who will use it;
- where it might be used;
- where it might be sold.

This will help you to think about the design of your product. It will also help you to write the specification. You will need to use the brief and the specification as references for your designing. By checking your design ideas against the brief and specification you will be able to see whether they are developing in sensible directions.

This checking is often called **reviewing** and it is very important. If you fail to review your work at the correct times you will almost certainly waste a lot of time and your design ideas are likely to be inappropriate and in some cases may not work at all.

First review

Once you have some ideas for your product in the form of quickly drawn annotated sketches, you should carry out your first review by comparing your ideas with the requirements of the brief and the specification.

Ask yourself the following questions for each design idea:

- Will the design do what it is supposed to?
- Will the design be suitable for the users?
- Will the design fit in with where it might be used or sold?
- Is the design likely to work?
- Does the design look right for the users and sellers?
- Have I noted any special requirements the design will need to meet later on?

Any design ideas that do not get a 'yes' to all these questions should be rejected or adjusted. In this way you can use the first review to screen out any design ideas that do not meet your requirements. You can do this screening in two ways:

- on your own, just thinking it through in your head and making notes against each design idea;
- working in a group and explaining your ideas to other students in your group who can check them out against the questions. This takes longer and you have to help the others in the group to check out their design ideas as well. But the extra time is usually well spent as other people are often more rational in their criticism of your ideas than you are.

Whichever way you choose it will be important to discuss your review findings with your teacher.

Second review

By screening your early ideas you will be able to focus your efforts on developing a single design idea and on working out the details of that design. You will present these details as a mixture of annotated sketches, rendered presentation drawings and working drawings (sometimes called **plans**).

To make sure that your designing is still developing in a sensible direction you need to ask the following questions before you begin making the product.

- Am I sure that the design will do what it is supposed to?
- Am I sure about the accuracy with which I need to cut out each piece?
- How long will it take me to make and assemble all the pieces of my design?
- Have I got enough time to do this?
- If not, what can I alter so that I have a design that I can make on time and that still meets the specification?
- Will the materials I need be available when I need them?
- Will the tools and equipment be available when I need them?
- Am I sure that I can get the final appearance that I need?
- Have I got enough time for finishing?
- Is there anything I can do to be more efficient?

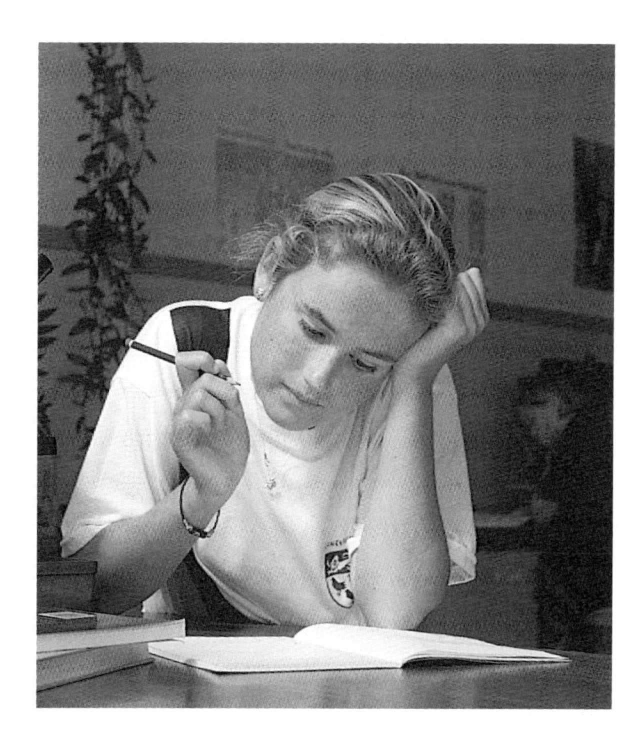

You are probably the only one who can answer these questions but it will be worth checking your answers with your teachers as they are likely to know about any hidden traps and pitfalls.

Evaluating the final products

Here are examples of the ways in which you can evaluate your design once you have made it. You can find out more about them in the *Strategies* section (pages 78–106). It will be important to use all these different methods in coming to a judgement about the quality of your design.

User trip

By interviewing the users Sally was able to find out what they did and didn't like about the game she had designed and made.

Performance specification

Gupta designed a mobile phone handset and made a model of it in a semi-resistant material. The specification for the equipment was as follows:

- it must be easy to use and hold, both when dialling and listening;
- it must appeal to the 'young executive' market;
- it will utilise new, miniature technology allowing it to fit in a thin pocket.

He was surprised to find how easy it was to accidentally depress two buttons at the same time. It is important to design your product to meet all the specification requirements.

Winners and losers

Jane designed some packaging for protecting growing seedlings during transportation. It was to be produced using card made from recycled paper using the latest computer-controlled cutting equipment that could cut 50 sheets at a time. It was faster, cheaper and used recycled paper. Who could lose? She found out that local pensioners were employed by the seed company to make similar packaging from scrap card. They met to do this once a week and it was an important part of their social life. Jane's new design would make all this unnecessary. By thinking about winners and losers Jane could see that it wasn't that simple.

Appropriateness

Fred designed a range of complementary wall panels and suspended shapes to decorate a nursery. The parts were simple to make and could be easily assembled. He hoped that their manufacture could be carried out in a depressed area as part of a regeneration scheme. By asking the questions on page 104 he was able to decide whether his design was appropriate.

Thinking about how well your product meets its specification

One way to do this is to discuss your product with some other students. Give your product a blob score for each part of the specification – 5 blobs if it meets that part really well, 3 blobs if it meets it moderately well, 1 blob if it meets it only poorly and no blobs if it fails to meet this part of the specification. The next part is the tricky bit. Explain to the other students in the group why you have given the scores you have. Their job is to question your judgements. Your job is to convince them that the judgements are correct. If you do this you will be in a good position to move on to looking at your own progress.

Looking at your own progress

At the end of a Capability Task it is important to look back at what you have done and reflect on your progress. The following sets of questions will help you with this.

Feeling good about what you have done

- Am I proud of what I made?
- Can I explain why?
- Am I proud of the design I developed?
- Can I explain why?

Understanding the problems

- What sorts of things slowed me down?
- Can I now see how to overcome these difficulties?
- What sorts of things made me nervous so that I didn't do as well as I know I can?
- Do I know where to get help now?
- What sorts of things did I do better than I expected?
- Was this due to luck or can I say that I'm getting better?
- Were there times when I concentrated on detail before I had the broad picture?
- Were there times when I didn't bother enough with detail?
- Can I now see how to get the level of detail right?

Understanding yourself

- Were there times when I lost interest?
- Can I now see how to get myself motivated?
- Were there times when I couldn't work out what to do next?
- Can I now see how to get better at making decisions?
- Were there times when I lost my sense of direction?
- Can I now see how to avoid this?

Understanding your design decisions

- With hindsight can I see where I made the right decisions?
- With hindsight can I see where I should have made different decisions?
- With hindsight can I see situations where I did the right thing?
- With hindsight can I see where I would do things differently if I did this again?

Part 2
Using other subjects in D&T at KS4

Using art

At key stage 4 you will need to use your understanding of art to help your design and technology. You will be able to use art when you are tackling Capability Tasks. This is different from using art in a Resource Task. In a Resource Task you will be *told* to use art in the Other subjects section. In a Capability Task you have to *choose* when to use art. The example below shows how some pupils have used art in developing the design for the interior of the room used for a school disco.

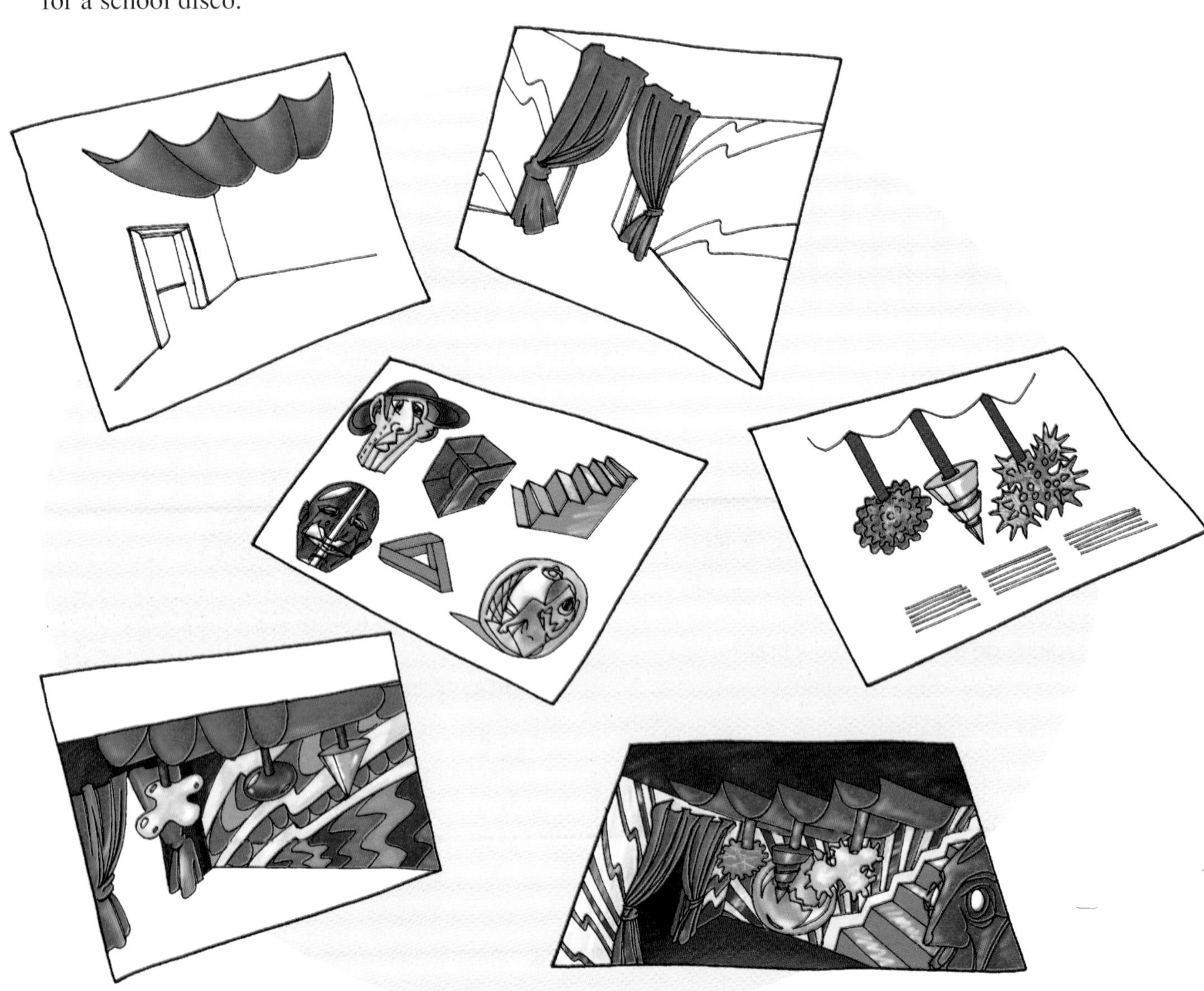

Using information technology

At key stage 4 you will need to use your understanding of information technology to help your design and technology. You will be able to use information technology when you are tackling Capability Tasks. This is different from using information technology in a Resource Task.
In a Resource Task you will be *told* to use information technology in the Other subjects section.
In a Capability Task you have to *choose* when to use information technology. The examples here show how pupils used information technology in the form of desktop publishing or computer-aided drawing packages to produce high quality, very professional results.

Desktop publishing packages can combine great graphics with your text to give very professional results

High quality vinyl shapes for logos or letters can be cut out using designing software linked to a computer-driven cutter

Using science

At key stage 4 you will be able to use science when you are tackling Capability Tasks. This is different from using science in a Resource Task. In a Resource Task you will be *told* to use science in the Other subjects section. In a Capability Task you have to *choose* when to use science.

Your science lessons will teach you two main things. First, how to carry out scientific investigations. If you need to find something out in a Capability Task, say the best type of mechanism to operate a moving part of a pop-up book, or the best material to choose for an outdoor sign, or the different strengths of structural shapes – then you can use your science to help you plan the investigation and design the necessary experiments. Second, in science you will acquire scientific knowledge which could be useful to you in a Capability Task. The information in the table will help to remind you of the science you are likely to find useful. Note that some of the science is from key stages 2 and 3 as well as key stage 4.

Uses of science in Capability Tasks

Capability Task line of interest	Science likely to be useful
Packaging	The properties and uses of materials (KS2) Stiffness of materials (KS4) Force and pressure (KS3)
Signs and signage	The properties and uses of materials (KS2) Stiffness of materials (KS4)
Interior design	Simple circuits, switches and dimmers (KS2) Power, current and voltage in circuits (KS4) Formation of shadows, reflection and refraction and dispersion of light, effect of coloured filters (KS3)
Card engineering	Simple levers (KS3) Springs and elastic bands (KS2) Force and pressure (KS3) Stiffness of materials (KS4) Simple circuits, switches and dimmers (KS2)
Information	The properties and uses of materials (KS2) Perception (KS4)
User interfaces	The properties and uses of materials (KS2) Planning experimental procedures (KS3 and KS4) Obtaining evidence (KS3 and KS4) Analysing evidence and drawing conclusions (KS3 and KS4) Considering the strength of the evidence (KS3 and KS4)
Games and pastimes	The properties and uses of materials (KS2) Magnets, magnetic field and magnetic poles (KS3 and KS4)

Using mathematics

At key stage 4 you will need to use your understanding of mathematics to help your design and technology. You will be able to use mathematics when you are tackling Capability Tasks. This is different from using mathematics in a Resource Task. In a Resource Task you will be *told* to use mathematics in the Other subjects section. In a Capability Task you have to *choose* when to use mathematics. Often you use mathematics without realizing it. The panel below shows some examples.

You use mathematics whenever you ...

... assemble anything

... use or make a working drawing

... plot a graph

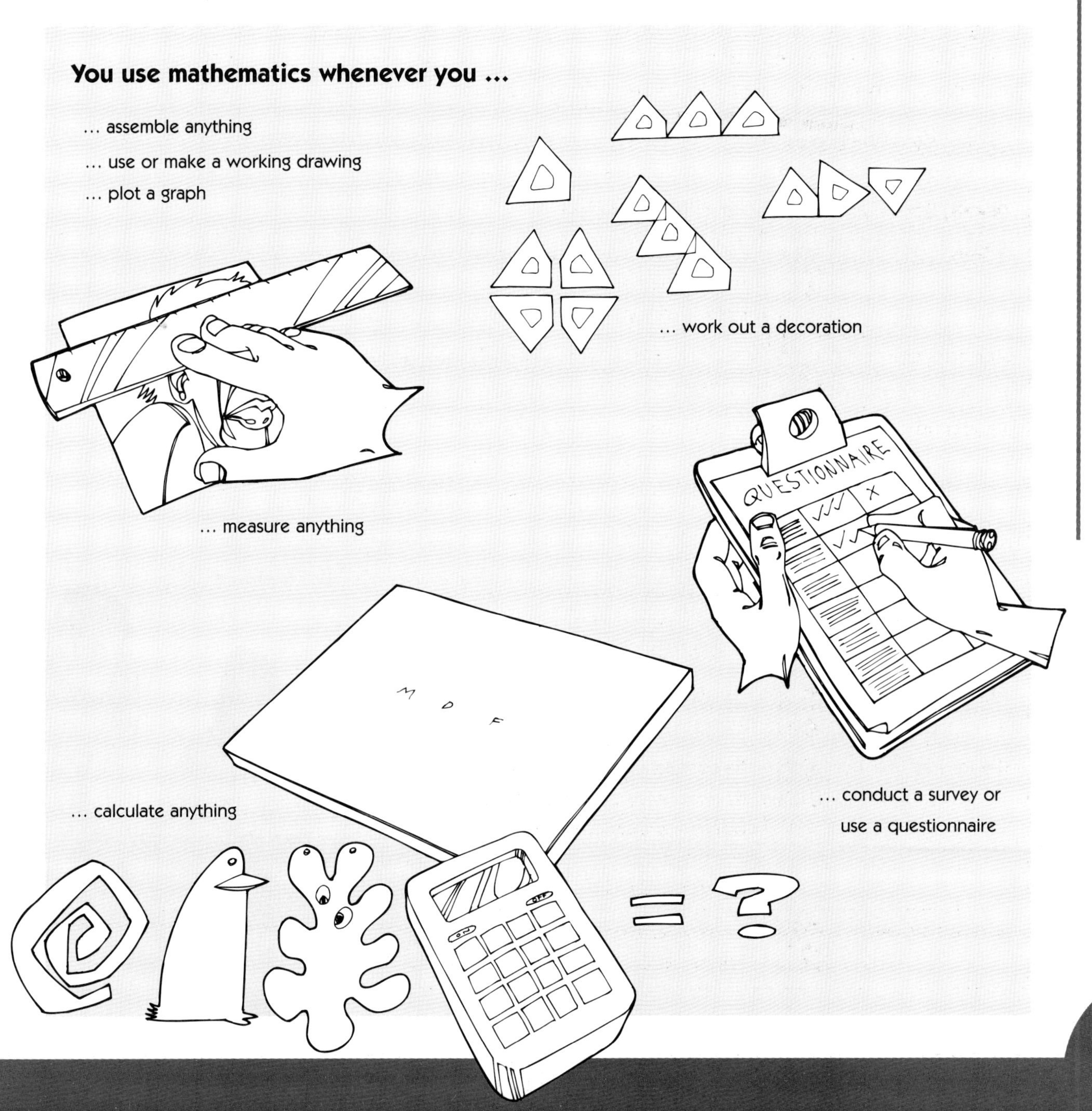

Part 3
How you will be assessed at GCSE

Writing your own Capability Task

It is likely that the Capability Task you tackle in year 11 will be the one that will be used for your GCSE coursework. This makes sense because you should be better at designing and making in year 11 than you are in year 10. Here are some guidelines to help you.

Designing the Capability Task

1 Deciding on the line of interest

Ask yourself these questions:

- Do you want to revisit a line of interest from year 10, or do you want to try something new?
- Which Resource Tasks did you enjoy most? Are these linked to a line of interest?
- Is there a group of students in your class who want to work on a particular line of interest?

2 Justifying your decision

Ask yourself these questions:

- Who will benefit from the product you are going to design and make?
- Will you be successful at designing and making this sort of product?
- Can you afford to make this sort of product?

3 Sorting out any extra learning that might be necessary

It is not difficult to identify particular areas of design and technology knowledge that are likely to be useful for your task. Discuss this with your teacher and identify Resource Tasks that could be useful.

4 Identifying any Case Studies that might provide useful background reading

Read and make notes listing those points that are relevant to your task.

5 Drawing up a 'Using other subjects' checklist

- Discuss this with your D&T teacher.
- Check with your other subject teachers if you think they can help.

6 Working with other people

There may be parts of your Capability Task that could benefit from a team approach – carrying out a survey, collecting reference materials, brainstorming ideas, for example. You will need to organize these carefully so that everybody's task is improved.

Tackling the Capability Task

7 Writing a design brief and developing a specification

You must remember that you are expected to design and make a quality product that meets demanding criteria. These should take into account how it could be manufactured, how it might be repaired or maintained and how it might be sold.

8 Generating design ideas

You will need to show where your ideas come from. Make sure you keep a record of your early thoughts.

9 Developing your ideas

You will need to keep a clear record of how your ideas have developed.

10 Making presentation drawings and working drawings

These should show what your design will look like and how it can be made.

11 Planning your making

12 Making your design

13 Evaluating the final product

Make sure you use a range of techniques.

14 Putting on a display

You should mount a display that shows your work to best advantage. It should describe the following:

- your ideas and where they came from;
- how they developed;
- presentation and working drawings;
- your schedule for making;
- your evaluation.

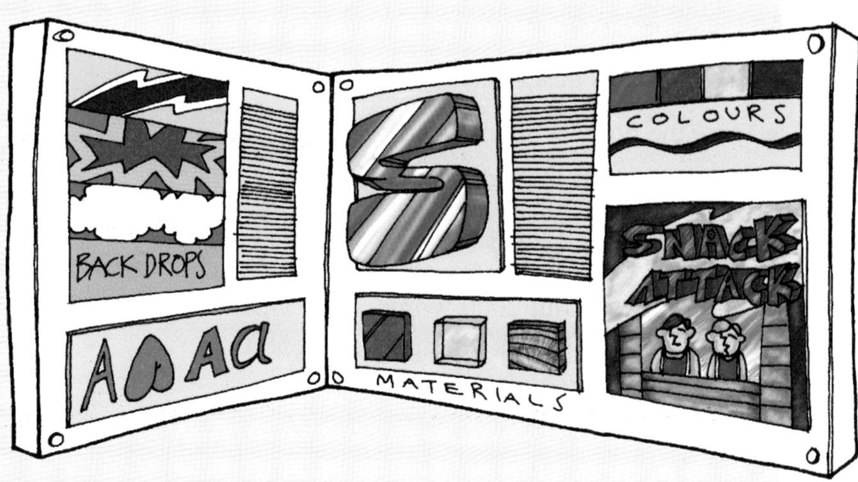

Writing your own Case Study

You may have to write your own Case Study as part of your GCSE assessment. Here are some guidelines.

Which product?

You should choose an everyday item that is manufactured. You should be able to examine it, use it yourself, see others use it and evaluate it. Here are some possibilities:

- pop-up cards
- corporate identities
- shop or restaurant signs
- a magazine
- a board game

What should it describe?

Your study should describe the following:

- what the product looks like;
- what the product does;
- how it works;
- who uses it and what they think of it;
- how it's made;
- the impact the product has made on the way people live.

You might also describe:

- how the product has changed over time;
- other products that do a similar job.

How many words?

No more than about 2000 words. (One side of A4 paper filled with typing is about 500 words.)

What about pictures?

It is important to use illustrations as well as text. You can use any of the following:

- your own illustrations drawn directly onto the page or pasted in place;
- illustrations photocopied from books or magazines and pasted in place;
- your own illustrations scanned onto disc and printed in place;
- illustrations taken from a library on CD-ROM and printed in place.

What about layout?

If possible use desk-top publishing (DTP) software to produce your Case Study. If this is not available use word processing (WP) software to lay out the text. If this is not available use a typewriter.

What about the overall length?

A reasonable mixture of text and pictures will give you a length of about 12 sides of A4.

What about special features?

You can make your Case Study:

- *attractive* by producing an illustrated cover;
- *easy to look through* by numbering the pages, using headings and producing a title page and contents page;
- *easy to understand* by using illustrations with notes and captions.

Examination questions

You may have to take a final written examination paper at the end of year 11 as part of your GCSE assessment. This paper will be made up of different sorts of questions. Here is a guide to some of these questions and how to answer them.

Interpreting a short Case Study

In this sort of question you will be given two or three paragraphs to read and one or two pictures to look at. The writing and the pictures will describe an aspect of design and technology from the real world. You will then have to answer a series of questions based mainly on what you have read. Some will involve finding a piece of information from the text. If you read the text carefully you can always get these questions right. Some will involve explaining something that is described in the text. These are more difficult as they will require you to use your design and technology knowledge and understanding. Some will ask you to make a judgement about the effects of the design and technology described. These are the most difficult but if you think carefully you will be able to use your design and technology awareness and insight to make judgements and give good reasons to back them up.

Presenting and interpreting information

In this sort of question you will be given some data from some design and technology research and asked to present it in a way that makes it easy to understand. The data may come from very different sources. It could be about consumer preferences, the results of testing a material or component, production figures for different manufacturing methods or sales figures for different products. Once you have presented the data you will be asked questions that require you to interpret the data.

Why is it like that?

In this sort of question you will be given information about a product in the form of annotated illustrations and text. You will be asked to explain different features of the design such as:

- what style has influenced the design;
- why a particular material has been chosen;
- why a part is the shape and form that it is;
- how particular pieces fit together;
- how particular parts work together to turn the input into the output;
- why particular fastenings have been chosen;
- what would happen if certain things were changed;
- how particular parts might be manufactured;
- how the design might be improved.

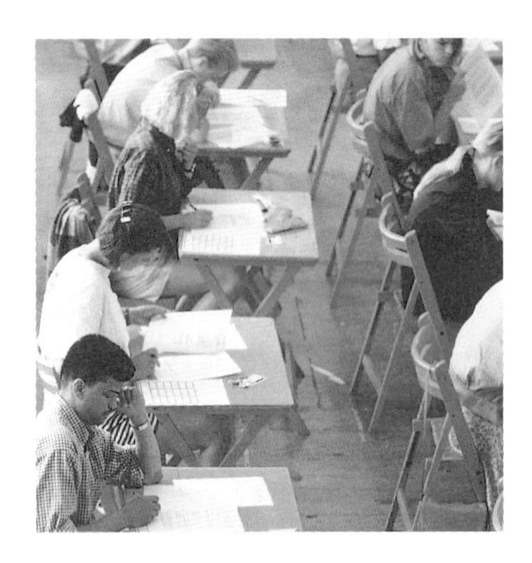

You will need to use the design and technology knowledge and understanding you have gained in years 10 and 11 to give correct answers.

What could you use for that?

In this sort of question you will be given a short technical design problem. You will be presented with an incomplete design to which there are several different possible solutions. Your task will be in three parts:

1. to describe some of the possible solutions by means of simple annotated sketches;
2. to compare these solutions;
3. to state clearly which solution you think is the best, with reasons.

Again you will have to use the design and technology knowledge and understanding you have gained throughout years 10 and 11 to give correct answers.

Exam questions 2

Questions 1 and 2 are taken from the RSA Examination Board GCSE Specimen Paper. They deal with writing a design brief, writing a specification, packaging and promotional material.

1 The product packaging shown here is for an 'instant' puncture repair system which uses self-adhesive patches.

(a) Suggest ONE suitable target market for this product. *(1 mark)*

(b) Give ONE reason for your choice. *(1 mark)*

When manufactured this product is blister packed.

(c) Comment on the suitability of this process of blister packing for this type of product. *(6 marks)*

Imagine that you were the designer who was given the task of designing this packaging.

(d) What is the purpose of the Design Brief for this product?

(i) Purpose of Design Brief:

(ii) List TWO items that must be included in the Design Brief.

Item One

Item Two *(4 marks)*

(e) List SIX points that would need to be contained in a detailed specification for this product. *(12 marks)*

2 The photographs below show two examples of graphics products; packaging and a picture from a promotional leaflet.

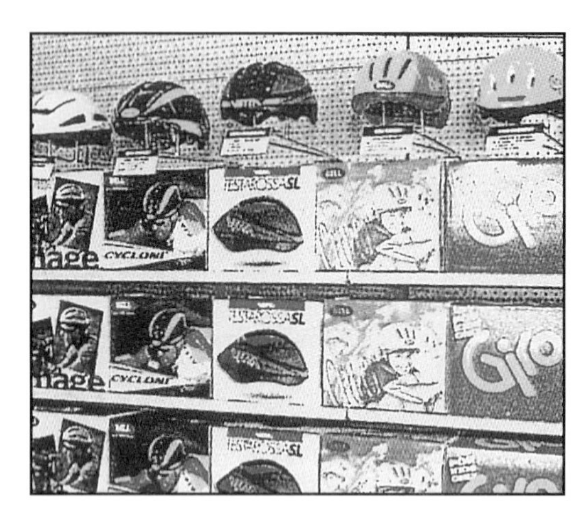

(a) Explain FOUR important considerations when designing the packaging for a cycle helmet. *(12 marks)*

50 000 copies of this promotional leaflet have been produced.

(b) Name the most likely printing process used for producing these leaflets. *(2 marks)*

(c) Give ONE explanation for your answer. *(4 marks)*

(d) Name THREE key requirements for any promotional leaflet. *(6 marks)*

Questions 3 and 4 are taken from the ULEAC Examination Board GCSE Specimen Paper. They deal with net design and information presentation.

3 A new triangular shaped chocolate is to be sold in boxes containing six portions. The drawing shows a pictorial view of one of the portions, together with a view of six portions arranged ready for packaging.

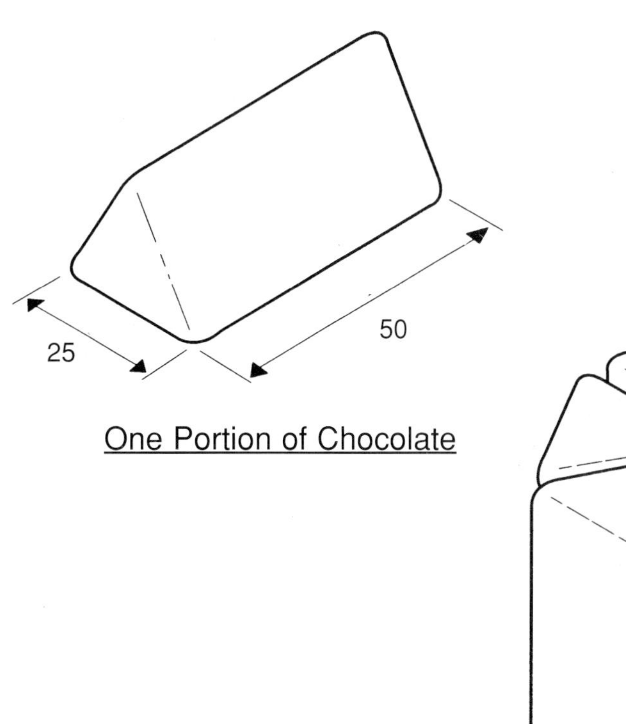

One Portion of Chocolate

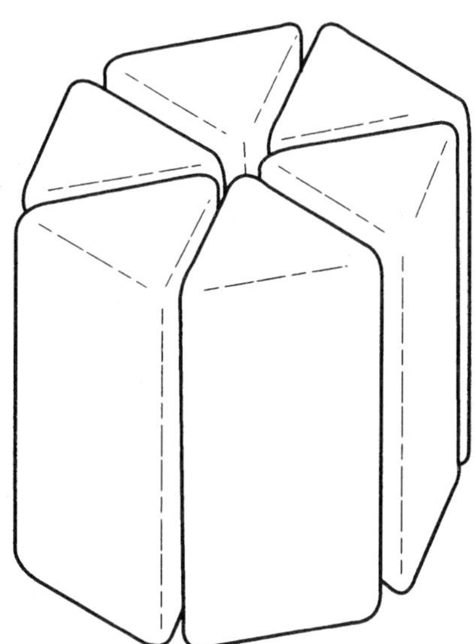

Six Portions of Chocolate

(a) Using freehand sketches and notes, design a net for the box based on the following specification:

- hold six portions of chocolate;
- be made from a single piece of card;
- have a lid that, when opened, allows chocolate to be removed one portion at a time. *(5 marks)*

(b) Using instruments, draw, full size, a development (net) of the chosen box. Clearly label all glue tabs, cut lines, fold lines, fold in flaps and lid. *(10 marks)*

4 The drawing below shows part of a design for a chess club knock-out competition results chart. The combined chart is to be stored on a computer and match results entered as data.

Match	1st Round	2nd Round	Semi Final	Final	Winner
1	Trish				
	Mike				
2	Gerry				
	Joan				
3	Robin				
	Andrew				
4	Jane				
	Ron				
5	John				
	Sheila				
6	Marge				
	Clive				
7	Larry				
	Ethel				
8	Viv				
	Malcolm				

(a) Complete the layout design of the chart so that match winners and next opponents are easily identified. *(3 marks)*

(b) Using the results of ALL matches played during the competition which are given below:

Ron	beat	Jane
Robin	beat	Andrew
Robin	lost to	Ron
Trish	beat	Mike
Trish	beat	Joan
Trish	lost to	Ron

Larry	beat	Ethel
Larry	lost to	Viv
Marge	beat	Sheila
Marge	beat	Viv
Marge	beat	Ron

(i) List the names of all players who failed to turn up for their matches; *(2 marks)*

(ii) Complete the chart by filling in the winners' names to identify who was the champion. *(2 marks)*

(c) State TWO advantages of using a computer for this task compared to a wallchart completed by hand. *(2 marks)*

General Case Studies

Information – the power to change lives

The way we communicate with other human beings and the speed with which we receive information have influenced dramatically the kind of world we live in today.

The start of books

Five hundred years ago most people were illiterate and relied upon word of mouth to receive information. Books were only available to closed religious orders and were laboriously copied by hand. In 1448 a German goldsmith, Johan Gutenberg, invented a way of printing whole pages using movable type. Gutenberg used this method to produce the first printed bible in 1456.

William Caxton was the first Englishman to develop a printing business. He printed his first book in the English language in 1474, called *The Recuyell of the Historie of Troye*.

As printing became faster, books were published on all sorts of subjects. As more books became available more people learned to read. It was also around this time that the first schools were opened.

How books shaped people's ideas

In France, the illegal and illicit distribution of cheaply printed books called 'Chap' books became commonplace by the late 1700s. One of these Chap books informed the ordinary people about the enormous excesses of the monarchy. Chap books helped to kindle a sense of national identity which ultimately lead to the French Revolution and the overthrow of the monarchy.

Pause for thought

Can you think of examples where the press is criticized for printing stories about royalty ?

Information from books added to the resentment that caused the French Revolution

Pause for thought

What is the possible connection between books becoming more widely available and schools opening?

Information becomes important for business

In 1605, the year of the Gunpowder Plot, the first newspaper was printed, in Antwerp, Holland. The first British newspaper was called the *Daily Courant* and first appeared in 1702. At that time newspapers were read mainly by businessmen and merchants because they contained stories from other parts of the world which were important to trade and politics.

Questions

Working in a group discuss the following.

1 With new industry new jobs develop. What jobs do you think were created to operate the newspaper industry?

2 How do you think newspapers got their news two centuries ago as compared with today?

3 a Who decides what news is printed in the newspapers?

  b What might influence their decisions?

Pause for thought

Despite technological advances news is still passed on by word of mouth today. Journalists often interview on-the-spot witnesses or experts before writing up the stories for the newspapers.

New inventions and discoveries for mass communication

By the end of the nineteenth century Sir Alexander Graham Bell, a Scottish scientist, had invented the telephone and Guglielmo Marconi had invented the radio. It was now possible to communicate rapidly with people across the world. Radio had such potential for mass communication that the government set up the British Broadcasting Company in 1922, later to become the British Broadcasting Corporation (BBC).

Radio made it possible for people to hear the voices of politicians and other important people for the first time. The people of Britain would have heard Neville Chamberlain's famous announcement that Britain was 'now at war with Germany' in September 1939 on the radio.

By the mid 1930s nearly every family had a radio – for many a major source of news and entertainment. Radio stars were as popular as pop stars are today

Radio with pictures

During the 1920s John Logie Baird, another British engineer, was working on the idea of talking pictures. The BBC immediately became interested in his idea and started to develop television, transmitting its first programme in 1929. However it was not until the coronation of Queen Elizabeth II was televised in 1953 that large numbers of people hired TV sets and started to watch television regularly.

In the 1970s satellite communications were developed so pictures could be transmitted as they happened from anywhere in the world.

Pause for thought

How much time do you spend each day listening to the radio and watching television?

Questions

Working in a group discuss the following.

4 Do you think that television and radio have changed our lives for the better or the worse?

5 Do you think television influences people's opinions?

6 Do you think it right that the government can censor what we watch?

Mass communication has changed our lives forever

Television is thought to have a very strong influence on people because of its power to shape our thoughts and ideas. The government regulates what we see on television and has the right to veto a programme if it thinks the content is not in the national interest.

At first there was only one channel and pictures were transmitted in black and white. By the 1960s ITV, the first commercial channel, had been given a licence to broadcast and later, in the mid 1960s, colour was introduced

Reporters covering wars, the World Cup or the Olympic Games all use satellite communications, so we can see events as they happen, wherever they are taking place in the world

Research activity

Find out about access to the Internet in your area by answering these questions.

1. Can you log onto the Internet at home?
2. Can you log onto the Internet at school?
3. Can you log onto the Internet in the local library?
4. Do your parents log onto the Internet where they work?
5. Is there an Internet users' service for hire in your town?

Use the answers to these questions to comment on how much the Internet is used in your area.

Information is power

Today almost everyone needs information for work, leisure, education and for the day-to-day running of our lives. We can access the information we need very quickly, almost instantly in some cases, through using information technology. A single CD-ROM can hold the information of many encyclopaedias, and high street banks' on-line computers can give instant information about personal finances at cash points throughout the country.

Having relevant information enables people to make decisions and to have more control over their lives. By using computers, phone lines and satellite links, the Internet allows people to exchange ideas and information with anyone in the world. It lets people communicate cheaply and rapidly without the information being edited or censored by a publisher, broadcaster or government. Communication via the Internet is a two-way process, meaning that anyone who transmits information on the Internet can have a dialogue with whoever receives the information anywhere in the world.

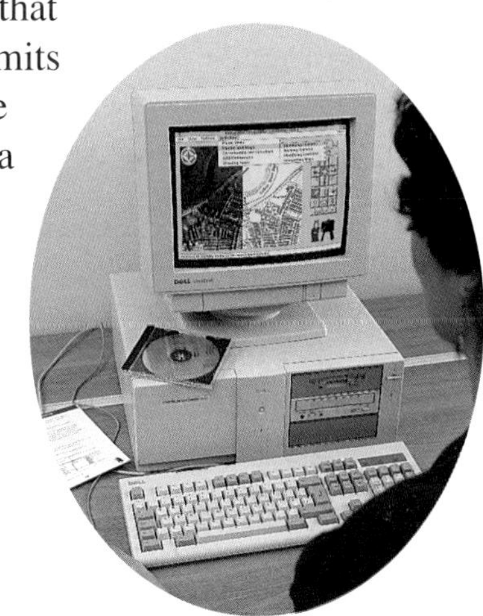

Using a CD-ROM to access information

DIY medical testing

Some products could not be designed if the designers didn't understand the science behind the way the product works. Obvious examples are motor cars, radios and televisions, microwave ovens and thermal blankets. The science behind these products is mainly physics and chemistry. Now new medical products are being developed which depend on an understanding of biology. For example, in the past a doctor would test for diabetes by sticking a finger into a sample of urine and licking it to see if it tasted sweet. Nowadays the doctor would use a chemical test strip developed specially to test for sugar.

Old-style medical testing

Some medical tests are so simple and reliable that anyone can carry them out. A new type of product has therefore come onto the market – do-it-yourself medical testing kits.

P

Pause for thought

What medical conditions might people want to test themselves for?

Testing for pregnancy

When a woman becomes pregnant she produces a chemical called human chorionic gonadotrophin (hCG). This chemical is present in a woman's urine when she is pregnant. In order to find out if she is pregnant, therefore, a woman can test for hCG in her urine.

Until fairly recently the only way to test for hCG was to inject the urine sample into a female animal such as a mouse or toad. If hCG was present then the woman's urine would cause the animal to produce eggs. If she was not pregnant there would be no hCG so no eggs would be produced. This test had many disadvantages:

- it had to be carried out by a laboratory technician;
- it took several days;
- sometimes the animals had to be killed to find out if eggs had been produced.

Biologists have discovered that our white blood cells produce antibodies as part of our defence system against attack by viruses, bacteria and certain chemicals, generally called antigens. The antibodies protect us by recognizing and combining with the antigens and rendering them harmless. The white blood cells produce particular antibodies to fight particular antigens.

In 1975 two scientists discovered how to produce large amounts of antibodies outside the body in a fermenter. This enabled scientists to produce a wide range of antibodies in large quantities, including one that could recognize and combine with hCG and nothing else. They knew this could form the basis of a reliable and accurate pregnancy test. Now it was up to product designers to develop an easy-to-use pregnancy testing kit.

Here's what they developed ...

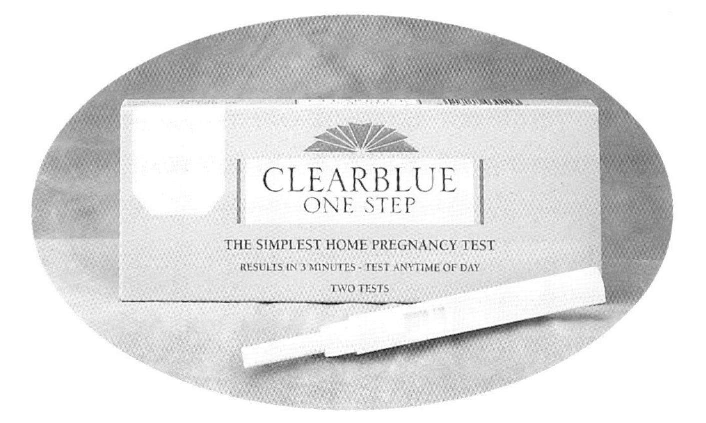

The Clearblue One-step pregnancy testing kit

The pregnancy testing kit

To carry out the test a woman urinates onto the absorbent sampler.

There are two windows in the test kit. A blue line appears in the smaller of the two windows to show that the test is complete and has worked correctly. If the test is positive a line will appear in the large window, showing that the user is pregnant.

How it works

How the test kit works is explained below.

Research activity

Find out the meanings of the following terms:
monoclonal antibodies
hybridoma cells.

Questions

1 Why is the small window important?

2 Why is urine used for the test rather than blood?

3 a What are the advantages for a woman in knowing that she is pregnant as soon as possible after she has conceived?

  b Are there any disadvantages in knowing as soon as possible?

4 Why is it important for the test to be reliable and accurate?

5 Why is it important for the test to be easy to use?

6 What changes would you make to the test kit if it were to be used in a hospital laboratory?

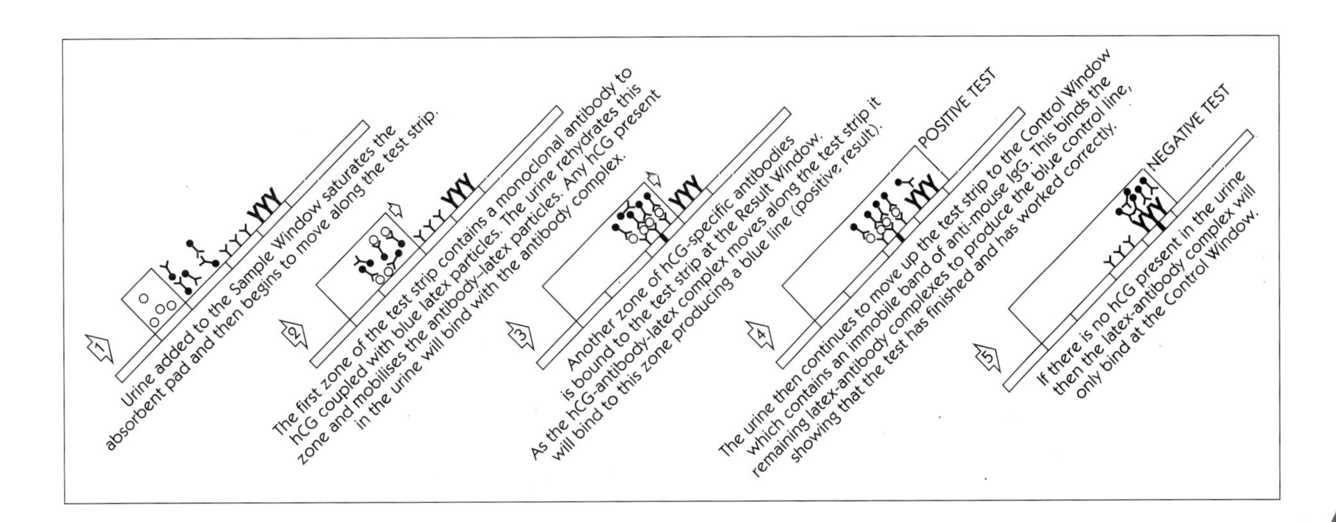

Manufacturing aircraft

Since 1901, when the American Orville Wright made the first flight in a powered aircraft, the aerospace industry has come a long way. Early pioneers, sometimes working in garden sheds, built their flying machines out of linen and wood – during World War I furniture factories were enlisted to meet the demand for aircraft parts.

By World War II most aircraft were made of aluminium alloy, and it was car factories which turned to aircraft manufacture. Since then the development of passenger aeroplanes and increasingly sophisticated technology have transformed the aerospace industry. It is now vast, encompassing the design and manufacture of military and civil aircraft ranging from microlights and gliders to Concorde.

Pause for thought

Why do you think it was car factories not furniture factories that made aircraft in World War II?

Multinational manufacture

Every aeroplane is made up of thousands of different parts or components, all of which have to be functioning perfectly to ensure the efficiency and durability of the aircraft, and the safety and comfort of its passengers.

From the engine and wings to the door handles and headrests, every component has to be painstakingly designed, developed, tested and made. Because of the enormous amount of work involved, the parts to make one aeroplane are often produced in different factories all over the world before coming together for final assembly as shown below.

Designing and making the wing flaps

Shorts is one of Britain's oldest and largest aircraft manufacturers. It has been in the flight business since 1901, when Oswald and Eustace Short started making aerial balloons. Today Shorts employs 7800 people in the design, development and manufacture of a wide range of aircraft and aerostructures (aircraft components).

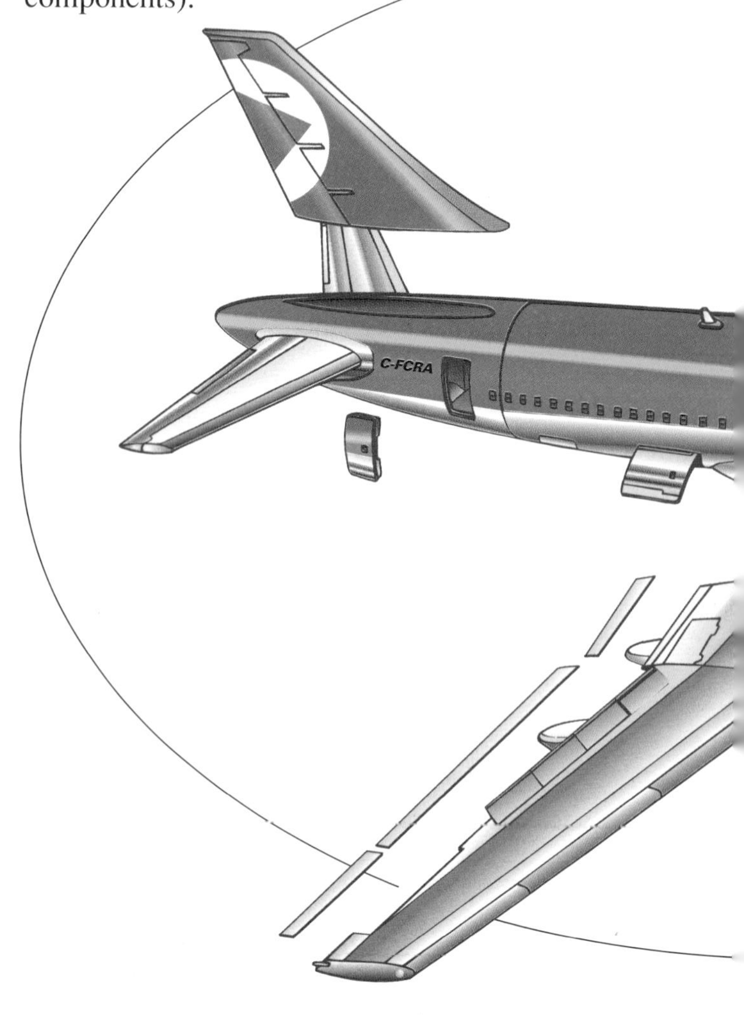

Shorts' aircraft and aerostructures are designed by Aero Designs Ltd on the Isle of Man. This is a special part of the company dedicated to designing aerostructures ready for manufacture and assembly at Shorts' sites. The designing is carried out using **computer-aided design (CAD)**. The results can be plotted out as 2D drawings, 3D wire frames or surface envelopes. From the design drawings the computer can calculate surface areas and volumes, and carry out stress analysis. All the members of the design team are networked to each other so that they can take into account how the others' designs are developing. For example, changes in the design of a wing will almost certainly require changes in the design of the wing flaps.

Once the final design for the wing flaps is complete and the designers are satisfied that it meets the specification, the information needed to manufacture the parts is sent via a telephone line to the manufacturing site in Belfast. The information is fed directly into computer-controlled machines which can then be set to work to make the parts. This process of designing and manufacturing with the aid of computers is called **CAD/CAM** (computer-aided design/computer-aided manufacture). Once the parts are made they can be assembled into the completed wing flap which is sent to the USA for inclusion in the aeroplane.

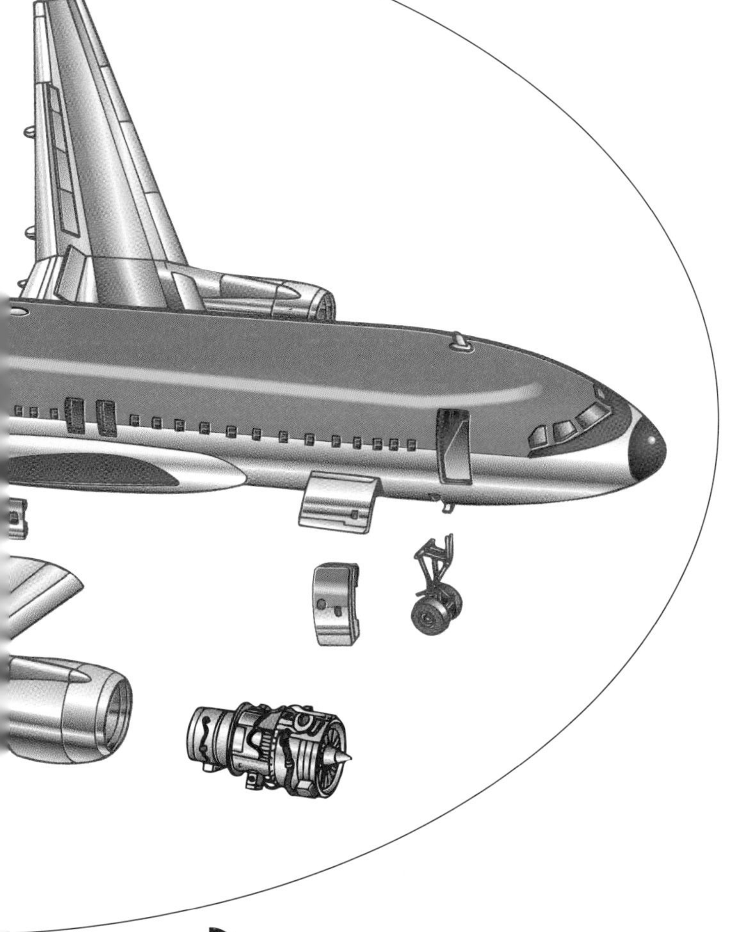

Parts for this airplane are made all over the world and assembled in the USA

Research activity

Find out if there are any manufacturing companies in your area. Make a list of them. Find out which ones use CAD to design their products, and which ones use CAM to make their products.

CAD/CAM in action producing parts for a Boeing 757

Public transport In London

The early Victorians had rutted and cobbled streets with poor drainage and no road system as such. Today we have crowded buses, trains and tubes as well as an increasing number of vehicles creating more pollution and slowing traffic down. Are today's London residents and commuters any better off than their Victorian predecessors?

Early victorian scene

Horses galore

The horse has played a key role in the development of public transport systems in cities across Europe. In 1829 the first regular horse bus service – carrying just 12 people – provided a fixed route service from the City of London to Paddington. It ran every three hours with a fare of one shilling (5p). This was a considerable sum of money at the time and so the service catered mainly for the wealthy. Its success encouraged other operators to set up services on other routes. This was the beginning of London's public transport system.

Pause for thought

What is the future for public transport in London or any of Britain's other major cities?

Competition and cobbled streets

More operators in the market-place meant they had to compete for passengers. This made operators invest in ways of carrying more people. This resulted in the introduction of back-to-back seating on the tops of buses in 1850. These seats were accessed by a ladder – it took another 30 years to get a proper stairway to the top of the horse-drawn bus!

The size of the bus and therefore the number of passengers it could carry was limited by the power of the horses. A significant advance was made in 1861 with the introduction of horse-drawn trams. These had wheels which ran on steel tracks laid in the road. This made it easier for the horses to pull their loads which meant that buses could be made larger or more passengers could be carried on the existing buses.

Travelling in 1870

Pause for thought

What else might be used to power buses and trams? Why weren't these used in 1850?

Trams provided a cheaper form of transport with lower fares. This meant that more people could afford to use them to get to and from work. By 1900 many suburban areas of London were served by tram routes.

Powering the way forward

In 1906 there were around 50 000 horses working in London, transporting more than 2 000 000 people per day. But the days of horse-drawn transport were numbered. Towards the end of the nineteenth century operators explored other power sources, such as steam, electricity and diesel fuel. Their aim was to become more competitive by making their vehicles either faster or able to carry more passengers. Experiments with steam-powered trams were short lived and electricity proved to be the ideal power source. From 1901 overhead power lines or road-embedded conduit systems were installed.

London electric tram in 1908

The main problem with electric trams was that they were not very manoeuvrable. The power lines and tracks were often laid down the middle of the road. People had to dodge the traffic passing on either side to get on the tram!

Horses could not compete with these clean, quiet, reliable and larger capacity vehicles, and with the simultaneous introduction of the diesel motor bus, the horse's demise was complete.

The trolley bus: more manoeuvrable than the tram because it did not need rails

Trolley buses were introduced in London in the 1930s. They had already been used successfully in other cities for over two decades. They did not run on rails, though they were powered using overhead electric cables in a similar way to the trams. This meant they were more flexible as their manoeuvrability was limited only by the reach of their overhead power links. After World War II, from 1945 onwards the diesel-powered motor bus became the dominant form of public transport above ground and trolley buses ceased operation in London in 1962.

Going underground

London pioneered the underground railway system. It began with railway carriages pulled by a steam engine in 1863. This system was dirty and noisy and was replaced in 1890 by a deep-level electric system – the first in the world. Most of the central part of London's existing underground system was developed between the two wars, the outer reaches being developed after World War II. The London Underground is still being developed today with links to the Docklands Light Railway and the Jubilee line extension to the south of the River Thames.

Back above ground

The tram has not been totally forgotten. European cities such as Amsterdam have operated tram systems successfully for many decades and cities in England are beginning to follow suit. Manchester and Sheffield launched new tram systems in the early 1990s. London Transport is exploring the possibility of a Tramlink between Wimbledon and Croydon using existing rail lines. As a virtually emission-free form of transport and one that can maximize the use of rechargeable power sources, tram systems are an attractive proposition for congested and polluted cities.

Question

1 As public transport became more comprehensive, reliable and affordable, London changed. People could consider living further away from their workplace, knowing that they could get to work by public transport.

What effect do you think this had on the areas surrounding London and in the Victorian slum sites within the city?

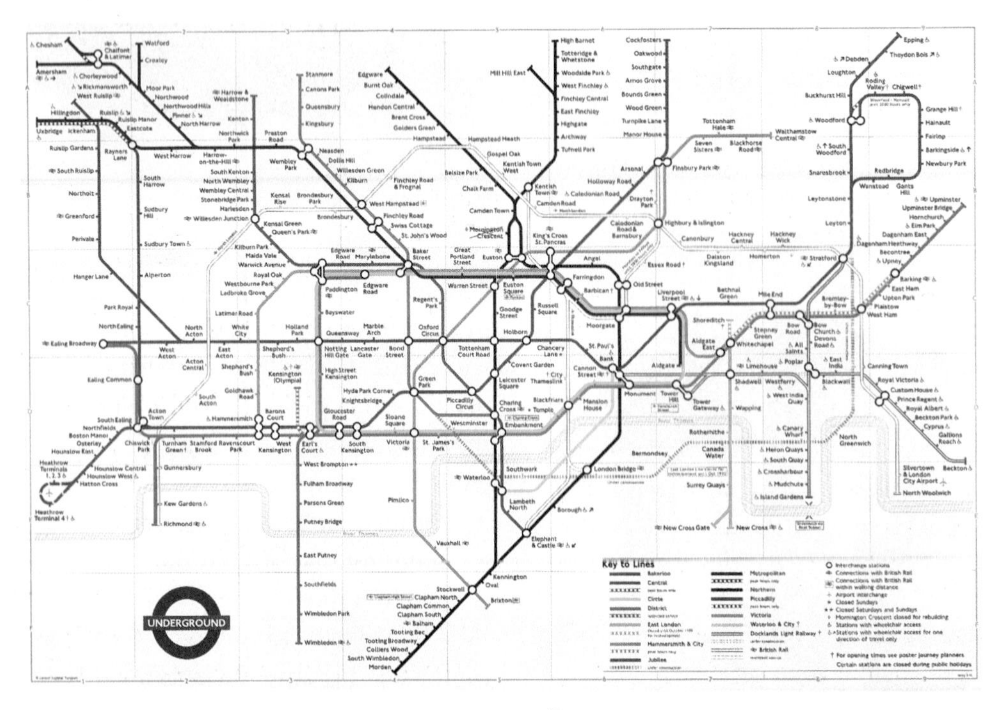

The modern tube map, first designed in 1933, shows only the sequence of stations and the connections

Ownership and intervention

Until the end of the nineteenth century individuals or companies owned various bus and tram routes. In 1891 London City Council started buying tramway companies and by 1899 they owned seven of the largest operations. By doing this the council was able to ensure that transport routes met the needs of the areas they served and the tram became the cornerstone of a public-owned transport system.

In 1933 the London Passenger Transport Board, a public body, was set up with powers to take over all bus, tram, trolley buses and underground services in London and adjacent counties. Today, bus routes are being offered for sale to private companies to manage. London Transport reported in 1994 'substantial savings of 15–20 per cent of previous operational costs … achieved from the tendering process.'

By the year 2001 it is planned that all bus routes will have been put out to tender to private companies. Over a period of 100 years public transport in London will have gone almost full circle, from private to public ownership and then back again.

Installing and managing the system

Public transport in London calls on all aspects of design and technology – civil engineering, mechanical and electrical engineering, large-scale manufacturing, advanced data capture and information handling systems, extensive maintenance and staff development.

London Transport has used the latest electronic and information technology to develop ticket vending machines and ticket reading machines linked to entry/exit points.

R

Research activity

Find out about the public transport in your area. Try to answer these questions:

1 What are the bus routes?

2 How frequently do the buses run?

3 What is the cost of a journey from the outskirts to the city centre?

4 What concessions are available?

You might present your information in the form of a display including an annotated map.

Modern designs keep improving transport in London

The 'look' of London Transport has been developed through corporate identity programmes that cover signage, uniforms, livery for vehicles, promotional materials and stationery.

Energy to make things work

The power rating of an appliance tells us how much energy is needed each second to make it work. The table on the right shows the power ratings of some appliances people use everyday.

Such amounts of energy have not always been available as the panel below shows. Note that the printing industry requires large amounts of energy for producing paper from wood pulp and operating printing machinery.

Appliance	Power rating
radio	10 watts
microwave cooker	650 watts
electric iron	1000 watts
2-bar electric fire	2000 watts (2 kilowatts)
washing machine	2500 watts (2.5 kilowatts)
family car engine	37500 – 450000 watts (37.5 – 45 kilowatts) under braking load

	Time	Power	Comment
Life without engines	prehistoric times	140 watts for a strong person	Even with simple machines and using animals life without engines is very hard work!
Wind and water power– the first engines			These low power sources are suitable for monotonous tasks like grinding corn and operating forge hammers.
	7th century for waterwheels in Europe after the Roman Empire	primitive water wheels 300/400 watts	Water power requires a suitable river and the power is only available at or very near the water wheel.
	12th century for windmills in Europe	late 18th century windmills 2-3 kilowatts	Wind power requires a windy place. The power is only available at or very near the windmill and when wind is blowing.
Atmospheric engines	18th century	Newcomen's engine 3.5 kilowatts	Can operate wherever engine can be built and fuel transported.
		Watt's engine 7-8 kilowatts	Power only available at or near the engine site.

	Time	Power	Comment
True steam engines	19th century	By the 1880s 5000 kilowatts	Can operate wherever engine can be built and fuel transported. Power only available near the engine site.
Generating electricity	late 19th century	100 kilowatt generators used for street lighting in New York in 1882	Principles of the dynamo and electric motor understood by mid 19th century. The scene is set for the generating and transmitting of electricity which can be used to power machines that work by electric motors.
Generating electricity using fossil fuel	late 20th century	Modern power station in the UK generates 500 – 1000 megawatts	Contributes to acid rain unless advanced technologies used. Contributes to greenhouse effect.
Generating electricity using nuclear fuel	late 20th century	Modern power station in UK generates 900 megawatts	Does not contribute to acid rain or greenhouse effect but concern over safety of power stations and disposal of radioactive waste.
Generating electricity using renewable energy sources	late 20th century	Modern windmill generates 3-4 megawatts Tidal barrier generates 240 megawatts	Do not contribute to acid rain or greenhouse effect but concern over other environmental impact.

Designing our surroundings

Our surroundings and the buildings we live and work in play an important role in how we feel about ourselves, and the world we live in. People work better if they have an environment which is comfortable and stress free.

Architects design environments to help people work better. When designing a new building the architect will consider factors that affect people such as:

- the air they breath;
- the opening and closing of windows;
- the temperature;
- the lighting, both natural and artificial;
- sources and level of noise;
- the closeness of other people.

Pause for thought

Try to remember an occasion when you felt uncomfortable in a room or building. What was it that made you feel that way?

Designed for work

When the architects were designing the Powergen building in Coventry they wanted to make it as energy efficient as possible as well as a good place to work. They decided to use a computer system to monitor the temperature, air flow and lighting. The computer uses the data it receives from sensors around the building to keep a constant check on all these things and to adjust them to save energy. It can open and close windows, turn on lights and so forth when the data it receives indicates that this is necessary. However, individual workers can override the computer, if they want to, at any time. This makes people feel happier because they are in control of their environment and the computer system is still able to save on wasted energy.

The architects were also asked to find ways to improve people's ability to work. Some modern buildings have been found to make people working there feel sick. **Sick Building Syndrome (SBS)** has been associated with factors such as air-conditioning systems, bad lighting and lack of building hygiene. Architects now know more about SBS and the subsequent rise in standards of materials handling during construction has largely eliminated SBS from new buildings today.

Questions

1. Make a list of the environmental factors that affect whether you can settle down to do your homework.
2. Make a list of the environmental factors that might affect whether an office worker can work efficiently.
3. Compare your two lists to identify the things they have in common.

The environment inside the Powergen Building is computer controlled

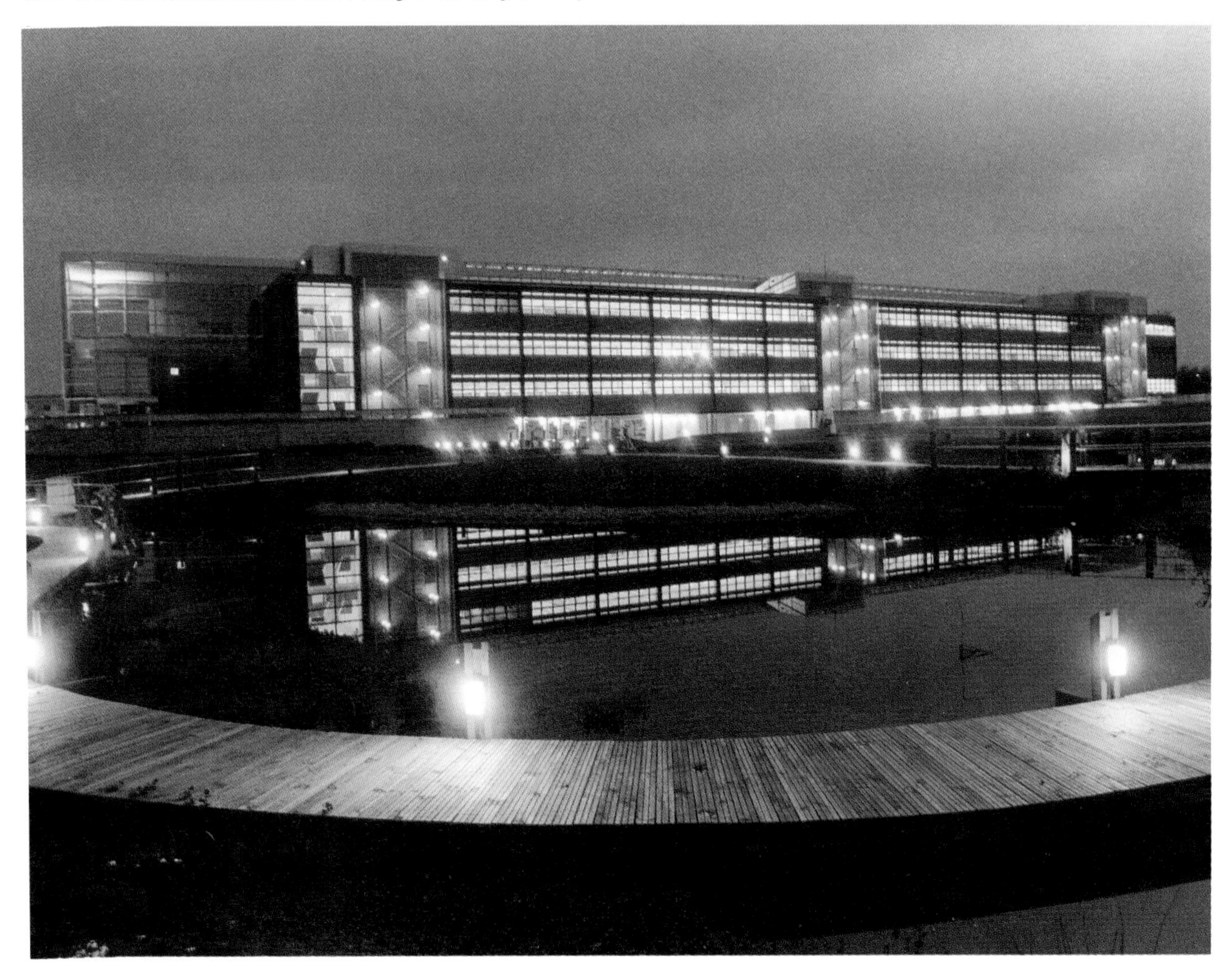

Designed to prevent crime and vandalism

When the Docklands Light Railway was being designed the architects knew that the railway went through tough, crime-ridden areas of London and that many of the stations were to be unmanned during large parts of the day. Any solutions they proposed would need to meet three targets:

- prevent crime;
- improve passenger safety;
- require minimum maintenance and repair.

Very little glass is used in the station designs as glass is often vandalized and needs replacing regularly. All the materials used in the construction of the stations have been chemically treated to make graffiti easy to clean off.

Research activity

Make a sketch (or take a photograph) of a building, and its surroundings, that is poorly designed or misused. Add notes to show what is wrong. List some of the ways which would improve the environment for everyone living or working there.

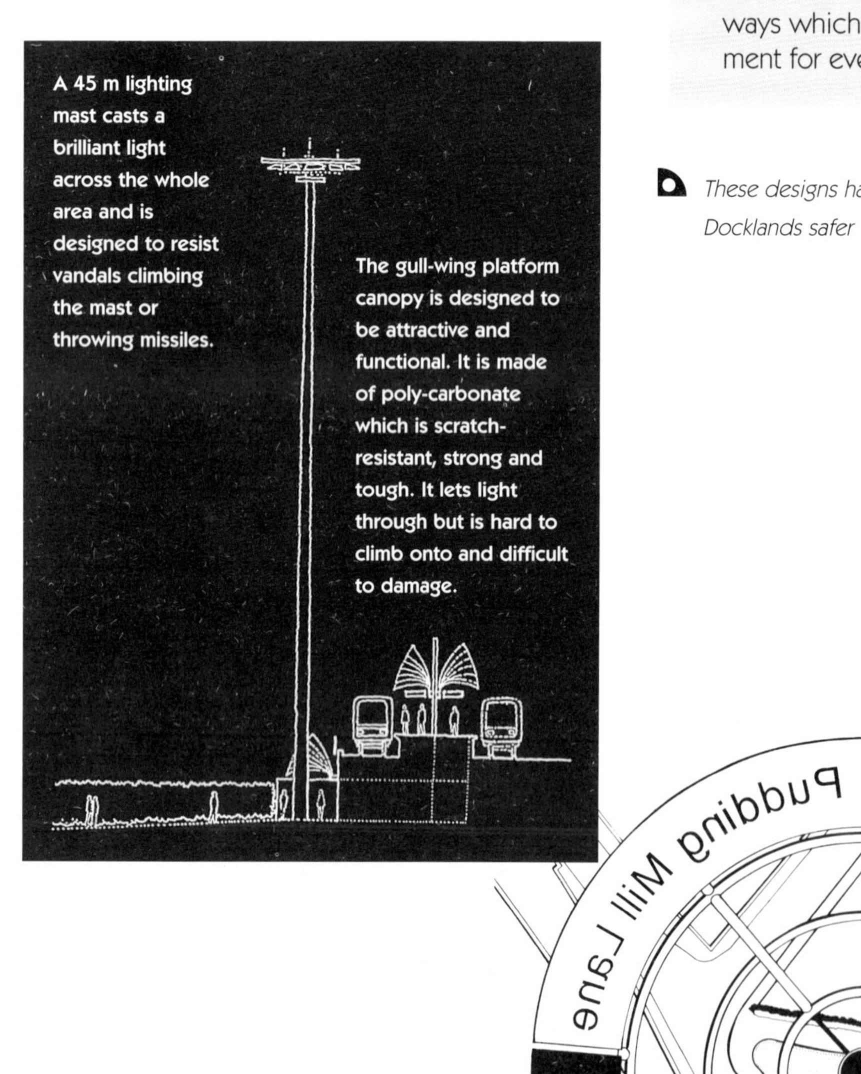

These designs have helped make Docklands safer

Looking down from the top of the lighting mast note the thorny hedge next to the path that leads to the ticket booth. This protects passengers from ambush by muggers. The ticket booth is designed to resist ram raiding even by a JCB.

Focused Case Studies

Packaging

Packaging serves three main functions:

- it protects the contents;
- it describes the product;
- it sells the product.

Particular sorts of products have additional requirements. Food products need to be kept hygienically clean and fit to eat; the packaging is often responsible for maintaining the shelf-life of the product and always contains nutritional information and instructions as required by law.

Pause for thought

Consider the Co-op. In 1958, there were 30 000 neighbourhood Co-op shops. By the early 1980s, the Co-op had only 9 000 shops – but:

- 1760 were supermarkets of over 4 000 square feet
- 43 were superstores of over 25 000 square feet
- 256 were department stores.

This change in the way we shop means that the shop assistants no longer select our products for us, we have to do this ourselves. Faced with many similar products, packaging has become a crucial sales tool. Packaging not only informs the customer about what is in the package (formerly done by the sales assistant), it also shows how the contents should be used.

Photographic films have to be kept in light-tight containers. Medicines and other potentially dangerous goods are often kept in tamper-proof containers and some skin-care products require special packaging to ensure they do not deteriorate. With the growth of information technology, bar-code placement and reliability is a pre-requisite for all packaging.

In this country, there has been a growth in supermarkets since the 1950s. They replaced many of the small neighbourhood shops.

Attitudes to packaging and waste disposal

There is a growing trend towards consumer preference for 'green' world and world-peoples friendly products. This may be largely due to a vast increase in the immediacy of international communications. For example, Live Aid (1985) made people aware of and aroused concern for people in difficult circumstances through music and pictures. Consequently people 'bought the product' by giving money to help change the situation in Ethiopia. This indicates the potential power of visual and audio images. However, if consumer awareness is raised, say, in the area of reusing packaging, this must be backed-up by systems that work well and easily. Otherwise people quickly become cynical. The EU has set up an infrastructure for an EU-wide symbol for eco-labelling. Such a label indicates that the product is environmentally superior to products without that label.

The German Green Spot is the symbol for the Dual System for collecting packaging. The spot can be any colour except red! It is used on a pack to show that a manufacturer has paid a fee. In Germany there is a responsibility for shops to receive back packaging for it to be recycled.

This symbol is used across Europe to indicate environmentally friendly packaging

In Germany this indicates that the manufacturer has paid a fee toward the collection of the packaging after use

This indicates that packaging is to be re-used

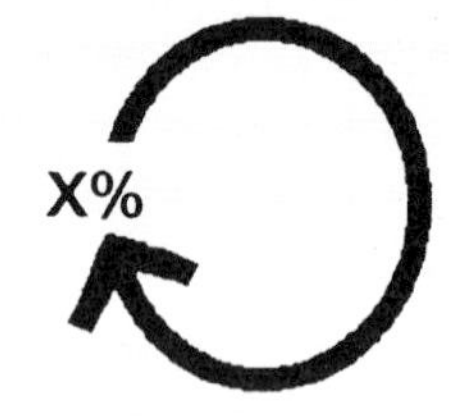

This indicates the percentage of recycled content within the packaging

These both indicate that the packaging is to be recovered for recycling purposes.

Symbols used on packaging to inform consumers about environmental effects

The Industry Council for Packaging and the Environment (INCPEN) has developed these guidelines.

In designing a pack, take account of all environmental factors especially:

Examples of returnable and refillable packaging

- energy requirements;
- raw material requirements;
- waste arising at all stages throughout the distribution chain;
- expected impact on waste after the pack has been used;
- avoid the use of excessive packaging;
- take positive action to reduce litter;
- examine opportunities for using secondary materials;
- support resource-efficient reclamation schemes;
- encourage repeated use where possible;
- assess potential for supplying your own packaging waste to a recycler.

Position in the market

The packaging designer needs to consider the position of the product, or product range, in the market. With a new product, positioning within the intended market is crucial for successful selling. With an established product, a change in package image can re-establish it within a different or changed market. Clearly, the whole identity of the product must be considered – including designs for advertising (TV commercials, radio, magazines and so on) and in-store promotional materials, display materials and so forth. Often, music will be a strong element in a corporate image.

Pause for thought

Levi's relaunch of 501 jeans in 1985/6 resulted in two of their commercials' soundtracks ('Stand By Me' by Ben E. King and 'When A Man Loves A Woman' by Percy Sledge) being numbers one and two in the charts in one week.

Budget lines – lower price goods – may well have very simple packaging and clean-cut minimum colour labels. This look has little to do with the cost of producing less fancy packaging – it has a lot to do with purchasers' expectations. However, recently – partly because of the 'green' factor – some very expensive (top-end market) packaging has become very simple. There is, of course, also a deep-seated mind-link between elegant simplicity and quality.

Position in the market is not as simple as it seems – these packages ***all*** *have simple, clean, even 'healthy', images, but are targeted at different markets.*

Questions

Discuss in a group the packaging of some make-up, skin care or body care products.

Use your discussion to do the following.

- Make a list of some products.
- Note down those examples where it is likely that the packaging costs more than the product contained.
- Decide whether this packaging is absolutely necessary to protect or sell the product.
- Note down examples of similar products packaged more cheaply.
- Decide whether or not these are aimed at different markets.

Research activity

Think about your local corner shop and the large food store where you normally shop. Make two image boards:

- one for the target consumer group of the corner shop
- one for the target consumer group for the big food store.

Question

It is possible to package water for sale. The container may be colourless or green-ish or blue-ish. The shape is usually similar to a bottle. The size and material used for the packaging will vary according to the market/target consumer group.

Do you think the consumer is buying the package or the contents?

Try asking yourself the following questions.

- What does the packaging tell us about the water it contains …

  … that it is just water

  … that it is a downmarket sort of water

  … that it is a quality water?
- Would you buy water if it was in a card carton, like orange juice?
- If not, why not?

Packaging & the nature of the product

Clearly, packages that emphasize ‘greenness’, ‘budget’ or ‘quality’ via their image are implying that the contents have similar qualities. Designers of packaging are therefore faced with a range of ethical dilemmas. Is it OK, for example, to show peas as bright green on packaging when the peas inside are not that colour? Would it be better to use clear packaging and containers so that consumers can see what they are getting? Is it a fair sell to package implied ‘added value’ – cartons that become storage containers, free figures in cereals, collectable tokens for free gifts? Does this, in a sense, lie about the nature of the product itself – the product is seen as extra ‘good’ because it has an added element – or does it imply a certain market?

Signs and symbols

Signs and symbols have a variety of functions. Some are intended to make you stop and look, some to entertain or decorate, while others make you move or act in a certain way.
In the majority of cases, a sign or symbol has a clear and direct function. It must convey information that we need or would like to know in the most simple and unambiguous manner. The designer has succeeded if the onlooker can answer these questions:
Do I understand? Do I like what I understand? Can I obey what I have understood?

Pause for thought

How many signs and symbols do you pass on your way to school?

A universal language

Signs and symbols create their own language. This is a visual and universal language that can be interpreted and understood by people within and across countries. The important elements that make up this language include colours, numbers, letters and simple illustrations. Sometimes elements of this language are combined in a sequence to pass on changing sets of information, for example traffic lights. The sequence of changing coloured lights informs drivers when they should stop and when they should go.

Research activity

Identify other signs and symbols that are internationally recognized. Why have they achieved this level of recognition?

Instantly understood

There are many examples of signs and symbols that are commonly used and recognized throughout the world. A sign that includes the drawn figures of a man and woman is instantly understood to stand for public toilets. When waiting to cross the road, the symbol of the green man indicates that the pedestrian should now be able to step safely off the pavement. The symbol of an ear indicates that there are facilities available for the deaf.

Questions

How would you convey these words using symbols:

- danger
- factory
- school
- fire
- zoo
- park.

 *Instantly recognized signs and symbols*

Road signs are a common sight

Traffic signals

Some of the most widely recognized signs and symbols used in the UK are road and traffic signs. They are present in every city, town, village and country area. They are understood by all those who use the traffic system.

A code

These signs serve a variety of purposes: they alert us to danger, they point us in the right direction, they provide us with information about distance and speed. The many symbols that make up the road traffic signage system form a language of their own. In fact, they form a code – the Highway Code. This series of visual symbols has become part of everyday life for all road users. It is given such importance that the inability to understand and interpret the Code prevents people from being granted a licence to drive a car.

The symbols and designs that make up the traffic signage system consist mainly of illustrations and numerical references. As recently as 1965, signs in the UK still contained a large amount of text – difficult and distracting to read when driving a car and impossible to interpret for those who do not speak English.

However, it is not just having the right type of symbol that is important when establishing a traffic signage system. European Ministries of Transport have established a clear set of guidelines, based on extensive research and testing, to ensure that sign designers and manufacturers produce signs that are clear and safe.

Size

The sign must be the right size so that it can be clearly read. This includes the overall size of the sign as well as the information included on it. The size and spacing of any type used is also extremely important if all the information is to be clearly legible.

A motorway sign has to include type that is clearly legible so as not to confuse the drivers of vehicles

The colour of signs has already been mentioned as a way of distinguishing types of information. Designers have to give the use and variety of colours within signs a great deal of consideration because if the signs contain too many different colours they can become distracting. However, if they are not clearly coloured, they could become indistinct from their background environment.

Materials

The materials used to manufacture road signs and the finishes applied to them are also of considerable importance. The signs must be sturdy and resistant to all forms of weather, particularly rain – rust and corrosion would interfere with the legibility of the sign. The signs need to be coated with a reflective finish to ensure that they can be clearly seen in the dark. The reflective coating picks up the light from a car's headlights, allowing the sign to be read and removing the need for lighting to be included as part of the sign's structure.

Positioning

Finally, the positioning of signs is extremely important. Signs must be clearly visible and always unobstructed. If signs are placed too close together, there is a great possibility that one sign will obscure the information on another. Signs must also be placed at a distance that gives the road user enough time to react before encountering the hazard, turning, roundabout or whatever the sign is telling them about. If the sign is placed at an inadequate distance or in an inappropriate position then it can become a danger.

The Olympic Games

Innovations in signs and symbols are frequently encouraged by competitions and international sporting events. One of the most interesting developments has been in the field of universally recognized pictograms.

A pictogram is a graphic device that conveys meaning by using an illustration of a specific action. Pictograms are now widely used in leisure centres, shopping centres and transport terminals across the world.

At the Olympic Games, where athletes and spectators gather from a large number of countries, the fact that words are not used on directional signage is a key factor in the success of the signage system. The team of graphic designers commissioned to design the signage system for the 1964 Tokyo Olympic Games are widely regarded as having set the standard for graphics at all future international events. They used clearly defined images, pared down to their simplest forms, to create figures in instantly recognizable postures relating to specific sports.

Examples of the pictogram signage developed for the 1964 Tokyo Olympics

Pause for thought

Why are pictograms such an effective method of conveying information?

Research activity

Find out how the signs and symbols used at the 1992 Barcelona Olympics reflect or differ from the examples provided here.

Otl Aicher's designs for the 1972 Munich Olympics clearly reflect the signs developed for the 1964 Games

What's in a name? To B or not to BT

Winds of change

BT used to be part of The Post Office, a public-sector industry. In 1984, it became a privatized industry known as British Telecom and identified with the yellow symbol and the 'yellow peril' vans – an identity that clearly separated if from the red of The Post Office, its former home.

Part of the privatization involved major restructuring of the company as it became more and more commercially driven and began to look to new overseas markets for its services and products. It aimed to be more than just a first-rate UK provider, it wanted to develop an international reputation as a leader within a high-technology industry and it wanted its corporate identity to reflect this.

The old-style image

How does the old-style image compare?

The international picture

In the international market the 'T' symbol was very similar to symbols and logos used by other companies. As a result, the 'T' could not be registered as a trademark. This meant there had to be separate identities for the UK and international markets – not a united image of a leading international company.

BT researched overseas markets and found that the name 'British Telecom', by using the word 'British' conjured up an unexciting, reliable but conservative image not associated with leading-edge technology. It also suggested to some that the company traded nationally not internationally.

Pause for thought

How many different logos can you bring to mind?

Designing the way forward

Wolff Olins, a UK design consultancy and world leader in developing corporate identities for all sizes of companies, was chosen to develop the new identity. To get a clear idea of the company's image among its own staff as well as with people outside the company, Wolff Olins' staff talked to customers, all levels of BT staff and opinion-formers in industry. It was not just about creating a glossy superficial image, the project had to reflect the company's vision of itself and how it wanted to be perceived in the world. To achieve its aims, the new identity would affect how the company functioned as well as the image on the phone box and the headed paper!

The Pied Piper

The piper figure in the logo represents two figures coming together: the listener in red, the teller in blue. The piper has been used as a symbol of communication for centuries and across many cultures. The final figure evolved from many sketches and boards showing different interpretations and possibilities.

Pause for thought

Who is the corporate identity for? Clients, users, suppliers, providers, staff?

BT particularly welcomed the use of a figure rather than an abstract design to express and reflect the important human element of BT's activities. The blue is the same blue that was used in the original logo with red introduced as a stronger supporting colour. Although the colours are normally blue and red, the piper may be used in other colours. For example, green has become identified with the phonecard and so that has been retained as the colour for phonecard call boxes with the piper figure being sandblasted into the call boxes' glass walls.

From initial ideas to finished design

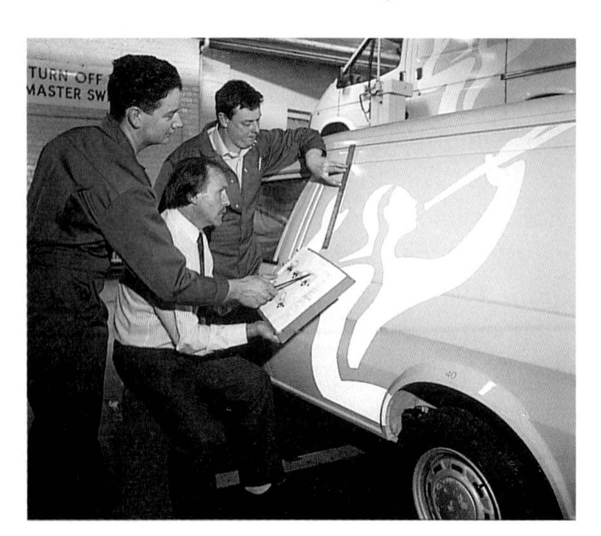

Checking the new logo on a van

Material considerations

The logo was part of a total identity package. It had to be able to appear wherever it was required. This involved testing and research into whether or not the colours could be matched across the range of materials to which they would be applied – paints, inks, plastics, metals, vinyls and glass and vehicle background colour, which had to ensure that the vehicle was conspicuous for road safety reasons.

Not just about graphics

Another aspect of the new identity involved coming up with new designs for telephones for the home as well as public spaces – the aim being that people should be able to look at a phone and know that it is a BT phone without seeing the logo! Following the product styling initiative in 1990, a detailed specification was developed for a new generation of telephone products. This said that one keypad should be the same as another, with digits and symbols always in the same place, that there should be common screen formats and a resemblance between all the different models.

Is this design in line with the new corporate image?

Putting all the pieces into place

The new identity has been introduced gradually since its announcement in 1991. It began with total introduction in Manchester and Liverpool, enabling BT to get a clear idea of any possible difficulties or potential hiccups over implementing the identity. Learning from this experience, they could then go about introducing it across all levels and geographical areas of their activities in the knowledge that they had ironed out any problems. Phasing the introduction of the new identity over a two-year period helped to keep costs down as this allowed major items, such as vehicles and phonebooks, which are distributed to every home in the country, to be updated at a time when they would normally need to be replaced.

Questions

Think of ways in which the design of a telephone can reflect BT's identity beyond the surface application of the logo. How can a product sum up or project a company's ethos – the things that are important to it?

You may need to consider use of colour, materials, shapes and forms in your analysis. Put together a hit list of issues and features that a designer might need to consider or include when designing a new domestic phone for BT.

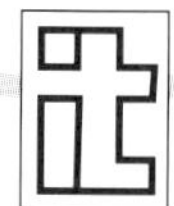

When words just won't do

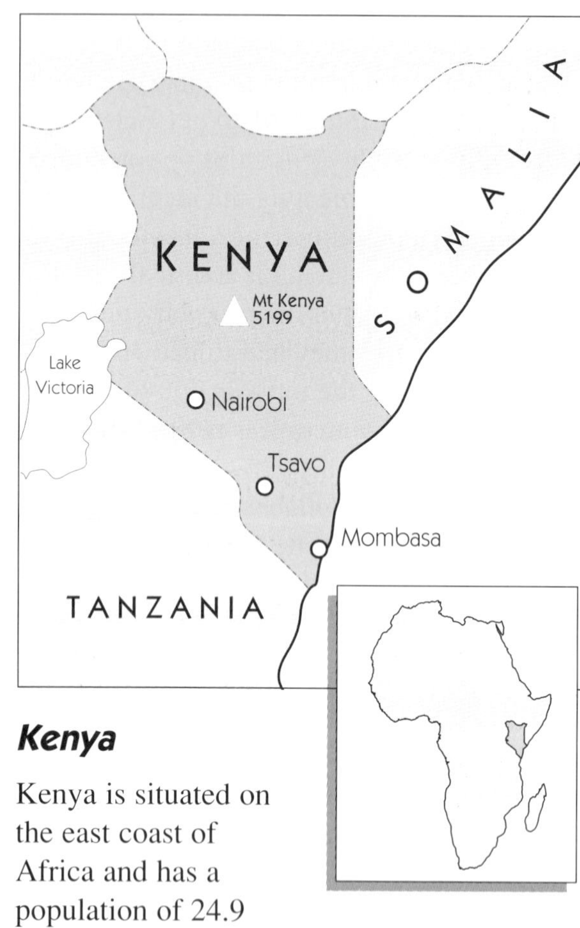

Kenya

Kenya is situated on the east coast of Africa and has a population of 24.9 million. The national language of Kenya is Kiswahili, the official language, English. Both are compulsory in schools. Kenyans divide themselves into about 70 ethnic groups who speak over 30 main languages. Other African languages include Kikuyu, Luhya, Luo and Kamba.

Attendance at school is not compulsory, although primary education is provided by the State. At secondary level, 70 per cent of children attend Harambees – self-help schools financed by local communities. Kenya has a literacy rate of around 45 per cent and there is an active programme to increase this figure. However, there remain people who are unable to have sufficient education to read and write.

The animal healthcare project

Maru is situated in the fertile central region of Kenya and Kimeru is one of the many languages spoken there. Many people are small-scale farmers and keep goats, cows and chickens. The farmers from Maru District were concerned about the health and productivity levels of their animals. Another concern of theirs was that government vets were scarce.

When Intermediate Technology, Kenya, conducted research in conjunction with a local farmers' centre, the team found that farmers needed improved access to medicines. They were keen to learn how to use basic medicines and wanted better veterinary care.

Training animal healthcare assistants

Local farmers selected 13 men and women to undergo a five-day training course in animal healthcare, organized by IT, Kenya, and the Kamujini Farmers' Centre. The newly trained animal healthcare assistants called themselves 'Wasaidizi wa Mifugo', the Kiswahili for 'helpers of livestock'.

It is against the law for animal healthcare assistants to use medicines such as antibiotics. However, their training in preventive medicine, use of local remedies and commonly available veterinary medicines means that farmers can now treat their animals for common diseases. The vet is now only needed for more serious illnesses.

Many of the animal healthcare assistants who run training courses are literate, but not all farmers who they assist can understand written instructions in English or Kiswahili. A range of languages is spoken in the area.

P

Pause for thought

Approximately 1 in 6, or 6.5 million (16 per cent), of adults in the UK have a low level of reading or writing skills. How do they find out about things they need to know?

Signs and symbols used on the training course

Some adults in the UK need help with reading and writing

The answer to this problem lay in formulating a common means of communication between different language speakers. The trainers achieved this by using commonly understood symbolic and pictorial language to illustrate, for example, how overgrown hooves should be trimmed, how goats and cows should be treated for fungal infections and in what dosages the drugs should be administered to different-sized animals and the different species.

Research activity

Find out how a medical manufacturer has used symbolic and pictorial language to depict a product and its use.

Pause for thought

There are many common packaging signs and symbols used to represent different instructions in Europe. Can you think of any?

The animal healthcare assistants returned to their respective communities equipped with a first aid kit of basic medicines, labelled with appropriate symbols, and equipment. They were able to treat their own and their neighbours' animals. 'Now I can take better care of my own animals as well as help my neighbours', commented one of the assistants, Mary Wachuka.

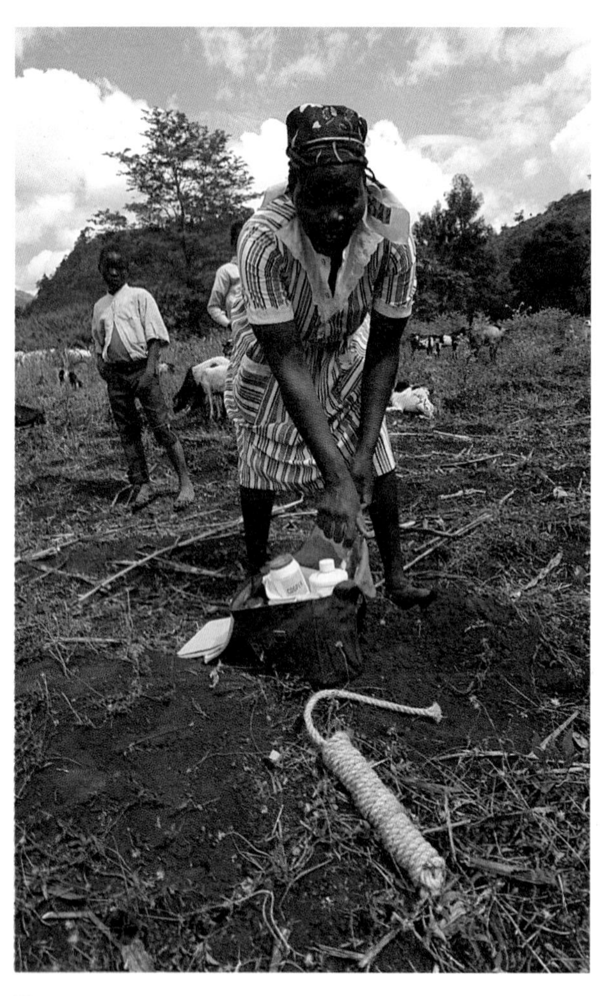

Animal healthcare assistant with first aid kit

Pause for thought

Animal healthcare assistants use labels on their products. Can you think of any appropriate system of replicating labels?

Research activity

Evaluate a range of medical labels. How are the needs and wants of users taken into consideration in their design?

When the medicines in the first aid kit run out, the assistant replaces them from small community-run shops or from distributors in larger towns and cities. Sometimes the assistants treat the animals immediately but on other occasions they dispense drugs in appropriate doses for the farmers to treat their animals. They decant them into available containers, such as jars, empty soda bottles and tins.

Practising one-to-one training skills

Interior design

Designing the interior of a nightclub, shop or fantasy environment often combines the skills of interior design, exhibition design and theatre design. The designer needs a good understanding of:

- how images and structures might look on a large scale and within a space;
- properties of materials – including likely wear-and-tear and cleaning aspects;
- how materials can be used well and cost-effectively in creating images and structures;
- how parts can be replaced cost-effectively or new installations created at low cost;
- how people may interact when in large groups;
- how people use spaces and artefacts;
- health and safety regulations.

Nightclubs

Nightclubs have been around for a long time. Since people have danced, performed or enjoyed socializing, they have met together in environments in some way enhanced to meet the needs of those occasions. You can think of dance palaces, jazz clubs and even barndances in this way.

Nightclubs are a commercial venture. They have to draw members in and persuade them to return over and over again. Therefore, the designer has to develop a series of designs that will help 'sell' the club. The exterior image of the club may be as crucial as the interior. There are some 'chains' of clubs and in these cases the design of the clubs may follow a theme, each varying slightly according to their individual locations and local competition.

Ronnie Scott's – a long-running, successful nightclub

Pause for thought

What factors might be important to the location of a nightclub?
How might a nightclub owner identify likely customers?

Knowing the scene and customers' preferences

The overall design may be based on a theme that is closely linked to the sort of music and fashions enjoyed by those who use the club. The designer therefore needs to be very aware of current influences and trends across the music and dance scene, as well as fashion and advertising/ promotional trends. The designer can also use an understanding of the local situation and the preferences of likely customers to produce a club particularly suited to their needs.

Most clubs have a strong identity, so the designer has to know what sort of people would go there and what the club would be like. However, there are often different events on different nights, so the designer must allow for this and design in what is required in order for this to be possible.

Clubs are usually targeted at:

- different groups of clients, for example younger or older, male or female;
- different interest groups, such as different kinds of music, live music or DJ;
- special themes or atmospheres, such as dressing-up nights, cabaret, party.

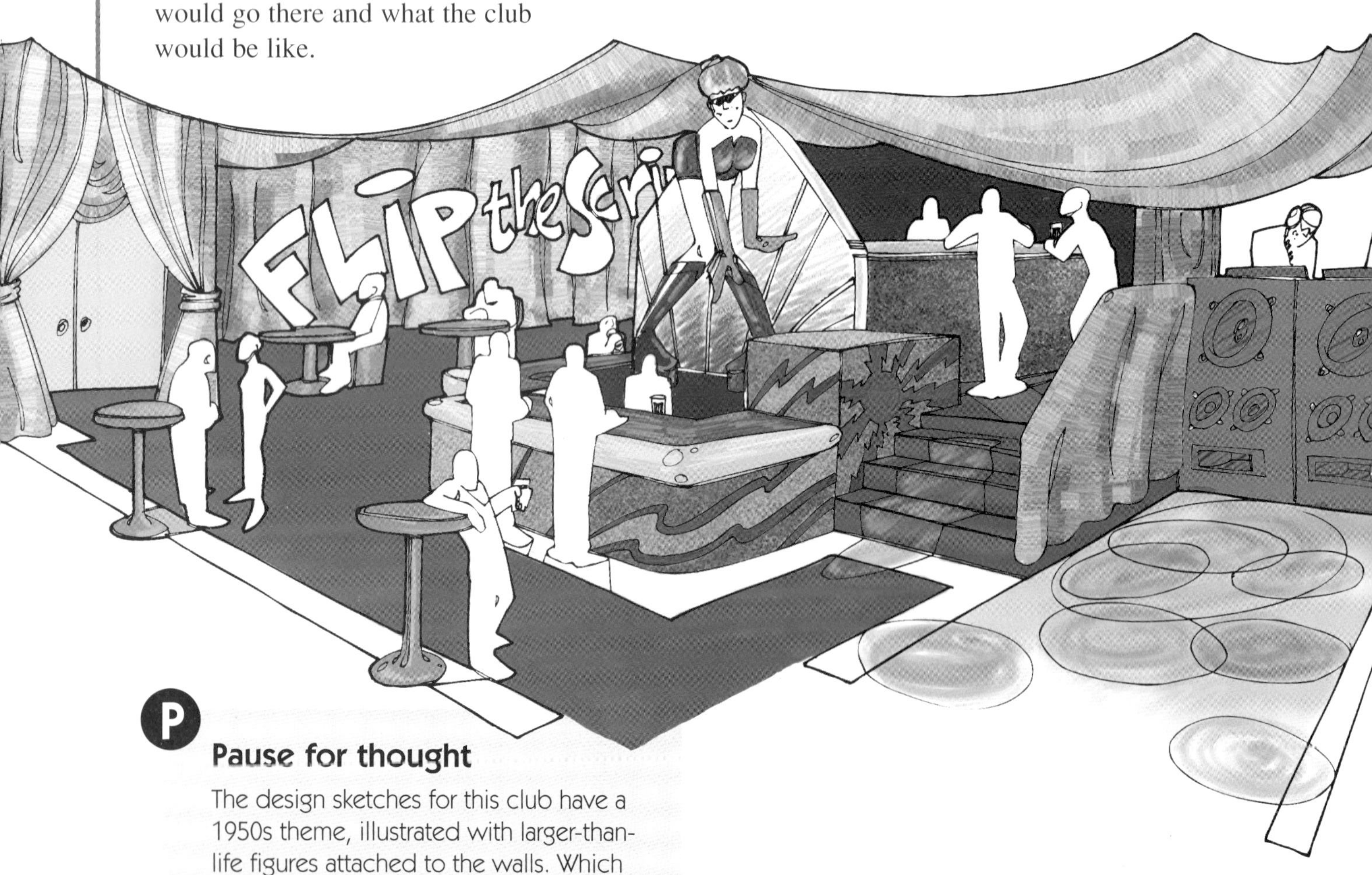

Pause for thought

The design sketches for this club have a 1950s theme, illustrated with larger-than-life figures attached to the walls. Which age group would find this appealing?

Lighting and sound

Lighting can be used to create an *overall* mood but can also create areas with different levels of light within the club. Often this is achieved by using interior structures that create regions of shadow. These structures can also create quiet areas, although overall the club may be quite noisy (the designer may have to consider sound insulation in the floor and ceilings to prevent sound escaping and causing nuisance). The lighting (along with sound) will usually be controlled by means of a central console, possibly computer controlled.

The designer's role in construction

In some cases, the interior designer will also construct the installations. They may have to work with a wide range of materials – plywood, MDF, plastic (vacuum-formed), glass reinforced plastic, foams and 'found' objects – and fabricate both two and three-dimensional constructions. Alternatively, the interior designer will provide the specifications for others to produce the constructions. In these cases, the designer may have to supervise the fixing and fitting and make on-the-spot decisions about necessary changes.

Dealing with conflicting requirements

The designer of any nightclub will be faced with conflicting requirements. Here are some examples:

- the club may need to be dark, but it is essential that people don't trip over and injure themselves;
- the club may become very smoky and sweaty during the night, but needs to feel fresh at the start of the evening;
- constructions and decorations that add to the atmosphere must not prevent cleaning;
- users may want access to both noisy, open dance floors *and* quieter, more secluded areas in the same club;
- owners of clubs may want 'quick change' structures and decorations so that they can appeal to different users on different evenings. These must therefore not be too heavy and they must be portable, but a compromise must be struck between these requirements and the stability and strength required for safety.

To ensure that a club stays looking attractive requires dealing with the matter of wear and tear. There are two extremes of approach – use a design that takes a long time to show wear or use a design suited to the rapid replacement of worn items.

Research activity

1 Find out about a local nightclub and answer the following questions.

- What kinds of people are its clients?
- What is the entry fee?
- What is the dress code?
- What are the themes?
- How does the club advertize?

2 Draw a rough map of where the club is and mark where the clients are likely to come from, how they will get there and then get home again.

The shop

The design of a shop interior (and image in general) is mainly about designing an environment that will successfully encourage people to buy the goods – and to return to buy more. The best designs invite people into the shop, providing an atmosphere where they feel relaxed, can choose which goods to buy and are encouraged to return and make further purchases. The design of Top Shop / Top Man (part of the Burton Group and a national retail chain) shown here meets these requirements in the following ways.

Style and image

- The designer has created an environment that is instantly recognizable across the country and which can be changed easily as required. The feel of the interior fits with the market level of the goods being sold and the likely customer group. It is neither overly plush nor too downmarket.
- The image is consistent across the country but some Top Shop and Top Man stores have "shops-within-shops" in them. For example, a Levi's Jeans area (a franchise arrangement) or, in the main London shop, a second-hand clothes market area.

Display of goods

- The display stands are modular MDF or pine wood with a satin finish. Stands are of varying heights and garments are folded in piles on the table structures. Hanging racks are metal and simple in shape and construction. Free-standing panels also display accessories and point-of-sale visuals.

Flow of customers

- The movement of the customers through the store is important in this sort of busy chainstore interior. If customers feel restricted, they get frustrated. On the other hand, wide-open spaces can be equally inhibiting for shoppers.
- There is room to move around, which makes it easy to mix and match garments from different rails, yet the general feel is of being surrounded by garments and visual images.

Sound and light

- The music is up to the minute – not too loud, but fairly lively. Lighting is around daylight level. The atmosphere is quite relaxed – which affects both shoppers and staff.

Payment and security

- Payment counters are long and so allow for folding and packing of garments as well as encouraging a one-directional flow of paying customers.
- Security is critical to the design if garments are freely displayed and there are lots of 'dead' spots. This is overcome by the use of overhead cameras, electronic security tags on garments and tag-sensitive barriers at the exits. The tighter spaces also preclude groups gathering within the shop.

Maintenance and safety

- By using sealed wood for the floor and smooth-surfaced fittings, the designer has produced an environment that is both safe and easy to maintain.

R

Research activity

1. Visit a local fashion goods chainstore.
2. Sketch the layout of the stands, units and spaces.
3. Indicate on your sketch where and how different goods are displayed.
4. Show how the flow to and from the payment counter works.
5. Notice how the security system works.
6. Notice the general style and feel of the environment.
7. Make some notes on the market level of goods sold, customer age range and how the design of the total environment meets, or fails to meet, the targeted customers' needs.

Fantasy environment

Alien War is a highly commercial venture. It is a fantasy environment based on the *Alien* trilogy of films from Twentieth Century Fox. The Alien War experience opened in October 1993 after three years of planning.

Alien War is situated within the Trocadero complex in central London, between Piccadilly and Leicester Square underground stations.

The designer of the environment for Alien War is a theatre designer who worked from the sets and costumes for the *Alien* films. Many of the installations are replicas of props that appear in the films and the sections of the total environment are based on the environments in the films. On the whole, therefore, it is futuristic but with a dull, dark, dank feel to it.

This is designing that has to take in all possible aspects of costume, set, props, lighting and sound in order to create the required atmosphere. The front-of-house 'sell' to tourists is perhaps the most well-known aspect of the total design – as the Marines move in on passers-by and footage of images and sound (mainly screams!) from the interior are blasted onto the street.

However, the ticket sales, merchandising and meeting area below ground are designed to feel 'secure', even 'reassuring'. Groups of up to 12 visitors are met by a Marine who then acts as their guide throughout the 20-minute experience. The Marine costumes stand out as 'noticeable' in the street or meeting area and also serve to distinguish them from the visitors while in the war zone environment.

Pause for thought

How are groups controlled:

- in a classroom
- in school corridors
- in small spaces – such as toilet blocks?

Questions

1. Have you seen any of the *Alien* films or anything similar?
2. What do you remember about the environments shown in them?
3. What do you remember about the sound or music in them?
4. How did any of the above affect how you felt while watching the film(s)?

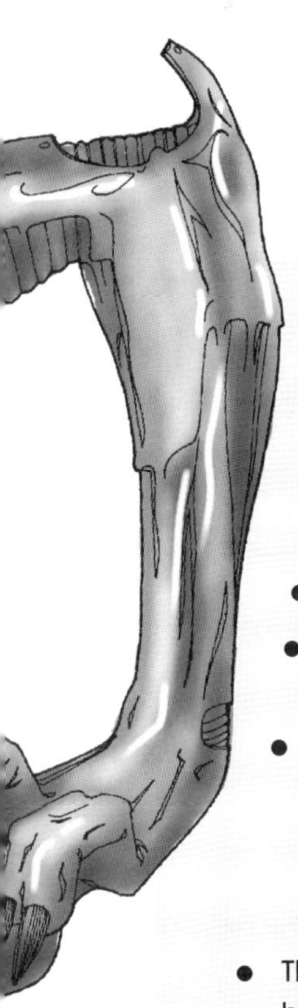

The following interior design aspects are crucial to the experience:

- False walls, false pipework, sliding doors, low-relief panelling, low lighting plus sound effects create the atmosphere.
- False pipework is used to provide some services.
- Metal flooring and stairs with non-slip surfaces and little bumps enhance the military feel.
- Some technical effects are very simple but give a futuristic impression. The light buttons to 'open' doors do nothing other than come on and off; the door is on runners and worked by the Marine, who simply pushes it!
- The finish on the surfaces and artefacts is very basic – giving an impression of things is all that is required, so rough painting with dark colours is sufficient.
- The role of the Marine is crucial. The Marine's job is to create controlled panic and provide fear and excitement without injury. The use of planted actors who scream and 'don't make it' adds to the experience.
- The *Alien* costumes are made mainly from Lycra with patched details. This makes them harder wearing and more comfortable as the wearer is constantly moving and liable to sweat in this very enclosed atmosphere. The heads are constructed from foam.
- The lift for the last part of the experience is controlled by hydraulics.

Would you trust her to get you out?

- Red strobe lighting creates an added eerie effect when the Alien appears.
- Wear and tear is considerable as the Marine orders people to rush here and there, to keep pressed against walls and so on, so many of the features are designed to be mass-produced and easily replaced.

Do as you're told and you might just survive

Making a magazine

The magazine market in Britain is vast – a recent survey found that no fewer than 10 152 are regularly published in the UK, with new magazines appearing almost daily. The products included in this figure vary enormously, from low-budget publications for specialist markets to glossy women's magazines like *Elle* and *Vogue*. Yet, whether well-known or unknown, expensive or cheap, every magazine has to be designed.

In this case study, we go behind the scenes at *Designing*, a magazine about design and technology for secondary school teachers and students, to find out how it is designed, produced and printed.

What makes a magazine?

Look at a range of magazines and you will find elements that are common to all of them.

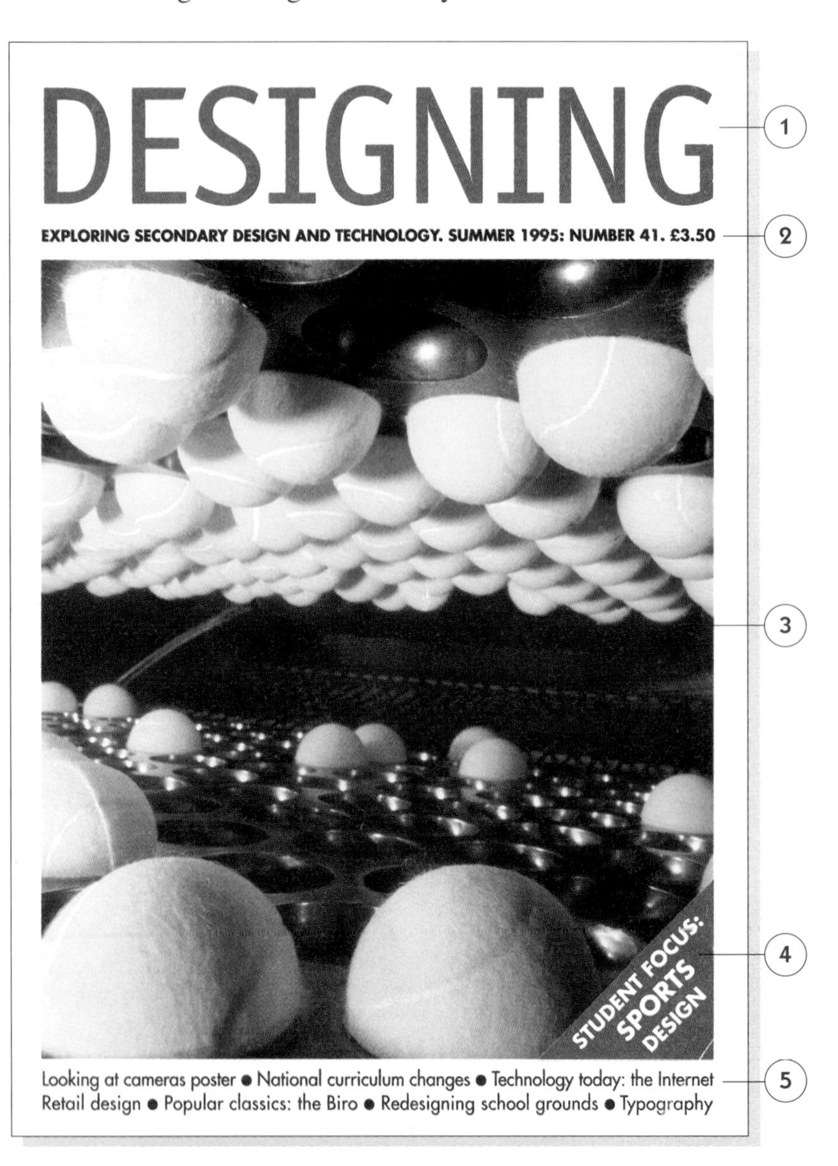

1. The magazine's title is the most prominent thing on the front cover, so readers recognize it quickly. This is called the masthead. In this case it is also the logo, which is used on letters and leaflets to give the magazine a strong identity. The designer chooses a colour for the masthead that complements the front cover image.
2. This is called the strapline. It sums up the publication's aims, and gives the issue number, publication date and price.
3. The image on the front cover plays an important part in attracting the reader's attention and must be of a good quality.
4. A flash across the corner of the image highlights one of the topics covered in this issue.
5. Coverlines give a taste of what is in store inside the magazine. They also help readers who are looking through back issues for a particular article.

6 The article's title is upper case (capital letters) to make it stand out on the page.

7 Underneath the title is an intro, which provides a brief explanation of the article.

8 Crossheadings are used to divide the text up into manageable chunks.

9 The basic text for the article is called body text. Although the print size of headings may change, body text print usually remains the same throughout a magazine. Here it is in a typeface called Futura.

10 Captions provide information to help readers understand the pictures.

11 Some of the pictures on the page have been borrowed from a museum and a credit is included.

12 A footer at the bottom of the page includes a page number, the logo and publication date. These are to help the reader identify and move around the magazine.

MATCH POINTS

Looking at the history of equipment and clothing used in one particular sport can show how designs have been influenced by developments in materials and technology. Here we take a closer look at tennis

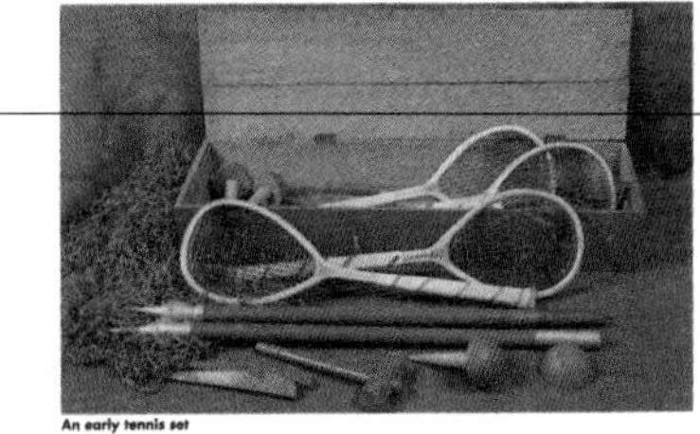

An early tennis set

TENNIS RACKETS

When lawn tennis first became popular in the 1870s, players used rackets with pear-shaped, often asymmetrical heads made from one piece of wood steam bent to shape. The wooden handles were fluted, grooved or combed to provide good grip, and the natural gut strings were coarse and loosely strung – some rackets were even designed with a parchment centre instead of strings. These rackets were made by craftspeople working in small workshops with basic tools like chisels, awls, tenon-saws and planes – it wasn't until after the First World War that a number of larger companies emerged and mass-production began.

By the 1920s the familiar shape of today's racket was already established and rackets became stronger in order to withstand harder hitting. Manufacturers began streamlining shapes to reduce wind resistance, slimming down shafts and making edges rounder. Laminated wooden frames replaced the one-piece frames of the past – some designers even began to experiment with aluminium frames, which failed because their piano-wire stringing wore out balls too quickly. In the 1930s leather grips were introduced to make the racket easier to hold.

Little changed for the next 40 years. Wooden rackets like the Dunlop Maxply (right) – made of ashwood cut into long strips and steamed, glued and pressed together – reigned supreme, although improved moulded aluminium rackets also came on the market in the 1970s. But it was when tennis racket manufacturers, inspired by aerospace technology, began experimenting with compression moulding graphite and glass fibres, that today's rackets began to take shape.

Today, players can choose from rackets made of combinations of materials such as carbon graphite, fibreglass, boron, titanium, Kevlar and ceramics – no top-class players use wooden rackets. The new range of materials, combined with the mathematical accuracy of computer-aided design, have resulted in rackets which are 30 times stronger than their wooden predecessors, up to 30% more powerful, yet 20% lighter.

HOW DOES A TENNIS RACKET WORK?

When a ball hits a tennis racket's strings they deflect, absorbing some of the ball's energy. They then spring back elastically, transmitting almost all the energy back to the ball and causing it to bounce off the racket. In the same way, if a racket's frame is flexible, it absorbs some of the ball's energy by bending, but this energy (and power) is lost, not transmitted back to the ball. Therefore racket frames are designed to be as stiff as possible. Lightness is also important, as players can swing light rackets faster, increasing the power with which the racket head hits the ball.

TENNIS BALLS

Lawn tennis is descended from a game called real tennis, which is played on stone floors with balls traditionally made of sheepskin and filled with sawdust, sand or wool. However, they did not bounce on grass, and as early as 1875 the rules of lawn tennis stated that balls should be hollow, made of rubber, and either plain or uncovered. In the 1920s the cloth cover, which had been sewn at the seams in the past, was cemented.

Although manufacturing and testing techniques have become much more sophisticated, tennis ball technology has changed little over the years. The rubber core of the ball is made in two halves, which are extruded and moulded together. The rubber is vulcanised – treated with sulphur to make it stronger and more elastic. A cloth cover, which is made of a mixture of wool and man-made fibres, is then moulded around the ball, and the seams are fused together. The balls are steamed to fluff up the cloth, and the manufacturers' transfers are applied after trimming and inspection.

Manufacturers like Dunlop Slazenger are constantly carrying out research to improve balls. Samples are carefully tested for wear, flight, deformation and precise uniformity of bounce. Balls for match play are usually pressurised to ensure an even bounce – the air inside the ball is at a higher pressure than outside. However, the air inside pressurised balls escapes over time, leaving them flat and soft. Temperature change and play affect the shape and pressure of the ball – this is why tennis balls at major championships are kept refrigerated before use and are changed regularly.

HOW DOES A TENNIS BALL BOUNCE?

When a tennis ball lands on the ground it comes to a sudden stop, and the rubber squashes up and stores the energy of the ball's movement. As the rubber springs back into shape it releases the energy and bounces the ball up again.

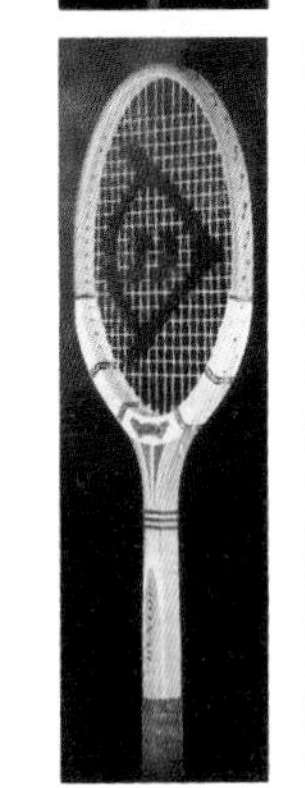

(Top) A racket of today, the Dunlop Revelation
(Above) The wooden Dunlop Maxply Fort – the most successful racket in post-war years
(Below left) 'The Demon' racket, popular at the turn of the century
(Below centre) Early racket-maker's workshop
(Below right) Testing the quality of tennis balls

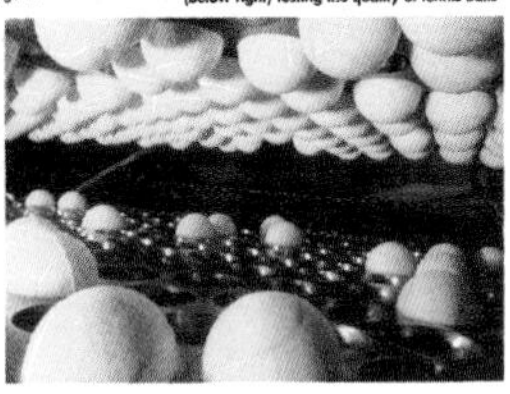

ALL HISTORICAL PICTURES COURTESY OF WIMBLEDON LAWN TENNIS MUSEUM

DESIGNING Summer 1995

Questions

Draw four columns on a sheet of blank paper and sketch different ways you could organize the text and pictures for the inside page. Could the pictures go at the top of the page? Does the title have to be at the top of the page?

Compare the pages from *Designing* with your school magazine. What do they have in common? Could your magazine be improved by adding some of the elements shown here?

Research activity

Designing has a style sheet, which shows examples of the masthead, strapline, coverlines, headings, intros, body text, bullet points, footers, captions and credits. This acts as a set of guidelines that the designer can follow to make sure the magazine looks consistent from issue to issue. Make a style sheet for a magazine by cutting out examples of different headings and text, sticking them on to a piece of paper and labelling them clearly.

Toni Anderson, a graphic designer, is the magazine's Art Editor. Here she talks about what this work involves.

More than meets the eye

'I work as a freelance graphic designer, which means that I'm self-employed and enjoy the freedom of working on a range of publications. I work closely with writers and editors, communicating by telephone, fax and the occasional face-to-face meeting. *Designing* is one of three magazines I design regularly from home.

My work begins when the magazine's Editor has prepared the contents for an issue. We hold a meeting to discuss the different articles and together produce a flatplan. This shows what will appear on each page, which articles will be in colour and where advertisements will go. I refer to this all the time when designing, to check progress and make sure that I'm putting the articles in the right order.

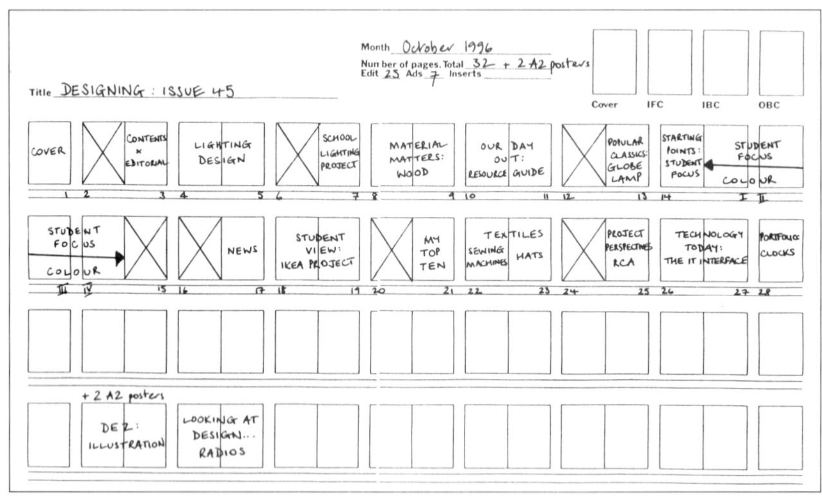

Toni works with the Editor to produce a flatplan showing what will appear on each page

Once the articles have been written and checked by the Editor, she sends them to me on disk, ready for design. The magazines are written and designed from start to finish on screen – the Editor writes and edits articles in Word (a word processing package) and I then load them into the Quark Xpress desktop publishing package. Before I start designing an article, I print it out and read it through so that I can make sure the words complement the layout and pictures I use.

Sometimes I need to find pictures for articles. This can involve ringing up companies for pictures of products, contacting picture libraries, which stock different images, or commissioning a photographer for a day and going along to art direct. I have to explain to the photographer how I want to use a particular shot, which angle I want the picture taken from, and I suggest possible backgrounds and lighting. For some articles I decide an illustration would work better than photographs and I commission an artist to produce an illustration. This all has to be done within constraints of time and budget.

Once I have the pictures and words to hand, I usually produce a rough sketch on paper of how I think the page could look before beginning to work on screen. Although lots of things about a magazine are fixed – the typeface, number of words, page size and so on – it's the designer's individual interpretation of them that matters. Working on *Designing* is varied and interesting – each page of each issue is different and I'm free to experiment with colours and unusual layouts. My computer has a large (21 inch) monitor, so I can view pages on a large scale.

Once I have designed the article and saved it on my hard disk, I copy it onto a floppy disk and send this back to the Editor, who adds captions, credits and cuts or adds lines to make the words fit the page. Then it comes back to me to make any final adjustments before it goes off for origination. I specify the sizes of pictures and the colours I want different sections and text to be (this is called colour mark-up), before sending my layouts, the pictures and any illustrations to the origination house (see page 68). Getting a batch of colour proofs (called Chromalins) back is always exciting – it's good to see how your design's worked out and to give everything a final check before it goes tothe printer.

Magazine design involves working on your own and as part of a team – you have to communicate well with editors, photographers and illustrators, and have a flexible approach to your work. You also need to be very organized – being an art editor often involves handling lots of pieces of paper, pictures and floppy disks. At the end of the day, I enjoy creating something and then seeing the final printed version.'

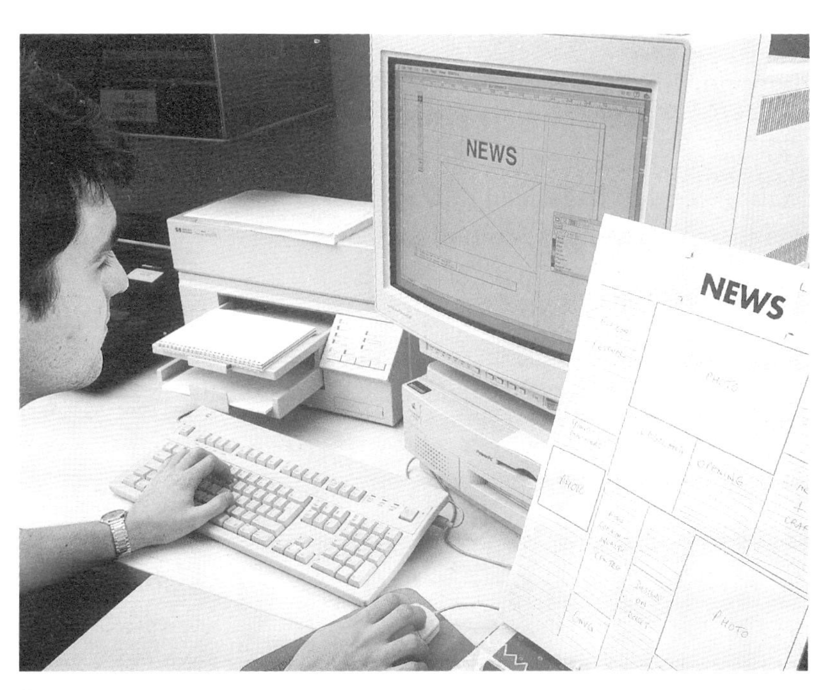

Before working on screen, a designer will produce a rough page-plan on paper

Questions

Draw a flow chart to show the different stages involved in designing a magazine.

Research activity

Magazine art editors are graphic designers. Find out what other types of work graphic designers do and write a report summarizing your findings.

Preparing to print

Designing is printed in colour and the pictures, text and disks that the editorial team have prepared have to be sent to an origination house before they are ready to go to the printing press.

Colour pictures and text printed in books and magazines are made up of just four colours of ink:

- yellow;
- magenta (a shade of red);
- cyan (a shade of blue);
- black.

By printing a combination of tiny dots in these four primary printing colours, almost any colour can be created. But first, the pictures need to be broken down, or separated, into their four different colour components. This is done at the origination house.

The images to be included in *Designing* are taped to the drum of an electronic scanner. The drum rotates at high speed and a beam of white light scans the illustrations, prints or transparencies and makes a pinpoint-by-pinpoint analysis of each picture.

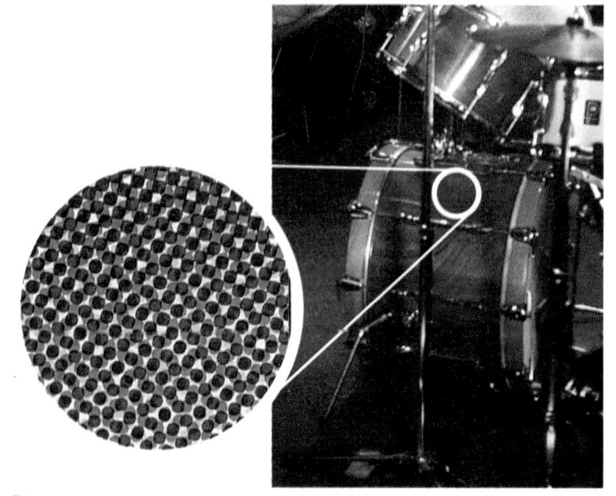

A close-up reveals the coloured dots

Signals are sent, via colour filters, to a computer and stored as digital information. This is then brought together with all the text and any graphics that the designer produced on disk, and is converted into light signals and exposed by a laser onto film. Four separate pieces of film are made, one for each colour.

To make sure that the film is accurate, colour proofs are made. For *Designing*, the origination house makes colour pre-press proofs by exposing each separate film onto a sheet of acetate with a photosensitized coating. The four acetate sheets (one for each colour) are superimposed and laminated and sent to Tony and the magazine's Editor to check. Tony makes sure that the pictures are the right size, the right colour and in the right position, and checks for blemishes, scratches and fuzziness (caused by the different colour films not fitting together properly). Once everybody is satisfied with the proofs, the film is sent to the printer.

The printing process

In order to print magazines in full colour, one printing plate is made for each of the four colours to be printed. Most printing machines print 4, 8 or 16 pages at a time, which are then folded into sections. *Designing* is printed in blocks of 8 pages.

In a process called stripping, 8 pieces of film are taped to a large sheet of clear acetate in the correct arrangement for folding. This process is repeated for all the four colours (i.e., 8 pages of *Designing* are produced by 4 x 8 pieces of film). The pieces of film are arranged on the acetate in perfect register to each other using pins that fit into holes punched in the film.

A large printing press at work

The acetate and film are laid on top of thin sheets of light-sensitive coated aluminium. These sheets are the printing plates, and they too are hole-punched to keep the film in register. The plates are exposed to a bright light which shines through the film and hardens the film's image onto the plate. When developing chemicals are then poured onto the plate, the areas that were not exposed to the light are dissolved away, leaving the hardened areas. The images of each page appear on the plate, and hold the ink during printing like the raised part of a rubber stamp.

The images are printed onto the paper via a series of rollers and cylinders. Each plate is fixed onto a cylinder with a trough above it and either yellow, magenta, cyan or black ink is poured into the trough. The ink is rolled onto the plate and the image is transferred from the plate onto a rubber blanket wrapped around a second cylinder, which in turn rolls the image onto the paper. Paper is loaded into one end of the printing press and is fed sheet by sheet through the machine (in newspaper production, one continuous roll of paper passes through the printing press). This process is repeated for each colour in turn, making sure that the colours are printed in register on top of each other. The first pages off the press are carefully checked to make sure the colours are right and the inks are adjusted if necessary. Large printing presses can produce thousands of pages in an hour.

The printed sheets are sent to a folding machine, which folds them into sections, and then to binder machines, which saddle-stitches (staples) each magazine down the spine and trims the pages to the right size. Completed copies are packaged up ready to be posted to schools, transported to shops or sent to a warehouse for storage.

Separated colour films and a proof of the fully coloured image

R

Research activity

How do yellow, cyan, magenta and black combine to produce any colour in the four-colour printing process? Find out by experimenting with paints and present the results as a chart.

Newsagents today sell hundreds of magazines for different age groups and interests. Each of these magazines has been carefully designed to meet its target audience's needs and preferences, and its publisher's budget. Some are printed in just two colours on low-grade paper, others in full colour on heavy, glossy paper. Some have few photographs and illustrations, others feature high-quality visual material on every page.

Just by looking at the magazines on this page, you can tell a lot about their audiences and aims. List the magazines in order of how expensive you think they are to produce (take into account paper quality, use of colour, number of pictures and size). Do you think the production cost of magazines relates to the people who buy them and their purpose?

a ***The Big Issue***
Cover price: 70p
(40p goes to the vendor);
number of pages: 48;
focus: housing and social issues, the arts

b ***Dialogue***
Cover price: free to Abbey National customers;
number of pages: 42;
focus: the home, financial products

c ***Take A Break***
Cover price: 52p;
number of pages: 64;
focus: competitions, human interest, family

d ***Private Eye***
Cover price: £1;
number of pages: 36;
focus: topical and political satire

e ***Micro Computer Mart***
Cover price: 60p;
number of pages: 184;
focus: computer advertisements

f ***The Beano***
Cover price: 38p;
number of pages: 24;
focus: cartoon stories

g ***Puzzler***
Cover price: 80p;
number of pages: 44;
focus: puzzles, including competitions

Questions

Write answers to the following.

- Who do you think is the target audience for each magazine? Can you tell by the cover designs?
- Why are some magazines glossier than others?
- What do you think affects the price of the magazine? Does advertising revenue play a part?
- How well do you think the front cover images work? *The People's Friend* and *Sega Magazine* both feature illustrations – how do they differ? Why do you think *Puzzler* has a photograph of a woman on its cover?
- Which masthead do you think is most successful? How well do the coverlines work?
- Why do so many computer magazines include free offers on their covers?
- Imagine the magazines on the shop shelf. Which do you think would catch your eye? Why?

(j) ***The People's Friend***
Cover price: 42p;
number of pages: 64;
focus: stories, British life

(h) ***Sega Magazine***
Cover price: £2.45;
number of pages: 100;
focus: computer games

(i) ***Vogue***
Cover price: £2.70;
number of pages: 354;
focus: fashion, style

(k) ***Just Seventeen***
Cover price: 90p;
number of pages: 64;
focus: teen interest, pop

Pop-up cards

People have been celebrating special occasions by sending pop-up cards since Victorian times. Greetings cards made in the last century were very ornate and delicate and were often kept as ornaments long after the occasion they marked had passed. Hours of painstaking work went into making them. Without the benefits of today's technology, they had to be cut and assembled completely by hand.

Although designing and making pop-up cards is a much more efficient business these days, it still demands detailed technical knowledge and complicated production processes. As a result, pop-up cards are quite expensive. People therefore tend to buy them less often than 'flat' cards, and there are only a few specialist card publishers who invest time and money in making them.

A cause for celebration?

The process of designing a pop-up card begins with the decision to publish a card for a particular occasion. Look around any card shop and you will see the enormous diversity of products on offer – cards to commemorate events such as birthdays and anniversaries; cards for special occasions, such as Valentine's Day; cards to wish people luck, congratulate them, apologize.... The list is almost endless. Within these categories there's a wide range of treatments of the subject matter – from humorous and cute to nostalgic and fine art.

Pause for thought

When did you last send or receive a card? What was it like?

Cards for every occasion

The three-dimensional challenge

Unlike designing flat cards, which simply involves an artist producing an image, designing three-dimensional cards means taking into account the problems of representing shapes in different planes at varying angles to each other. In order to do this, card publishing companies enlist the help of both an artist and a paper engineer.

Once the company has chosen the subject matter for the card – for example, a heart, a wedding cake or an animal – the paper engineer considers how the image can be represented in three dimensions. It is important to take into account the graphic style of the artist who is going to paint or draw the image, as this can influence the complexity of the shapes that need to be cut.

After discussing possible ideas and forms, the artist produces a sketch of the main parts of the image, which the paper engineer then converts into a working mock-up of the three-dimensional card. The dimensions and shapes of the pop-up pieces are checked to ensure they fit neatly and the card opens and closes smoothly.

From this mock-up, the different elements of the card are drawn in outline on tracing paper or clear acetate. This forms the basic pattern or template for the card and is called the cutter guide. Following the outlines on the cutter guide and looking closely at the mock-up, the artist produces the final artwork ready to go to the printer. At this point, it is essential that the paper engineer specifies the correct weight, strength and grain direction for the paper or board – the material chosen must be rigid, hold a crease well and not tear easily.

Once the image has been printed, it is cut out, perforated, and creased or scored by a die-cutting machine. The cut out pieces are then sent to a factory for assembly – a slow and expensive process that involves hand folding and gluing. Increasingly, companies are sending the cards for assembly in developing countries in the Far East and South America, where labour is cheaper than in Europe. Fully assembled, the cards are packed and transported to a warehouse, where they are stored until they reach the shop shelf.

Questions

On what kinds of occasions would you send someone a pop-up card?

When wouldn't it be appropriate and why?

Look at the cut out shapes shown in the picture. If you were printing them on a sheet of paper or board, how would you position them to avoid waste? (Remember to bear in mind the grain of the paper.)

Present your ideas as scale drawings.

Research activity

Find out about recycling paper and board. How is it done? How energy efficient is it in comparison to making new paper? Produce a flow chart showing the processes involved, marking points at which energy is saved.

When recycled paper is used to make greetings cards, what would it have been used for before? And what could it be recycled for again?

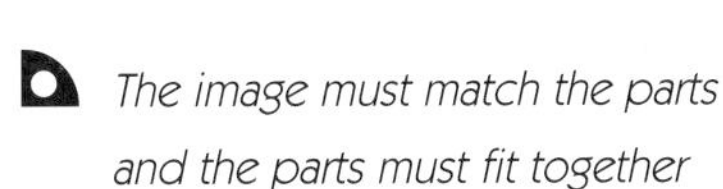

The image must match the parts and the parts must fit together

Polaroid – the camera which developed in ten months!

At the end of 1993, multinational manufacturer Polaroid asked the British Design Council to recommend design groups that could help them redesign their instant camera. The product was losing market share and reaching the final quarter of its sales life. Polaroid needed to:

- extend its sales life;
- continue to supply dealers.

Old camera, designed by William Draffus Associates in the early 1980s

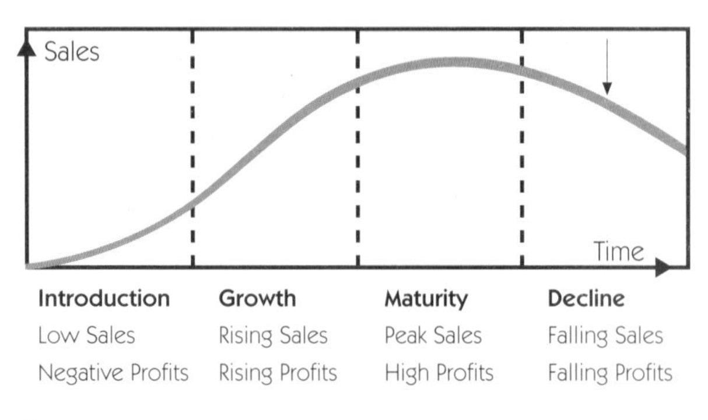

The sales graph indicating that redevelopment is needed

The design needed to revitalize the market area, raise the product's image and excite the market. Pankhurst Design and Development Limited (PDD) were chosen by Polaroid to develop the new camera.

The main focus of the design was to:

- restyle the main casing of the camera;
- eliminate several components;
- address problems with fit and assembly.

The timescale was formidable – full-scale production in ten months in order to capture the Christmas sales market of 1994. The product relaunch graph shows how the timing of the redevelopment is crucial if the profit of the product is to be extended.

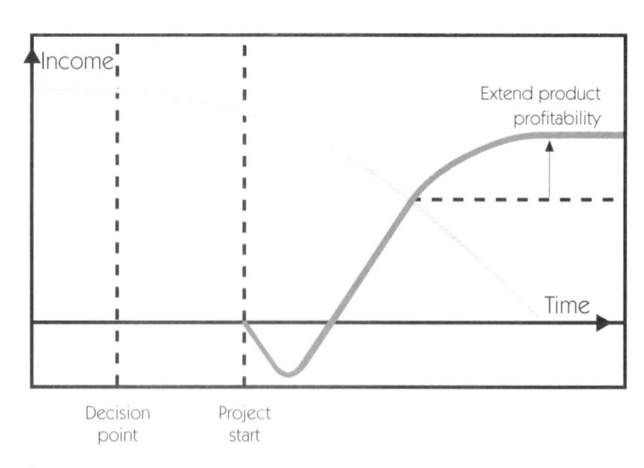

Product relaunch graph showing extended life of product

Pause for thought

Why do the sales of a product eventually decline?

Stereo lithography: an important modelling tool

Part of the success of this venture depended on stereo lithography. This process is based on the use of a computer image that has been cut into many horizontal slices 0.125-0.75 mm thick. The information about each slice is transmitted to a laser. The laser draws the first slice on the surface of resin. Once the laser hits the polymer fluid, it sets and becomes a solid. This layer is supported on a platform. When the first layer is complete, the platform moves down to enable another layer of fluid to cover the top of the solidified skin and the process is continued. The layers build one on top of another and so the three-dimensional computer image literally 'grows' in the vat of resin. The process is summarized in the diagram opposite. The stereo lithography prototype for part of the Polaroid camera case shows how detailed such models can be.

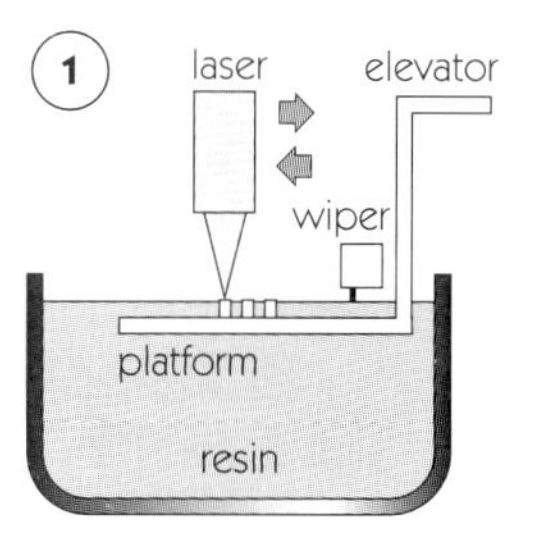

Start: elevator platform at surface. Laser draws first support layer on platform

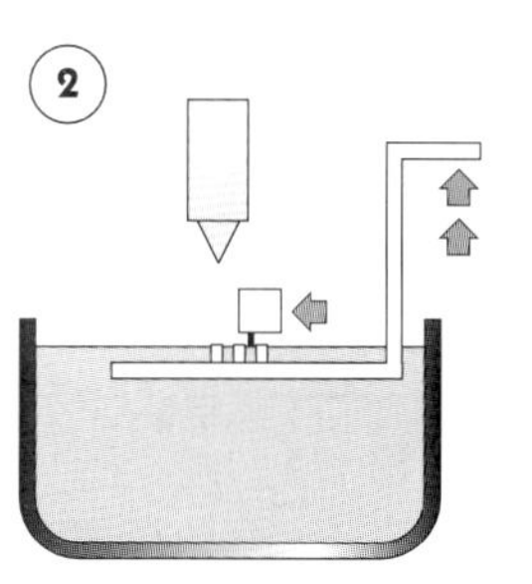

Elevator positions part one layer for wiper. Wiper traverses part to create an even layer

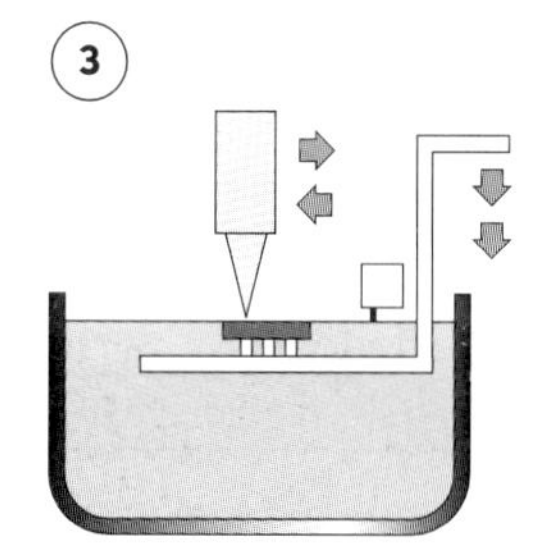

Elevator dips part in resin, positions it one layer from surface and laser draws next section

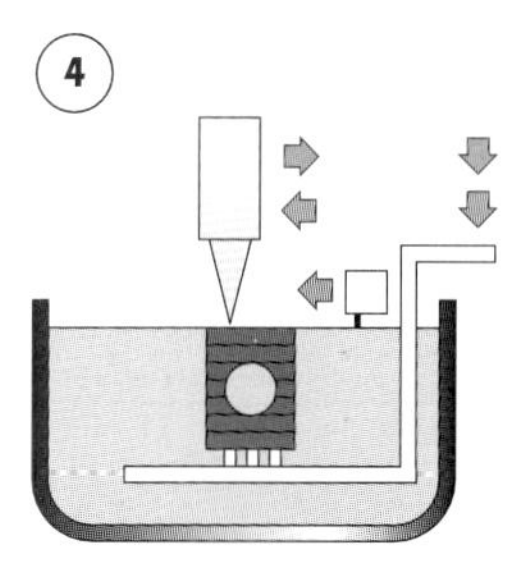

Process continues until all sections are produced

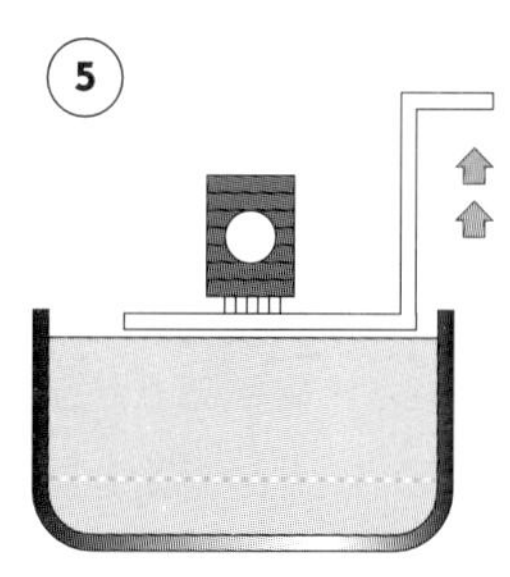

End: completed part is withdrawn from resin vat

Pause for thought

Can you see what would happen if the project start is delayed?

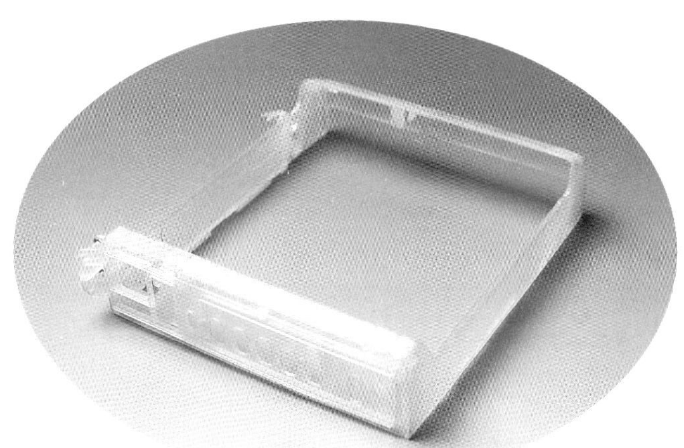

This prototype for part of the Polaroid camera case was made using stereo lithography. Can you imagine trying to make this by hand or by using a milling machine?

The project time schedule plus comments is shown as a Gantt chart in the panel below. Notice one very important feature – lots of different activities are happening at the same time. This is sometimes called parallel processing or concurrent engineering.

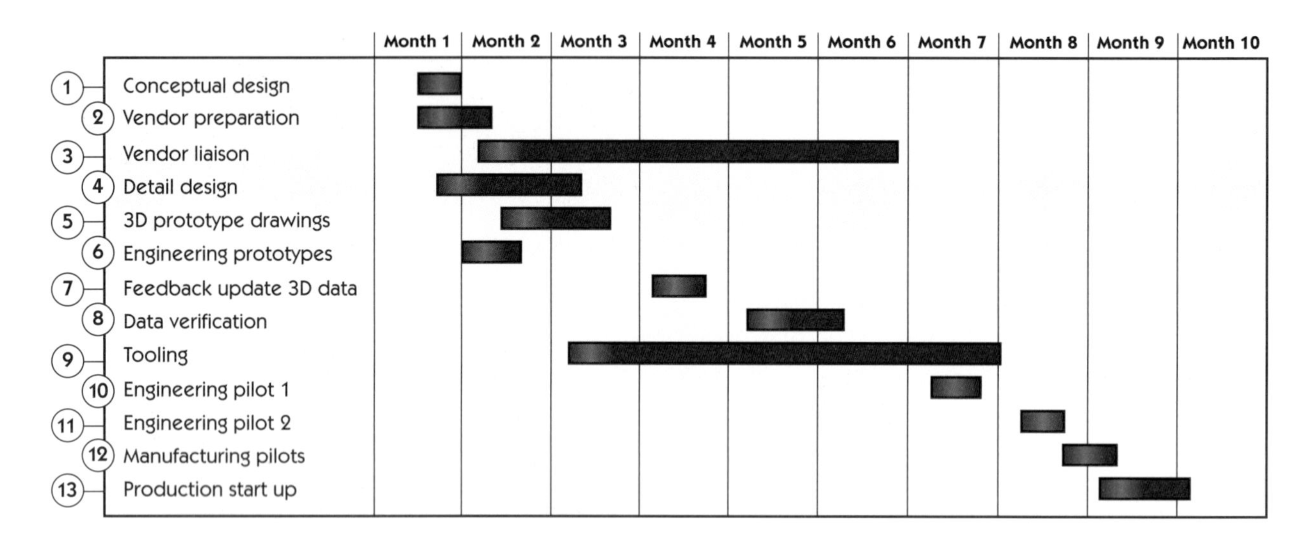

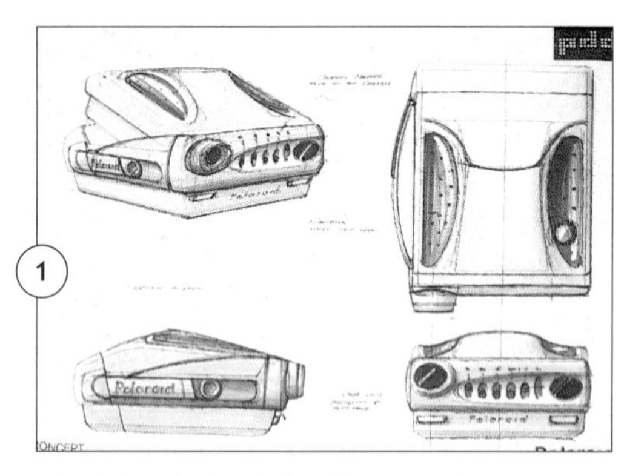
Initial ideas by hand sketching (month 1)

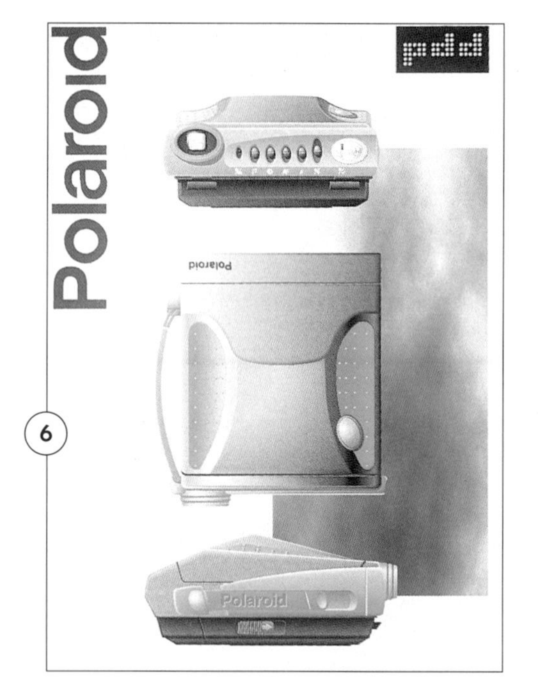

Computer generated images and a hand-held model convince Polaroid to give the go ahead for the next stage (month 2)

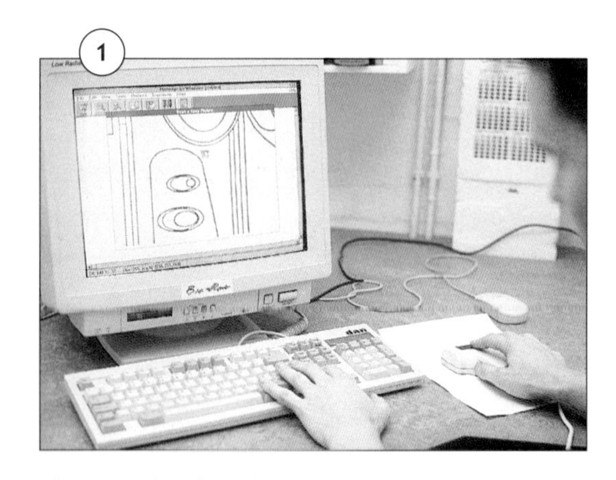
These are developed using CAD software (month 1)

(3) USA market research results in reappraisal and redesign (month 2)

(4) 2D and 3D information for internal and external structure developed using computer software (month 2)

(8) Major design review by involving design team, programme manager, marketing staff and production staff (month 5)

(9) Tool makers make preliminary moulding (month 3)

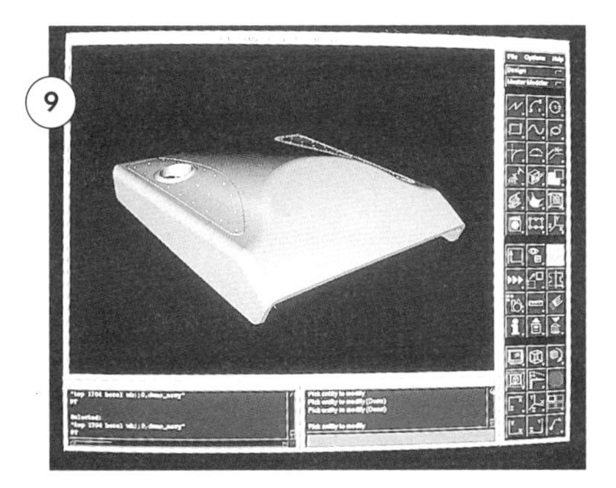

Stereolithography prototypes produced from computer data (month 4)

(9) Tooling developed to high tolerances and surface textures (months 6&7)

(10/11) Engineering pilots ensure that the mouldings will fit together correctly (months 7&8)

Pause for thought

How long would the project take if all the parts were done in sequence one after the other?

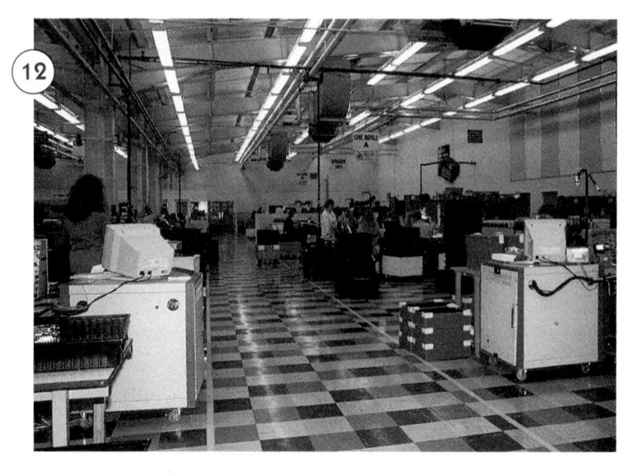

Manufacturing pilot with workers on the assembly line (months 8&9)

(13) Approval for mass production (month 9)

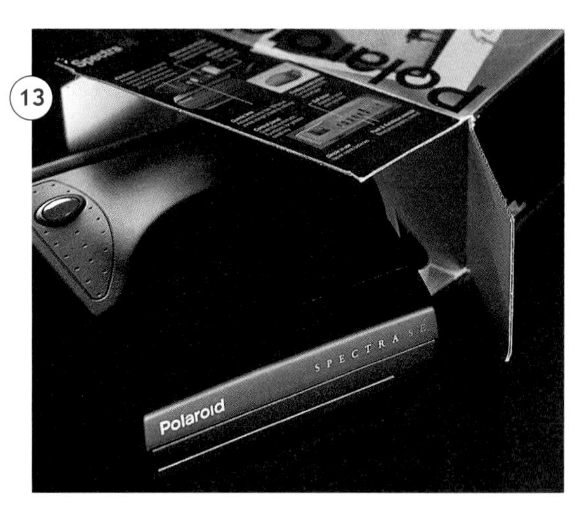

Finished product in the shops before Christmas! (month 10)

What does the future hold?

It is likely that the use of computers to develop accurate prototypes rapidly through detailed design information (as in the Polaroid case study) will become more possible as the cost of the required facilities falls. This will enable a wider range of designers to use these facilities in more and more innovative ways. An additional feature that will promote international concurrent engineering is the Internet, through which designers, production engineers and marketing staff can keep in touch, even though they may be in different countries across the world.

Identifying needs and likes

You can revise strategies for identifying needs and likes from key stage 3 by thinking about these people who visited a busy shopping centre on Saturday morning.

Georgie 3-year-old boy shopping with his Mum, Jo.

Maisie 13-year-old girl looking at the bus timetable.

Jo 28-year-old pregnant woman, Georgie's Mum.

Jack 39-year-old man, looking at guide book.

Dot 72-year-old woman in wheelchair looking for the Age Concern drop-in centre.

Thinking about what people might need

The people visiting the shopping centre will have different needs and likes. You can try thinking about these by using the PIES approach. PIES stands for **p**hysical, **i**ntellectual, **e**motional and **s**ocial. Each of these words describes a type of need that can be met by products that have been designed and made.

Observing people

You can find out a lot about people's needs and likes by watching them. It is important to record your observations in a way that doesn't affect what the people are doing. The illustration shows several different recording methods. Can you explain which ones are suitable for use in a shopping centre?

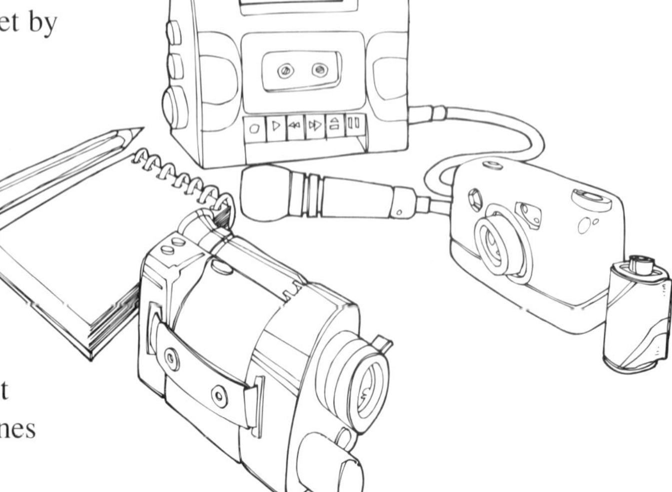

Asking questions

You can find out about people's preferences by talking to them and asking questions. This is sometimes called **interviewing**. It is different from using a questionnaire as you will only interview a few people. It is important to ask the right sorts of questions. To find out what each of these people shown want from their shopping centre you would probably need to ask them different questions.

Using books and magazines

Sometimes you need to find out something by looking things up in books and magazines. Some magazines might tell you about the preferences of the people using the shopping centre. Where would you find these magazines? Some books would tell you about the rules and regulations governing shopping centres. Where would you find these books?

Image boards

You can make a collection of pictures of things that a person or group of people might like, places they might go, activities they might do. This is called an image board. An image board for Georgie will look very different from one for Maisie. Making image boards will help you understand what different people might like. It may also help you understand the style of products that would appeal to different people. For example, Jo and Dot may both read magazines but they will almost certainly be very different.

Questions

Here is the beginning of an image board for Jo.

1. What does it tell you about her?
2. What other images could be added to give a fuller picture?

Who is Jo?

Using questionnaires

A questionnaire is a carefully designed set of questions. It is often used by businesses to find out what different groups of people like or would buy. A questionnaire will usually try to get information about the sort of person who is answering it — their occupation, how much they earn, and so on. This information enables businesses to provide goods and services that people want at a price they are prepared to pay. It also shows where and when these products could be sold and how best they might be advertized.

Designing your own questionnaire

You need to be clear on what you are trying to find out. Target your questions to obtain the information you want. Avoid leading questions that suggest the answer. Avoid questions that don't discriminate, such as 'Do you like sunny days?'. Everyone always answers yes!

Sometimes you will use the questionnaire in face-to-face questioning when you record people's answers. At other times people will fill it in on their own and return it to you. In this second case it is particularly important that the meanings of the questions are clear as you won't be there to explain these.

Advice on writing questionnaire questions is given in the panel on the right.

Questions

Notice how newspapers and magazines use so-called questionnaires to attract the readers' interest rather than provide useful information.
What sort of information do these questionnaires reveal to the readers?

Questionnaire question guide

- Use closed questions. These require a yes or no answer or give people a choice of answers.
- Make it easy to fill in the answers. Use tick boxes where possible.
- Each question should be short and simple.
- Use words people will understand.
- Write questions which only have one meaning.
- Each question should ask only one thing at a time.
- A scaled choice of answers is a good way to find out people's attitudes.

What sample size should I use?

It is important to present your questionnaire to as many people as possible. This will give you a large number of responses from which you can draw reasonable conclusions.

A hundred responses would be an ideal number, but this would be a huge task for one researcher. If the research is shared amongst a group of people the task becomes manageable both in terms of collecting responses and collating data. If each member of a class of 20 students took responsibility for 5 questionnaires the sample size would be 100.

Collating the results

Once you have the returned questionnaires you will need to analyze the information. Here's how to do it.

- Draw up a summary results table or tally sheet of the possible answers to each question.
- Count how many of each possible answer you got for each question and write this in the table or on the tally sheet.

When you have done this for each question on each questionnaire the table is complete and you can begin to think about what the results mean. You will find that putting the information into a database or spreadsheet may help you collate it more quickly.

Using spreadsheets and databases

The database will organize the information so that it is easily accessible and can be displayed clearly. The database can be 'interrogated' for statistical information and thus provide a picture of user needs and likes.

Statistical information from the database can be put into a spreadsheet. The spreadsheet displays the information as rows and columns of numbers. You can analyze the information in a variety of ways and present your findings in graphical forms like pie charts and bar graphs.

Here is an example of a survey of comics and magazines. The completed questionnaires provided information on the comics and magazines read by students. This information was recorded on a tally sheet. It was then analysed using a spreadsheet to identify user preferences. The results were presented visually.

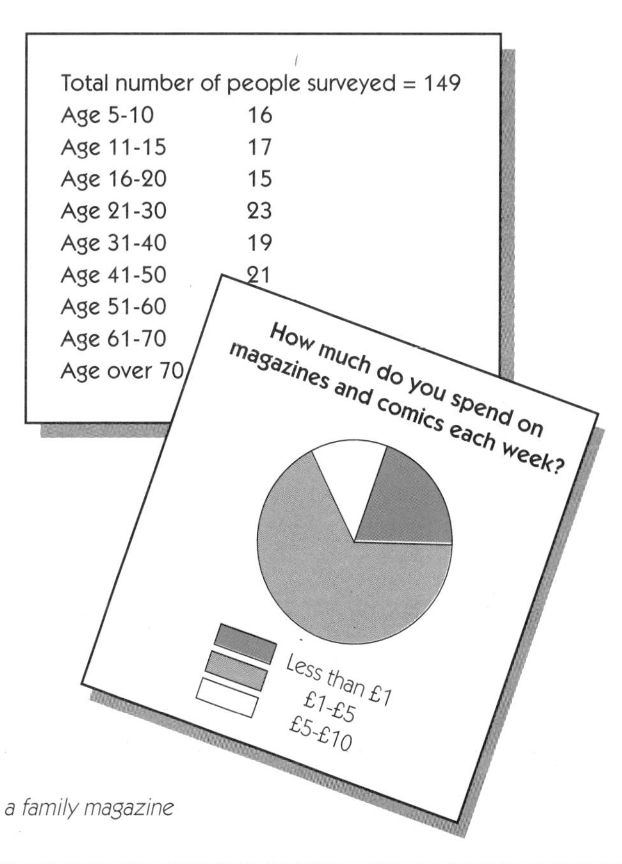

Total number of people surveyed = 149

Age	Number
Age 5-10	16
Age 11-15	17
Age 16-20	15
Age 21-30	23
Age 31-40	19
Age 41-50	21
Age 51-60	
Age 61-70	
Age over 70	

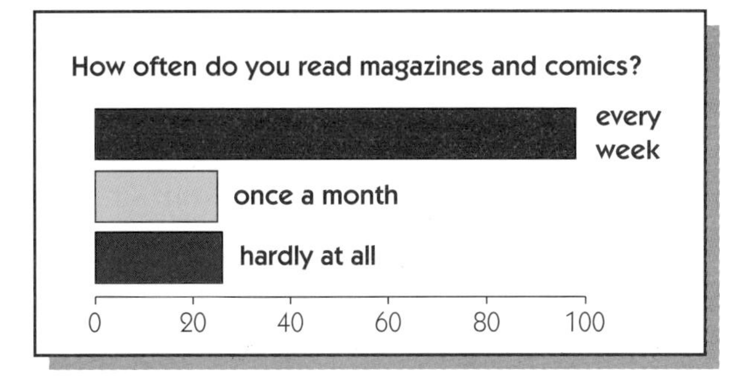

This information was used by students who were designing a family magazine

Design briefs

A design brief is a short statement which describes some or all of the following:

- the sort of product to be made and its purpose;
- who will use it;
- where it will be used;
- where it might be sold.

An **open** brief provides general guidelines and offers the opportunity for a wide range of possible outcomes. A **closed** brief is more specific and detailed in its requirements. Here are examples of open and closed briefs for two lines of interest.

Interiors

Open design brief: Design a mural for a new café called Good Vibrations to be opened in a seaside town. It will seat up to 80 people at 20 tables. Overall, the interior has the 60s as a theme with an accent on the 'surfin' sound' and it aims to attract young couples during the day.

Closed design brief: Design a mural for a new restaurant called Bloomsbury that aims to attract couples and small parties for 'special occasion' evening meals. It will seat up to 30 people at 10 tables. Overall, the interior should feature memorabilia of the Bloomsbury Group including paintings, prints, decorations and writing. It should include pictures of members of the Group with newspaper-type headlines indicating the controversy associated with their lives.

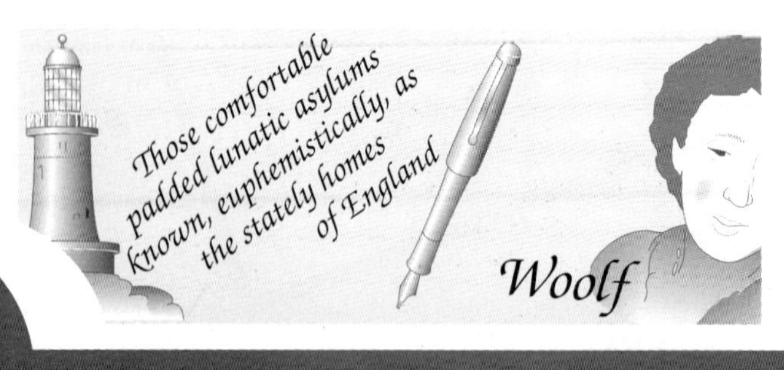

The open brief provides the designer with freedom to explore a wide range of possibilities to create different interior effects. The closed brief provides the opportunity to produce different solutions, but the nature of the interior is more clearly defined so the range of possible outcomes is limited. A particular style is required and there are fewer ways in which this can be achieved.

Paper engineering

Open design brief: Design a range of pop-up cards suitable for children of primary school age to be sold in a wide range of outlets, such as specialist card shops, department stores and W. H. Smith.

Closed design brief: Design a series of press-out scenes based on stories from traditional nursery rhymes for children at infant school to be sold at craft shops that specialize in handicraft kits.

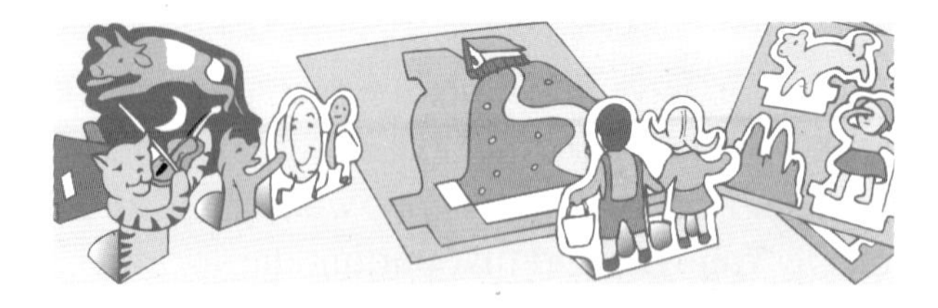

For the open brief different styles of cards are possible. They could be traditional or modern in appearance, linked to toys and games popular with young children, and even use special effects, as in 'exploding' cards and cards that play tunes on opening. Different complexities of card are possible, from simple stand-up figures to mechanisms with moving parts. In the closed brief the product and its style are specified and the end user is more clearly identified. This provides a more detailed picture of what is required.

Specifying the product

You will need to develop the design brief into a **performance specification**. This will provide a list of criteria against which you can assess your design as it develops.

The performance specification will always:

- describe what the product has to do;
- describe what the product should look like;
- state any other requirements that need to be met.

For example:

- how it should work;
- how much it should cost to manufacture;
- possible production levels – one-off or batch production;
- what materials it should be made from;
- what energy source should be used if it needs to be powered;
- ergonomic requirements related to end user;
- legal requirements to be met in its development and use;
- environmental considerations and requirements.

Here are two examples of performance specifications and products that meet their requirements.

Local music scene guide specification

What it has to do:

- provide information about local bands, gigs and playing venues (clubs) on a monthly basis.

What it should look like:

- be attractive to young people in the 15-30 age group
- indicate the wide range of music styles available.

Other requirements:

- have a recognizable house style, as it will be produced monthly
- use one colour ink only
- include a summary of information in the form of charts as well as more in depth information
- be made from easily recyclable materials as it will be used and thrown away
- be suitable for inclusion in a free community newspaper
- contain adverts for playing venues, to cover the cost of design and production.

Packaging specification

What it should do:

- protect and promote an expensive special occasion / anniversary celebration sparkling wine from Italy.

What it should look like:

- the surface decoration be based on fresco-style art depicting wine drinking in ancient Rome
- reflect the special occasion nature of the wine in a way that appeals to a wide age range from 25-55 years.

Other requirements:

- be easy to manufacture for batch production
- use low cost materials, recycled if possible
- be seen as part of a range of packaging that can be used to promote wines from different parts of the world.

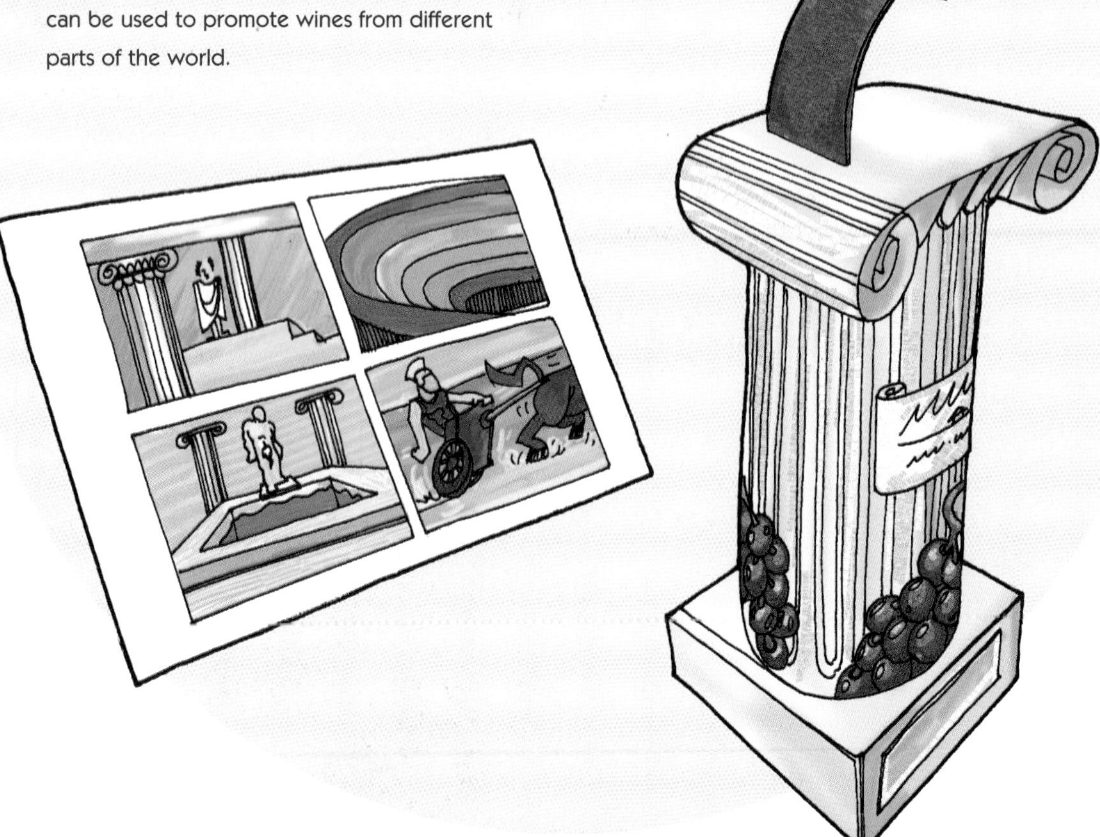

Generating design ideas

Brainstorming

You probably did some brainstorming at key stage 3. Here is a reminder.

Brainstorming is:

- a process for getting ideas out of your head!
- a process for getting ideas you didn't know you had!
- a process which uses questions and associations and links ideas to actions;
- a process you can do on your own, but it is usually better in a group.

Brainstorming an idea can help you to identify a wider range of options for your designing and making and to work out how best to develop these ideas.

How to brainstorm

- First state the problem or need.
- Record every idea suggested as words, phrases or pictures.
- Produce as many ideas as possible.
- Don't make judgements until the brainstorming pattern is complete.
- Allow enough time for new and diverse ideas to emerge, but agree a time limit so that ideas remain fresh.
- Sort out ideas by considering which are unrealistic, inappropriate and unachievable and removing them. What is left will give you a focus for action.

What can I use for this?

By asking this question you can identify design options. You can give each possibility a yes/no verdict based on specific criteria – availability, cost, effectiveness and feasibility. You can refine the remaining options using similar criteria until you are left with a 'best' solution. Here is an example.

A small shop which sells memorabilia from the 1950s to the present day has decided to revamp its image so that it appeals to a more up-market clientele. It has changed its name from Granny's Attic to Past Investments. The design of the shop sign is the focus of the brainstorm.

This brainstorming session gave full details of the overall image, font, material and fixings for the sign. Notice that the brainstormers used image boards plus Font, Materials and Fixings Chooser Charts to answer some of the questions.

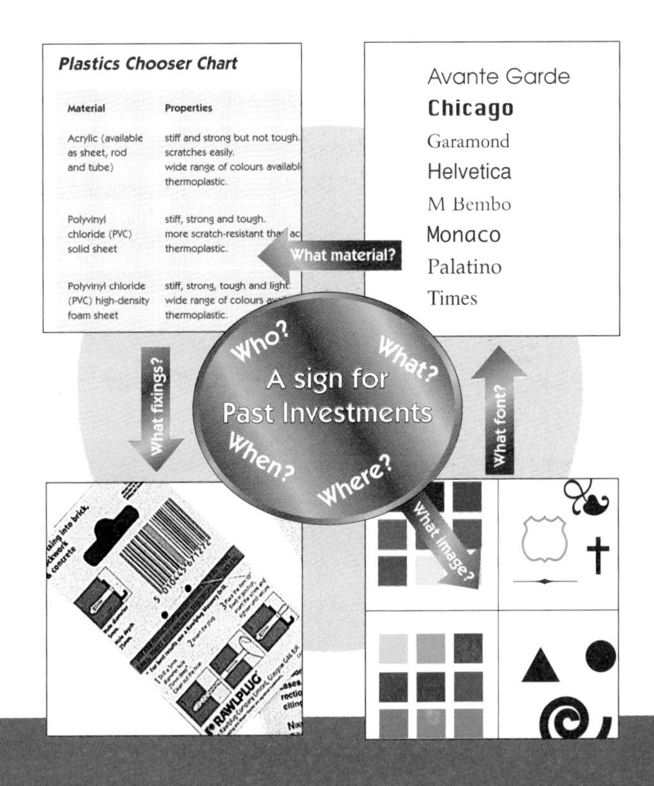

What can I use this for?

This is the sort of brainstorming that you use when you have some technical capabilities and aren't sure what to do with them.

Imagine that you live in a historical town and you have an ion camera that can take 'digital' pictures. These pictures can be fed into your computer and used with desk-top publishing software to produce illustrated printed material. You can use brainstorming to find something useful to do with all this knowledge.

Here is an example. Notice how the brainstormers have used the PIES approach within their brainstorming approaches.

Where?
at home, at work,
whilst travelling on public transport,
whilst out walking or cycling,
in zoos, museums or art galleries,
in shopping malls and town centres

Who?
tourists with special interests
tourists in general
resident population
young, middle aged, elderly

ION CAMERA
DESK TOP PUBLISHING

Why?
Physical, Intellectual,
Emotional, Social needs

What?
flyers, posters,
broadsheets, pamphlets

When?
leisure time, work time,
domestic time, travelling time

Who?	What?	Where?	When?	Why?
Tourist with special interest	Pamphlets	Whilst out cycling	Leisure time	*Physical:* cycling *Intellectual:* finding out new things *Emotional:* security

Attribute analysis

You may have used attribute analysis at key stage 3. Designers and engineers use it to help them produce new designs for familiar products.

Here is an attribute analysis table for an interior. The headings of the table describe attributes which will affect the final design. You can read across the columns and combine different words from each column to create new designs. Some combinations will be totally inappropriate, while others will offer viable design ideas. In the examples shown both combinations give interesting and worthwhile designs.

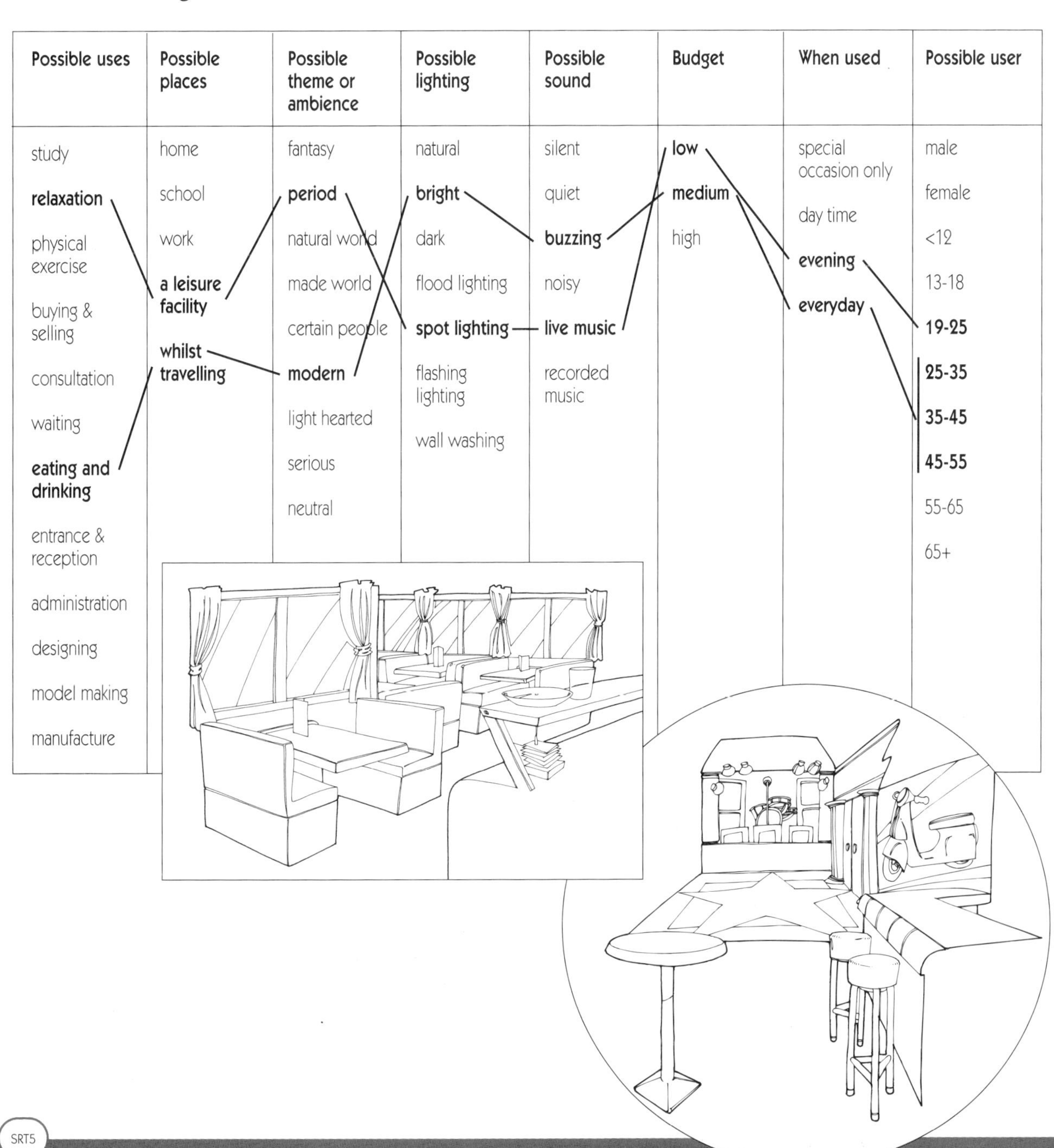

Possible uses	Possible places	Possible theme or ambience	Possible lighting	Possible sound	Budget	When used	Possible user
study	home	fantasy	natural	silent	**low**	special occasion only	male
relaxation	school	**period**	**bright**	quiet	**medium**	day time	female
physical exercise	work	natural world	dark	**buzzing**	high	**evening**	<12
buying & selling	**a leisure facility**	made world	flood lighting	noisy		**everyday**	13-18
consultation	**whilst travelling**	certain people	**spot lighting**	**live music**			**19-25**
waiting		**modern**	flashing lighting	recorded music			**25-35**
eating and drinking		light hearted	wall washing				**35-45**
entrance & reception		serious					**45-55**
administration		neutral					55-65
designing							65+
model making							
manufacture							

Observational drawing

You can use observational drawing to give you a reference for what things look like and to help you get ideas. Here are some examples showing where observational drawing has been used to help with designing.

Observational drawing	Resulting design
These drawings of Islamic patterns provided ideas for the sort of lettering to use in the sign for a shop. 	
These drawings of car silhouettes helped with the design of icons to go in a 'best buy' chart. 	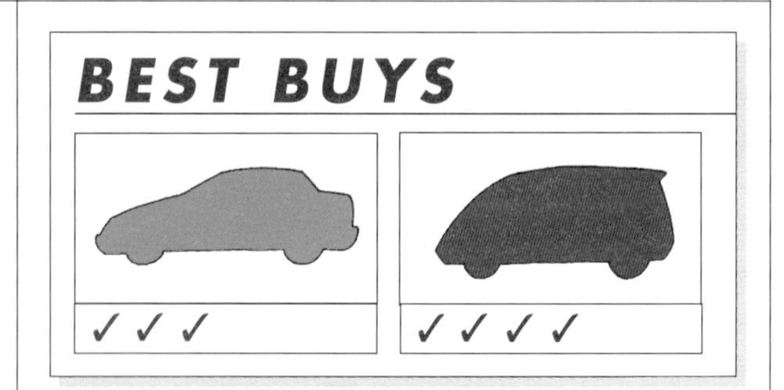
These drawings of leaves helped with the design of a child's ecology board game. 	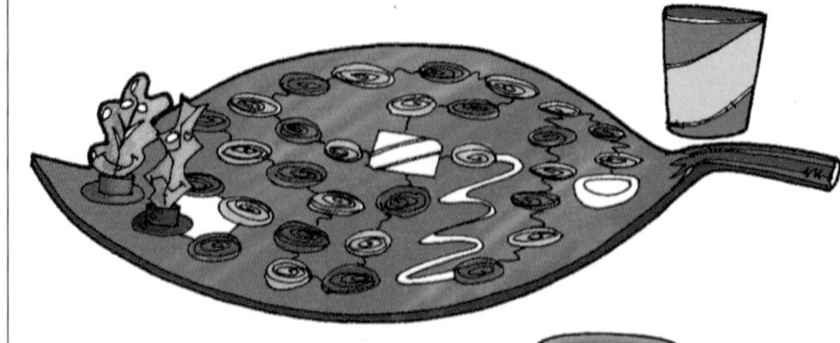
These drawings of fish helped to provide ideas for packaging products to be sold at a sea world park. 	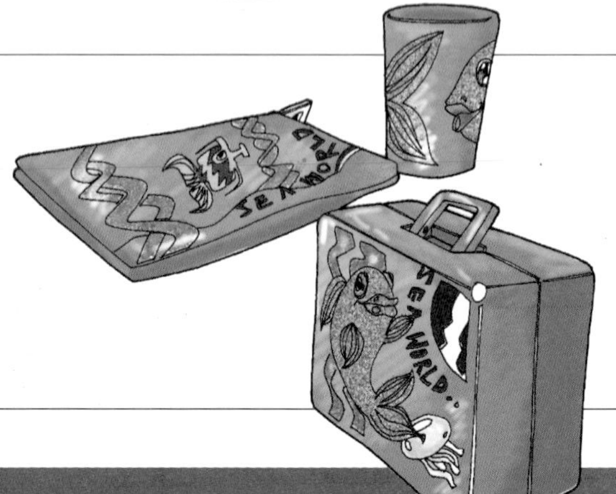

Investigative drawing

You can investigate the way something works by doing careful drawings that try to explain how it works. Here's how to do it.

- First find out how it works by using it and looking at it quickly.
- Write down what you have to do to make it work and what you think might be happening when it works.
- Then investigate how it works by looking more closely. Use a hand lens for close-up views. Look inside and if necessary undo parts to get a good view.
- Draw the parts you can see and add notes and other drawings to show what the different parts do.

An investigation of Easter egg packaging produced this series of drawings. By looking closely at the different parts, trying to understand how they make a 3D form from a 2D shape, and how they fit together, you can gain a better understanding of the way the packaging works

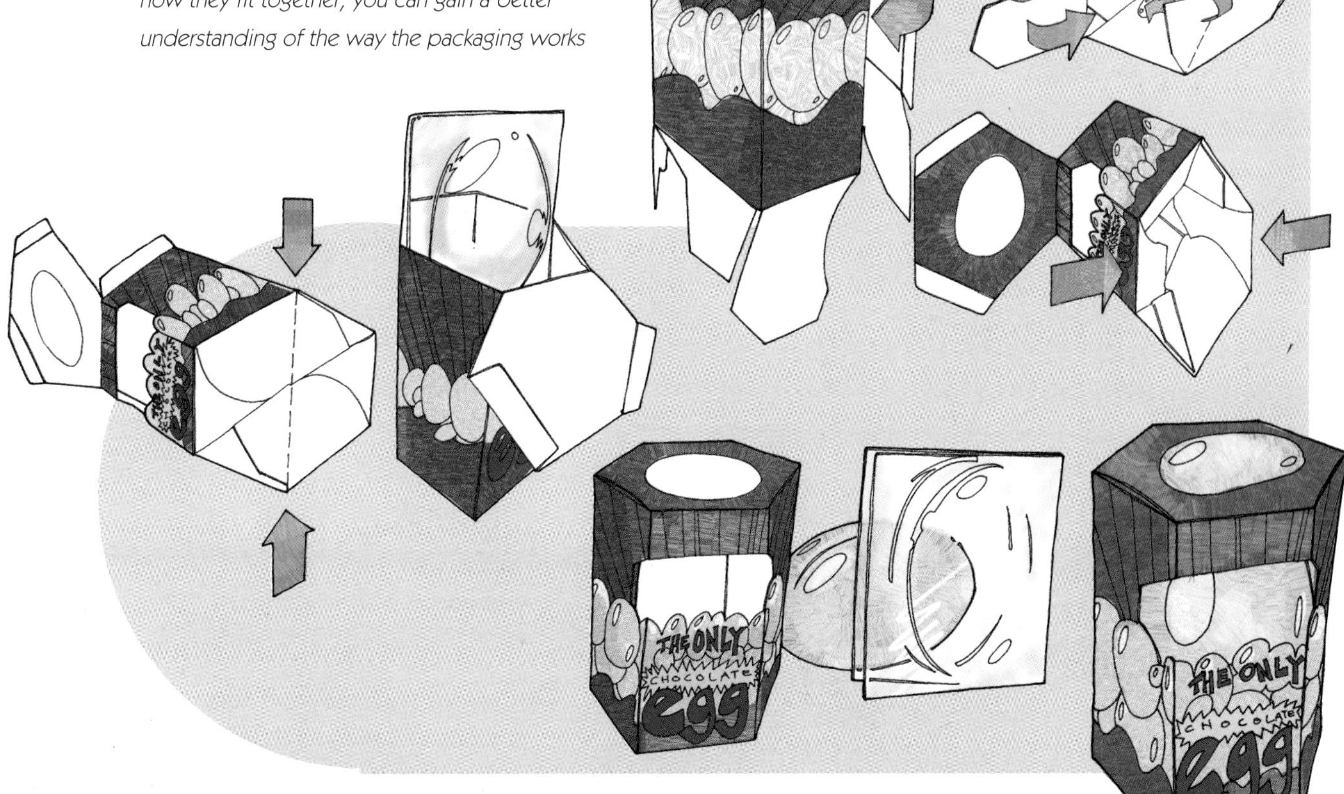

Modelling

It is often difficult to imagine what a design idea will look like or how it will work. Modelling your design ideas gives you something to look at, think about and test.

Modelling will help you:

- clarify and develop your design ideas;
- evaluate them;
- share them with others.

Modelling appearance

There are many modelling techniques, some of which you will have used at key stage 3. Here are examples of the way modelling techniques have been used to develop the designs for a fantasy board game.

1 **Talk through**
Talking about what you want to do with other people will help you clarify your design ideas.

2 **Thumbnail sketches**
This is a quick way of getting your ideas into a visual form. You can also make notes to explain things which you cannot draw.

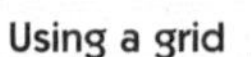

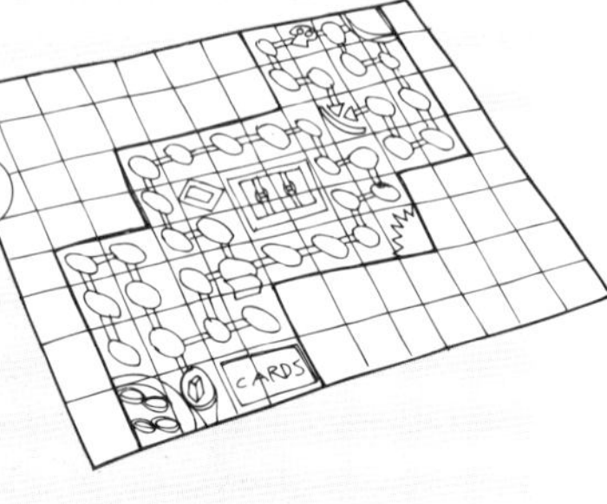

3 **Using a grid**
This is a useful way to get the overall layout of the game and the relative sizes of the figures.

4 **Annotated sketches** will provide detail of the design of the figures.

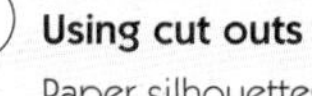

5 **Using cut outs**
Paper silhouettes can be used to explore the shapes of figures.

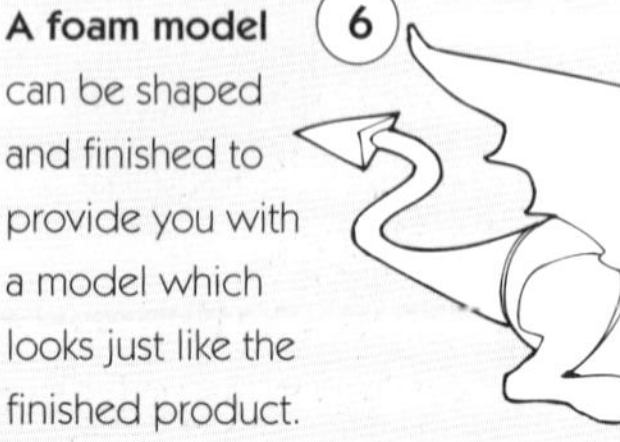

6 **A foam model** can be shaped and finished to provide you with a model which looks just like the finished product.

Modelling appearance is a useful process for assessing design ideas for development into real products

Modelling product performance

Modelling not only describes the way a product will look, it can also describe the way it will fit together and how it will work. You can use a range of modelling techniques to develop design ideas about product performance. Talking about the design, thumbnail sketches and detailed drawings will help you to model how a product might work.

But you will need to use a more sophisticated approach for products that involve some form of movement or control.

Simple card modelling techniques are shown here for developing designs for the mechanisms in a pop-up book.

Whenever you design products that people will use you will need to think about sizes and shapes (**anthropometrics**) and movements (**ergonomics**). Tables of data are available and you can use this information to make your product easier to use. The handheld remote control on page 92 was informed by anthropometric and ergonomic information.

Modelling how graphic products will work

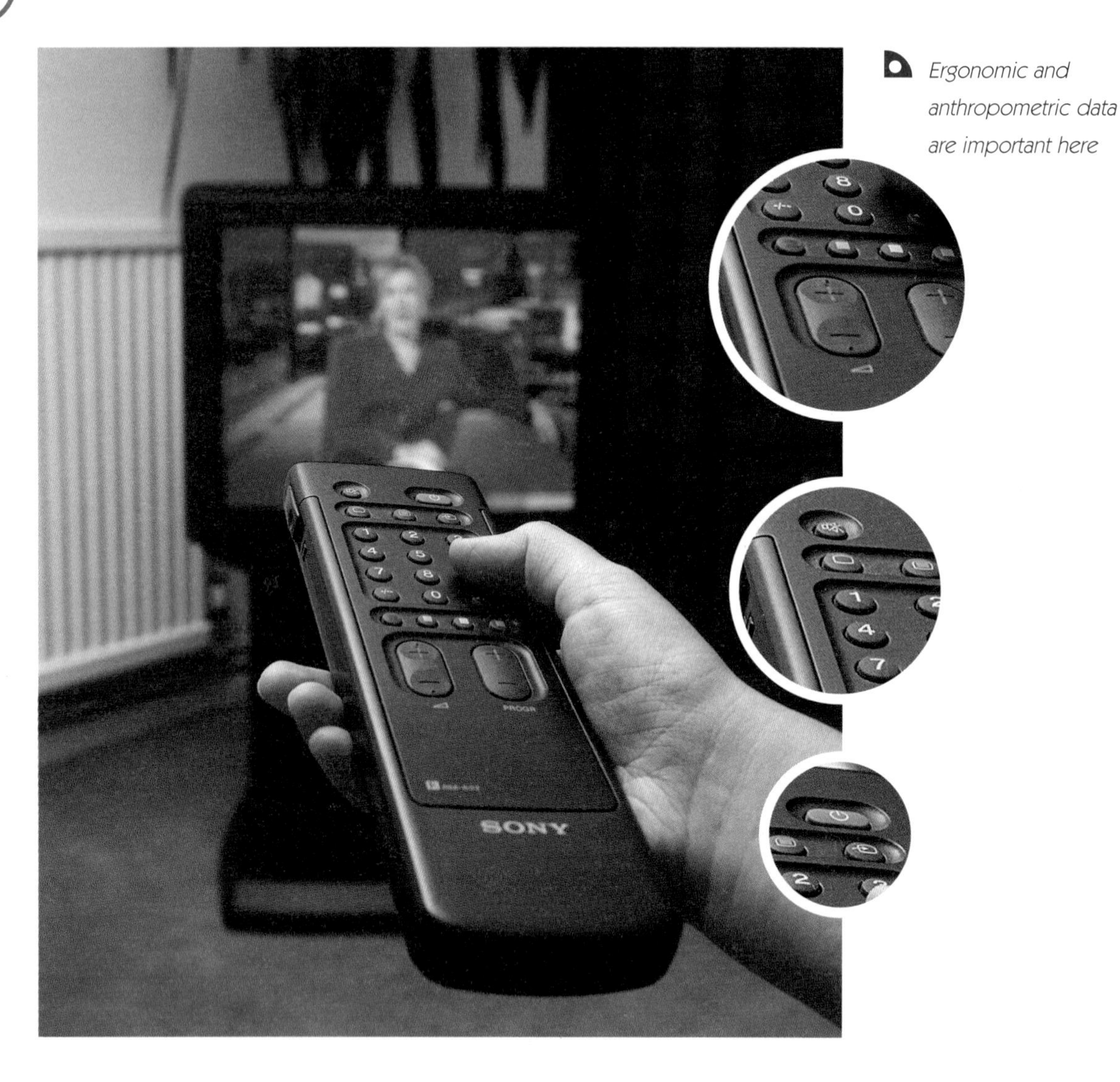

Ergonomic and anthropometric data are important here

You can assess some of the effects of a product on a place where it will be used by modelling both the product and the place. For example, scale models of the wall and floor decor placed in a scale model of a hotel reception provided an opportunity to assess its appropriateness and performance in that environment. You can find out if it looks right, if it takes up too much space, and if it fits in with any other decor and surroundings.

Modelling with computers

Modelling appearance and form

If you use computers properly they can help you model your design ideas so that you can explore many more possibilities than if you were working just with pencil and paper. There are several ways to start using computers as these designs for a computer games club show.

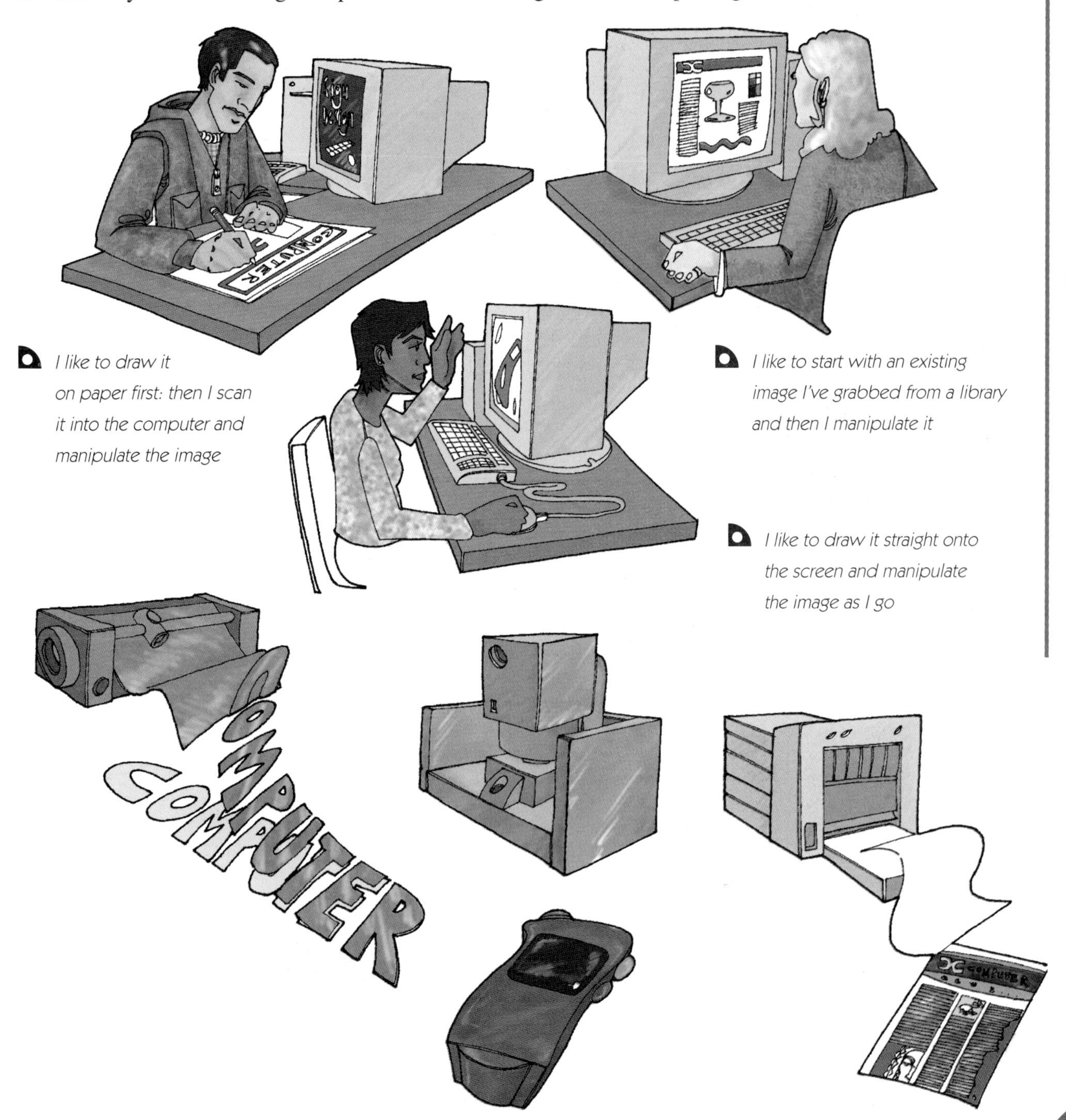

Modelling function

You can use a computer to model the way a product might work. You can make changes to the design 'on-screen' and see how this affects the performance.

The design for the interior of a clothes shop involves a wide range of products, lighting and decoration. Modelling the interior on computer will help you get the details of each part right so that they work well together.

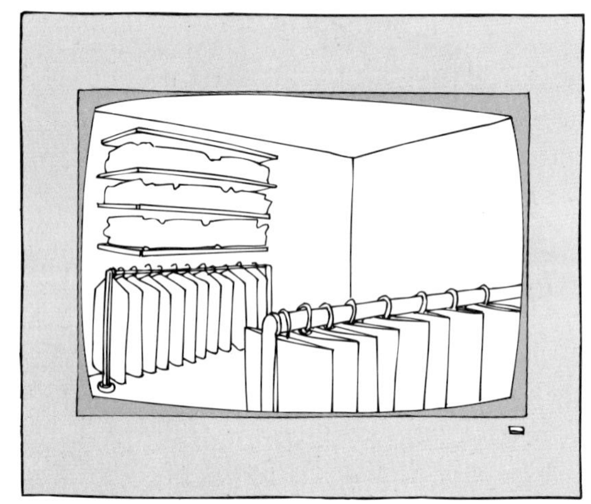

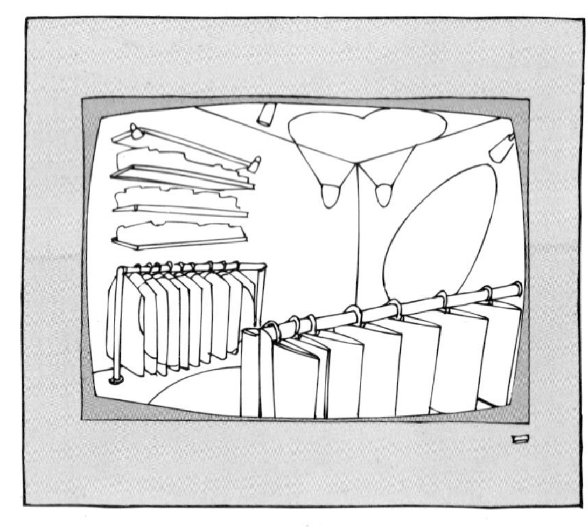

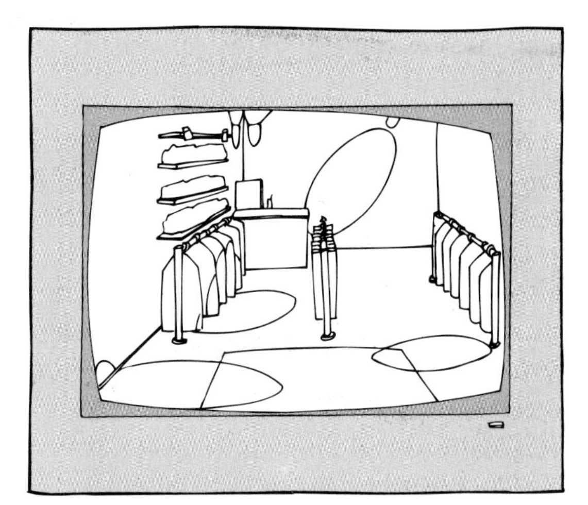

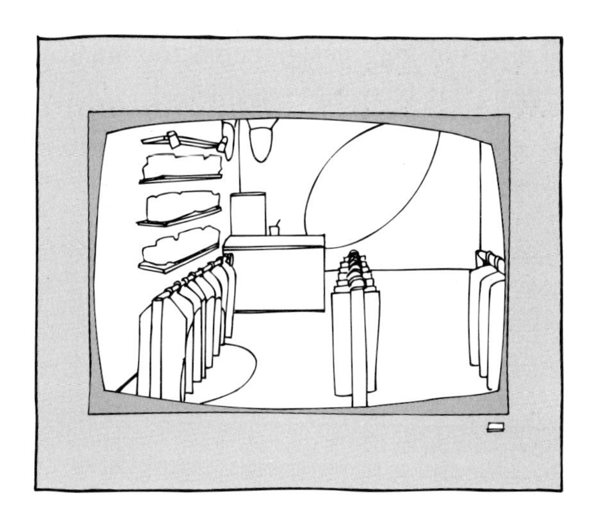

Applying science

Checking on your choice of material

Most materials will react with their surroundings in some way. Some will react only slightly and it will take a long time for them to corrode or rot. Others will decay quite rapidly. The time taken will depend on the material and the severity of the conditions. You can check on the durability of materials by looking them up in the Materials Chooser Charts on pages 177–179.

You can improve the durability of your design in two ways:

- use a finish on the material which protects it from the surroundings;
- choose a more durable material.

This is a problem faced by sign makers. The attractive scenes on many inn signs have to be repainted quite regularly as the wind, rain, frost and sun cause the paint to fade, crack and flake off. The plastic letters used for many shop fronts are much more weather resistant although many people find them less attractive.

Choosing a material with the correct strength and stiffness is important. Just imagine if the plastic chosen for a large tiddlywinks counter was not strong enough; it would break when used to make the smaller counters jump. If the plastic was too elastic it would bend out of shape when you pressed it onto a smaller counter, making it difficult to get the counter to jump.

Strength is one of the properties of all solid materials. If the strength of the material is high then it will be difficult to break. If the strength of the material is low then it will be easy to break. Elasticity is another important property of solid materials. The elastic property of a material is often measured as Young's modulus of elasticity. An elastic material is easy to stretch or bend. You may find that a material is strong enough but too elastic; it doesn't break under the load but it does bend. You can find out about the strength and elasticity of some materials by looking them up in the Materials Chooser Charts.

If a part of your design isn't strong enough you can do one of two things:

- change the design so that the cross-sectional area of the part is greater — if there is more material there it will be stronger
- make the part from a stronger material.

If a part of your design bends too much you can do one of two things:

- change the design so that the part has a cross-sectional shape that is less bendy
- use a material that is less elastic.

The most weather-proof may not be the most attractive

What would happen if the counters were rubbery?

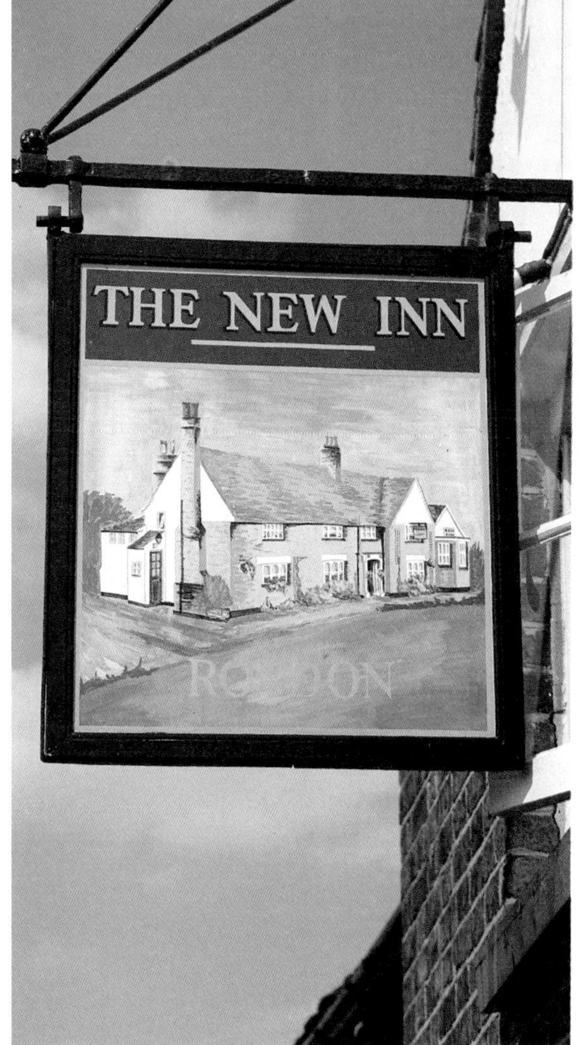

Systems thinking

During your key stage 3 work you may have been introduced to systems thinking. You can use this to help you understand the way graphic products might be produced.

Feedback and control

When a designer is beginning to design a newsletter production and distribution system, she only needs to consider what goes into the system and what comes out. She does not need to worry about what happens inside the system just yet. All the things that go into the system are called inputs and all those that come out are called outputs. For a newsletter production and distribution system the designer might identify the inputs and outputs shown here. The designer will then break down the system into sub-systems and see how the inputs and outputs need to be arranged. A system diagram showing these inputs and outputs is also shown.

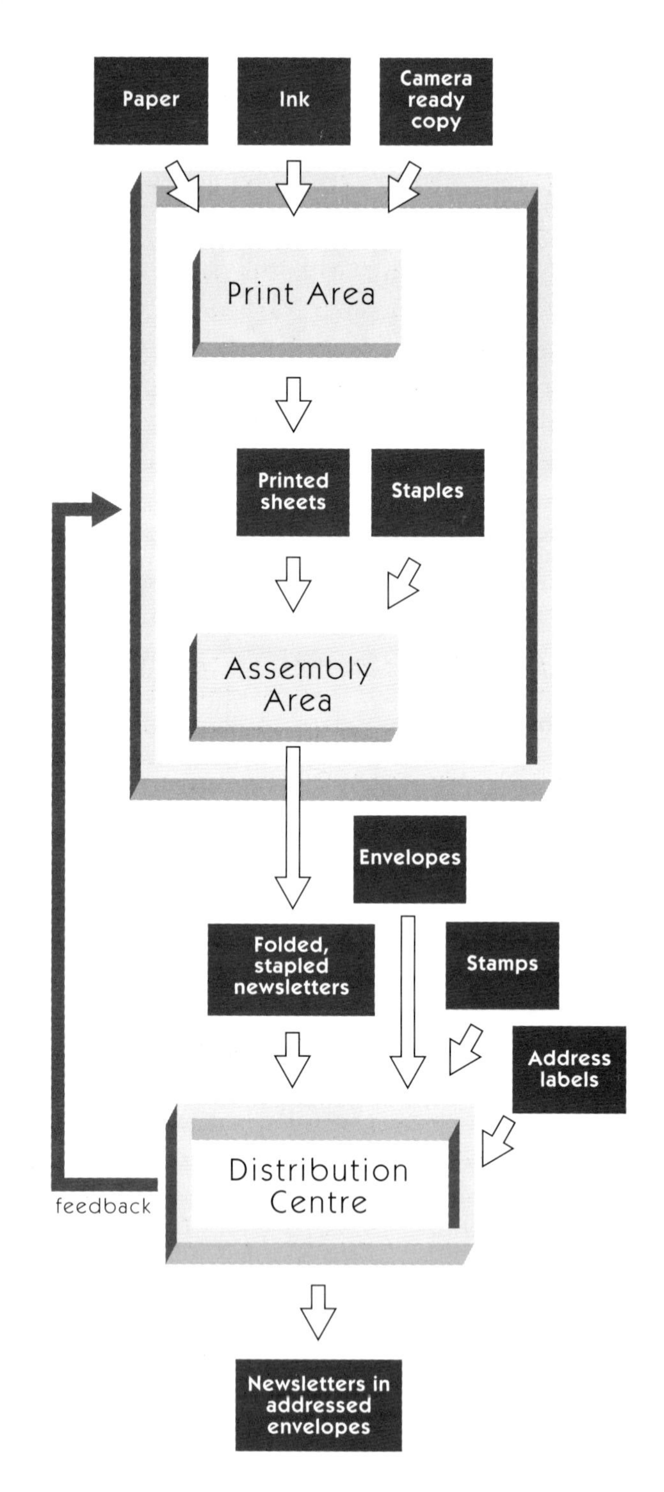

Systems diagram for newsletter production and distribution

You should note the following:

- It doesn't look like a print room and a mail room but it does help you understand how they work.
- The output of one sub-system becomes the input of another.
- There is **feedback** of information from one sub-system into another. This allows the system to be controlled. For example, if the number of people wanting the newsletter increases, there is feedback from the distribution centre to the production centre telling the printer to produce more copies. If the number of people wanting newsletters decreases, there is feedback telling the printer to produce less copies. Systems with this type of feedback are called **closed-loop** systems. Without feedback the system cannot be controlled. A system without feedback is called an **open-loop** system.
- The designer has drawn the system boundary so that it includes the printing and distribution centre but not the writers, illustrators and graphic designer who produce the newsletter on disk, nor the postal service that delivers the newsletter. These are serious omissions. If the disc containing the camera-ready copy does not arrive on time, then the production of the newsletter is held up. Special arrangements for collecting large amounts of mail should be made with the postal service – if not, the newsletters could be delayed. To address these issues the designer could redraw the system boundary to include sub-systems that deal with the writing, illustration and design of the newsletter as well as the postal service.

Left outside the systems boundary

User and operator interfaces

The parts of a system used by people are called **user interfaces**. For the customers of a bank the user interface may be the counter where they pay in cheques and discuss their accounts. This interface is a human interface but machine interfaces are becoming increasingly common in banks, providing a range of facilities – cash withdrawal, information about the amount of money in a customer's account and requests for statements. Human interfaces are friendly and can explain things if a user is unsure. However, they require special training and are not usually available 24 hours a day.
A machine interface has the advantage of always being available but it can appear unfriendly and difficult to use. Machine interfaces should be designed to be self-explanatory and user friendly.

The parts of a system operated by the people who help run and control a system are called operator interfaces. They are usually more complicated than user interfaces. Operators need more information and have to be able to do more things than users. Operators are usually trained to operate the system while users are not. The operator must be able to put information into the system through easy-to-use controls. The operator interface should be as easy to use as possible. The information systems used by the personal bankers at high street banks are a good example of an operator interface. They allow the banker to record large amounts of information given by the customer in a short time in a form the bank can use to give the customer advice and financial services.

A combination of human and operator interfaces where graphics play an important part

Planning

Flow charts and Gantt charts

You can use flow charts and Gantt charts to help you plan your way through a Capability Task. In year 11 you may spend two whole terms on a single Capability Task as part of your GCSE assessment. It will be important to ensure that things like school holidays, public holidays and sports days don't upset your plans.

You can use the headings in the flow chart shown here to get the order of the task right. Once you have the order right you can use a Gantt chart to think about how long each part should take and to make sure that you get the task done on time. A Gantt chart will give you an overview of the whole task, showing both what needs to be done and when it should be done.

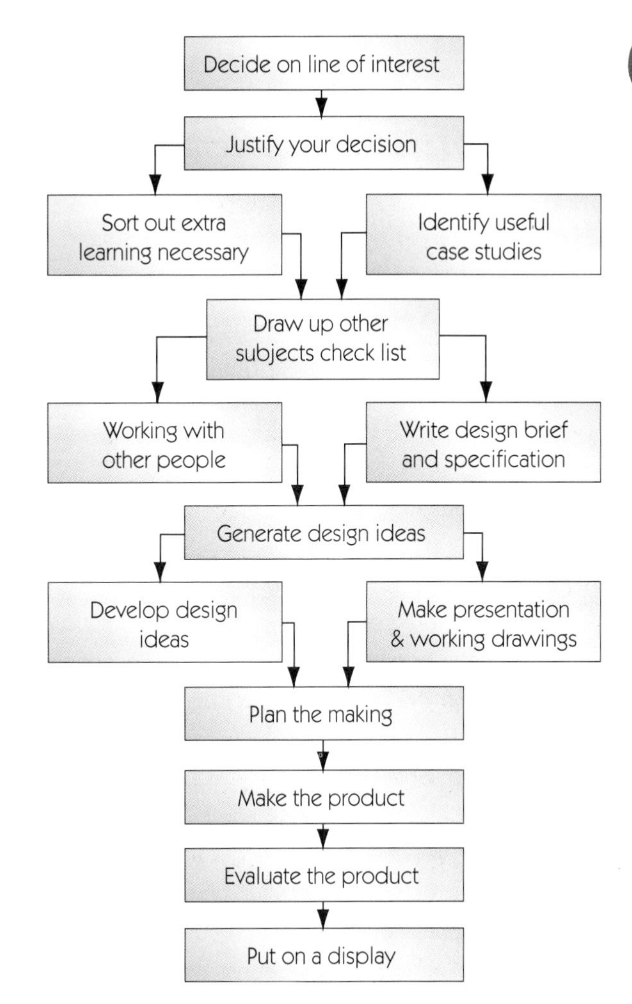

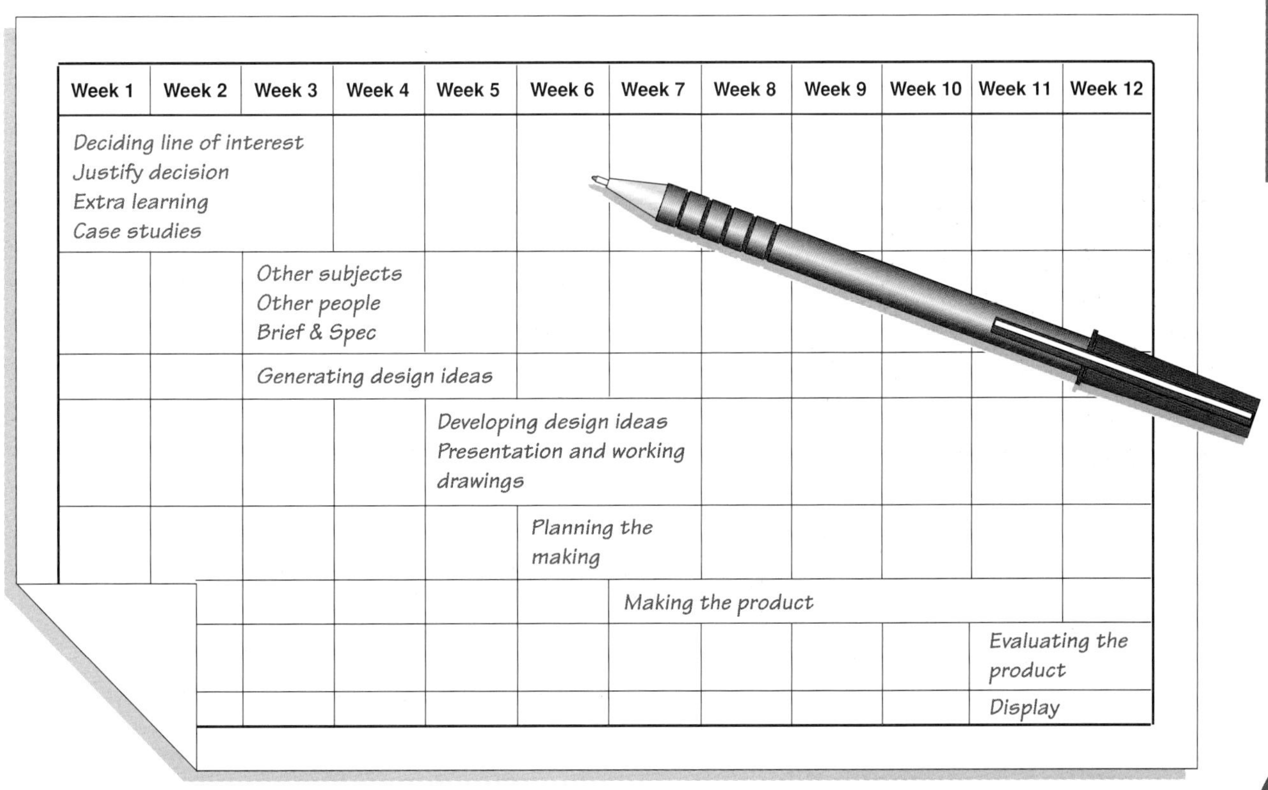

Evaluating

User trip

The simplest way to evaluate a product is to take a user trip. This involves using the product and asking a few basic questions:

- Is it easy or convenient to use?
- Does it do what it is supposed to do?
- Do I like it?
- Would I want to own or continue to use it?

A large telephone company has decided to modify public telephone boxes so that the user simply speaks the number into the receiver rather than dialling with push buttons. But will the public support this change? Our user group, Georgie aged 3, Maisie aged 13, Jo aged 28, Jack aged 39 and Dot aged 72 have been asked for their views and are taking a user trip. Their thoughts about the new phones will be expressed when they respond to the user trip questions.
How do you think they will respond to the change?

Winners and losers

The outcomes of design and technology will provide benefits for some and disadvantages for others. Designing and making a product will affect a lot of people directly and indirectly.

Maisie's brother, Wayne, has worked hard doing odd jobs around the house for his parents to raise enough money to buy himself a fantasy adventure game. Within four weeks he has raised enough money. Wayne is excited that all his hard work will allow him to buy the game and have lots of fun. His parents are pleased because, for the first time, Wayne has helped keep the house tidy. The toy shop owner is pleased because he will sell another game. Maisie, however, is not sure. Wayne has been too busy to bother her for the last four weeks and that has been good, but now she is concerned. He and his friends will monopolize the living room for hours when they play a large battle. She is not sure that war games encourage Wayne to treat other people well.

The Winners and Losers chart helps you identify those people affected by Wayne's purchase of the fantasy adventure game.

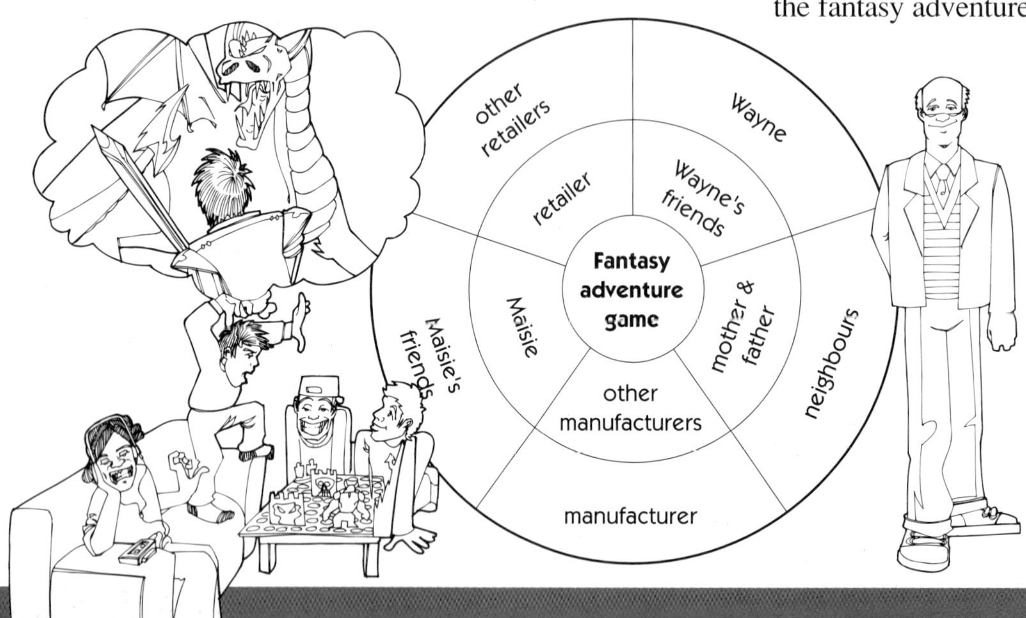

Performance testing

Evaluating a product will involve comparing how well it works against its performance specification. You have to ask, does it do what it was designed to do? Here is an example.

Pop-up greetings cards are becoming more complex and innovative. There are now cards for different ages and celebrating different events. To be successful such cards have to meet a demanding performance specification.

Here is the design specification for a pop-up card.

What it has to do:

- present a greeting celebrating an event for a particular age group
- contain pop-up elements which will surprise, intrigue and amuse those receiving the card.

What it should look like:

- be in a style that is appealing to the target age group.

Other requirements:

- must fit into an A5 envelope
- must not weigh more than 25 g (suitable for first or second class letter post)
- must not cause offence when on display.

These questions will help you to compare the performance of the product against the specification.

- Does it celebrate an event for a particular age group?
- Does it contain pop-up elements?
- Does it appeal to the target age group?
- Does it fit into an A5 envelope?
- Does it weigh less than 25 g?
- Does it cause offence?

You can find the answers to some of these questions by investigating the product for yourself. For others you will need to observe the reactions of different people to the product; those who might buy it and those who might see it.

Is it appropriate?

Appropriate technology is suitable technology. You can use these questions to find out if a product or technology is appropriate.

- Does it suit the needs of the people who use it?
- Does it use local materials?
- Does it use local means of production?
- Is it too expensive?
- Does it generate income?
- Does it increase self reliance?
- Does it use renewable sources of energy?
- Is it culturally acceptable?
- Is it environmentally friendly?
- Is it controlled by users?

It is unlikely that any product or technology will score highly against all these questions. Many will seem appropriate in one context and inappropriate in another. Here is an example.

Injection moulding is a process which has revolutionized the plastics industry. Our life is made easier by the production of cheap plastic goods which cater for our everyday needs. These include food containers, general household goods, toys and shoes. Millions of children have benefited from hours of constructive play using injection-moulded building bricks. Chess pieces which once had to be made by hand by skilled craftsmen have been replaced by injection-moulded plastic pieces which are cheap and can be produced using unskilled labour.

This technology has created employment and wealth in many communities throughout the world and clearly benefits manufacturers and consumers in those communities. However, in one community the advantages of injection moulding have not been so obvious to the local people. The community produced both chess pieces in boxes and playing boards by traditional means and made a successful living by selling these for export. With the introduction of the injection moulding process the market for the traditionally made pieces became much smaller. For this group of people the introduction of injection moulding led to unemployment. The small timber processing business that supported the wood carvers also closed down. The injection moulding equipment that produced the new style chess pieces was sited in the main industrial city over 100 miles away and employed just 20 of the people who had made the pieces by traditional methods. The synthetic materials for manufacture had to be imported and there was a greater need for energy to power the machines and a consequent increase in pollution. As the new plant was owned and run by a foreign company, much of the profits created by the industry were not shared with the local community.

It is clear from this example that for many people in this community injection moulding was an inappropriate technology.

Whether a product or technology is appropriate will depend upon the situation in which it is used.

Modelling Materials Chooser Chart

Here are some suggestions to help you choose which modelling material to use for modelling design ideas for each line of interest.

Line of interest	Modelling techniques	Model
Packaging	Paper or card networks 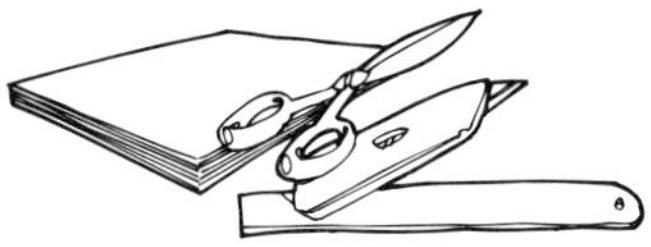	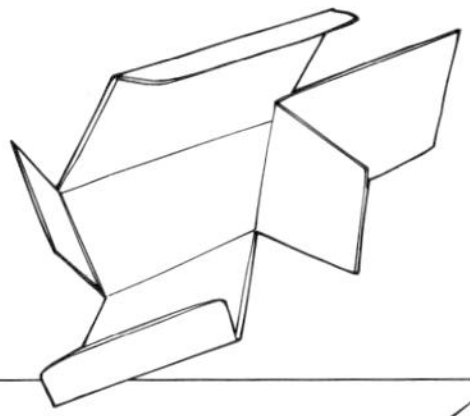
Information	Rapid visualisation 	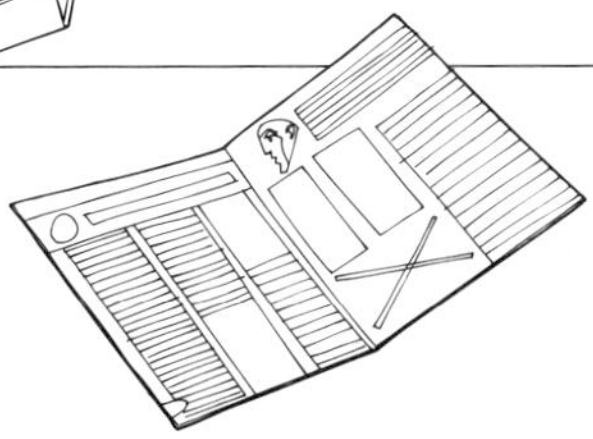
Signs and signage	Paper and card cut-outs 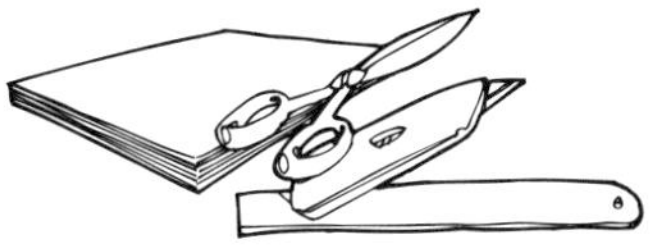	
Card engineering	Paper cut-outs and nets 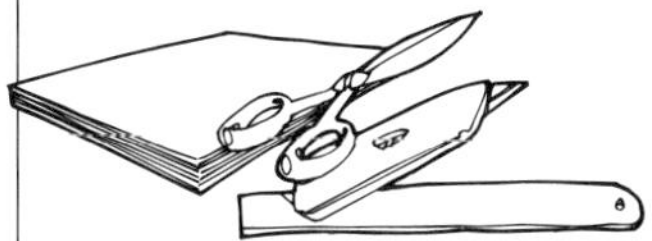	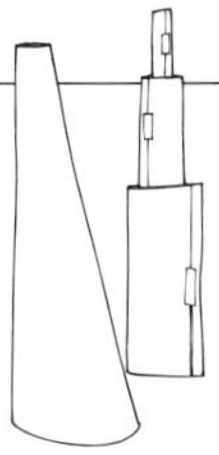
Interior design	Corner of room simulation 	
User interfaces	Block models with surface details 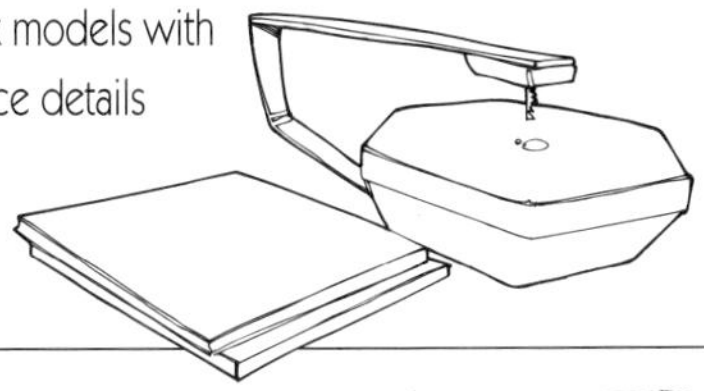	
Board games & puzzles	Rapid prototyping 	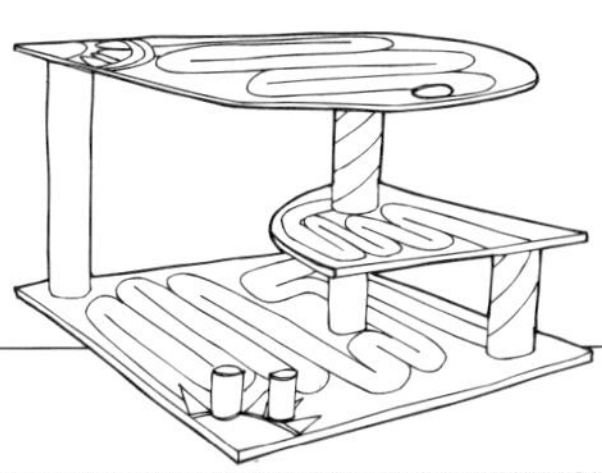

Strategies Chooser Chart

This Chooser Chart gives you information about strategies:

- when to use a strategy in a Capability Task
- how long the strategy will take
- how complex it is
- whether it involves other people.

Use the key to find out what the icons mean.

Key to icons:

When: beginning middle end

Time: short to long

Complexity: simple to complex

Other people: one other to many

Strategy	Comments				
Identifying needs and likes					
PIES	beginning		short	simple	
observing people	beginning		short	simple	
asking questions	beginning		short	simple	
using books and magazines	beginning		short	simple	
image boards	beginning		medium	simple	
questionnaires	beginning		long	complex	many
Design briefs	beginning		short	simple	
Specifications	beginning		short	medium	
Generating design ideas					
brainstorming	beginning	middle	medium	simple	two
attribute analysis	beginning		short	simple	
observational drawing	beginning	middle	medium	simple	
investigative drawing	beginning	middle	medium	medium	
Modelling					
modelling appearance	middle		medium	medium	
modelling performance	middle		medium	complex	
modelling with computers	middle		long	medium	
Applying science	middle		short	simple	
Systems thinking	middle		medium	medium	
Planning	beginning	middle	short	simple	
Evaluating					
user trip	end	beginning	short	simple	one other
winners and losers	end	beginning	short	simple	one other
performance testing	end	beginning	short	simple	one other
appropriateness	end	beginning	short	simple	one other

Communicating your design proposals 5

In the business world, ideas can only be turned into real, manufactured products if the designers can communicate their design proposals effectively. Graphic designers have to communicate their design ideas to clients and manufacturers, and us as the users.

The designer

I run my own graphic design studio and I employ a small team of designers. Clear communication with the client is essential at all stages of a design. It is important that we know exactly what is required, and that the client understands, and is happy with, our proposals.

The client

I am in the music industry and I manage a recording company. I rely on the work of the graphic designers to promote musicians as well as to advertize and package new music. I have to be sure that the designs they create will present the right image to the public and will help to sell our music.

The manufacturer

When a designer brings work for printing, I need to have clear information and the details of the design job. Then I will know exactly what materials and manufacturing processes to use for a successful product.

The user

When I buy a new CD I think the graphics on the package are important. I like to read about the band and the words of the songs. The style of the images and pictures also give the 'feel' of what the music will be like. Sometimes I've bought music by a band that I've not known much about, just because I thought that the CD cover looked really interesting.

In your work you may be both the designer and the manufacturer. You might even be the client too. Do not fall into the trap of thinking you don't need to communicate your ideas just because you know what you are doing! You have to communicate your ideas so that they can be understood by other people. You can then ask them for their advice and opinions about your proposals. You will also be able to judge more clearly whether your design is exactly right, before you start making. You can use techniques in this chapter to help you communicate ideas.

Rough sketches

Your first thumb nail sketches of ideas probably only make sense to you. To help you explain your ideas to a client, you will need to make clearer rough sketches. These are sometimes called **scamps**. They are drawings that are made quickly, but give a closer impression of the final product. Rough sketches are usually drawn on thin paper with a pencil or felt tips. The standard required for these drawings depends on the type of person with whom you are discussing your ideas. If the client is familiar with how designers work, sketchy drawings may be adequate. People from outside the world of design may only understand more precise coloured sketches.

Key points

- Rough sketches should not be too time consuming to produce. Draw with something that you find quick and easy to work with.
- Decide on the level of detail that you will need to give an impression of your idea.
- Use notes and arrows to explain your ideas more fully.
- Only add colour if it is an important part of your design.
- Make these sketches clear enough for other people to understand your design proposals.

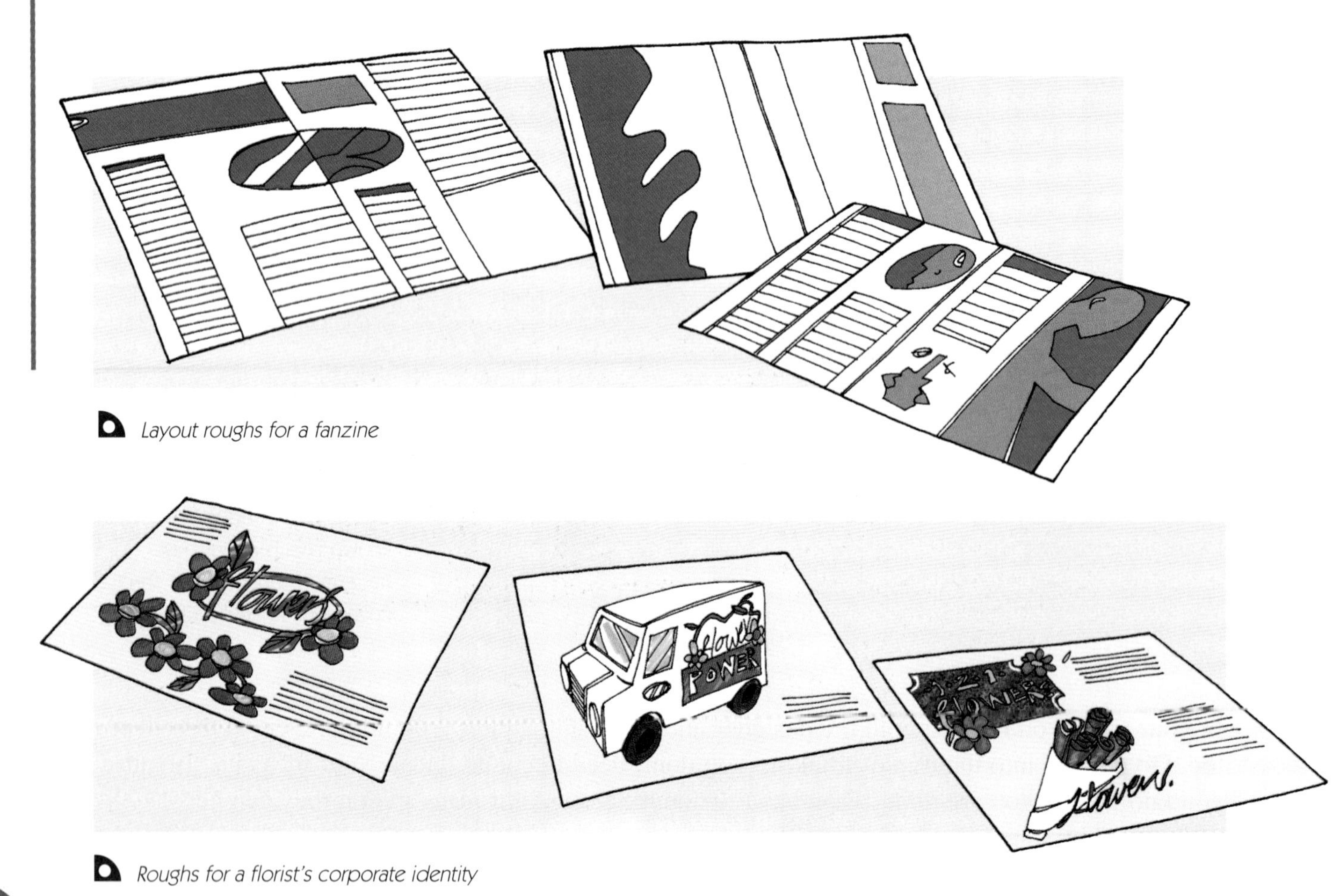

Layout roughs for a fanzine

Roughs for a florist's corporate identity

Sketch models

These are three-dimensional versions of a rough sketch or diagram. They are useful when you are planning space or proportions, as in interior design, or to show how something works, such as a pop-up card mechanism. For this type of design, a sketch model will give the client a better understanding of your idea than a two dimensional drawing.

Key points

- Sketch models should be very simple and quick to make. They do not need to show detail, but should act as a talking point for your early ideas.
- Use materials that are easy to work with and that can be quickly changed and adapted. Paper, card, polystyrene foam and found materials such as cardboard tubes and boxes can be quickly assembled with double-sided tape, paper fasteners and staples.

Simple mock-ups

If you are designing a three-dimensional product such as a package or display stand, it is useful to show your client a simple mock-up of your idea. A mock-up is a rough three-dimensional model that is made full size and will show the graphics that will be used on the final product.

A 3D mock-up will allow you and the client to view the design from all sides and judge if the colour, scale, proportions and graphics look right. You may decide to make changes to your design at this stage, as ideas often look quite different in three dimensions.

Guide to making mock-ups

- Choose materials that are quick and easy to work with, such as card for packages or display stands. Block models can be sculpted from polystyrene foam.

A dummy

A dummy is an accurate drawing or a three-dimensional model of the final design. It should be the correct size and look exactly like the final product.

You can use a dummy to:

- show the client a precise imitation of the product. If the client is not satisfied with your design, changes can still be made before production. However, if your design is accepted, the client may use the dummy to advertize the new product.
- show the dummy to the printer or manufacturer as a guide for the production methods and costings of your design solution.

- You should give a good impression of the final design, but you do not need to use too much detail. Simple mock-ups should give more information than sketch models as your ideas should be more developed.

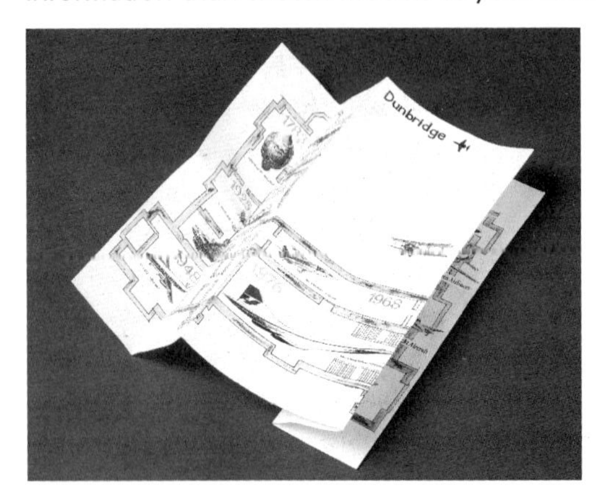

Working drawings

When a three-dimensional product is ready for making, the designer will present the model maker or manufacturer with a working drawing. These are drawings that contain all the instructions necessary for making.

A working drawing must include:

- accurate dimensions of all parts;
- details of materials and the colours or surface finishes required;
- construction and assembly instructions.

Working drawings show information using British Standard Institution (BSI) conventions. This provides a standard visual language that is recognised throughout the world of industry. The panel and drawings beneath it show some examples of useful BSI conventions for drawings. For further information refer to BSI 308 or PD 7308 (Engineering Drawing Practice for Schools and Colleges).

Line	Use
continuous thick	for visible outlines and edges
continuous thin	for dimension and projection lines
continuous thin irregular	limits of partial or interrupted views
chain thin	centre lines, lines of symmetry

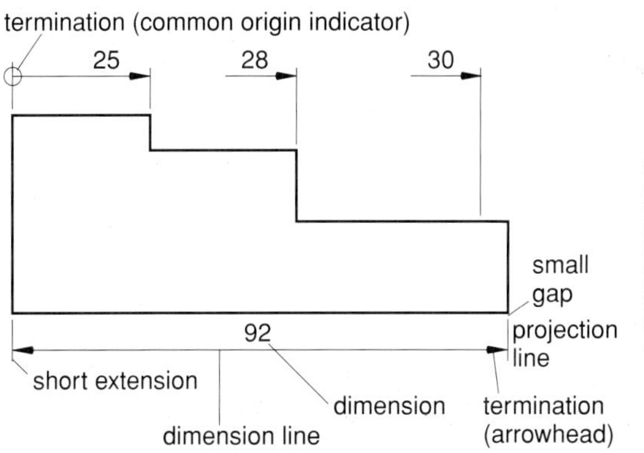

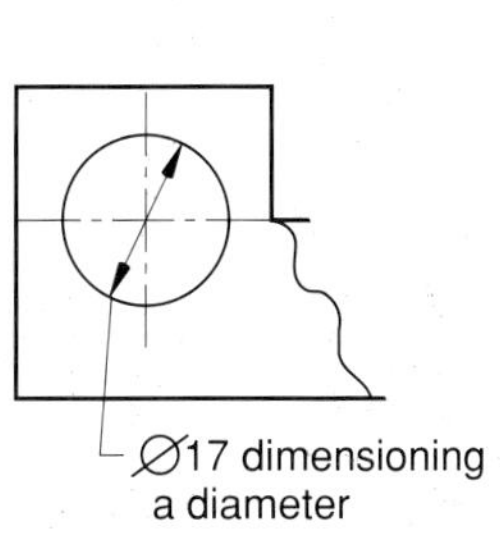

Measured orthographic projection

These are accurate scale drawings that show elevations (square-on views) of the product. They should give all the construction information about the design. Usually all the details can be shown using three views: the plan view, a front elevation and a side elevation. The drawing is set out in a clear, organized arrangement as shown in the **first angle projection** below.

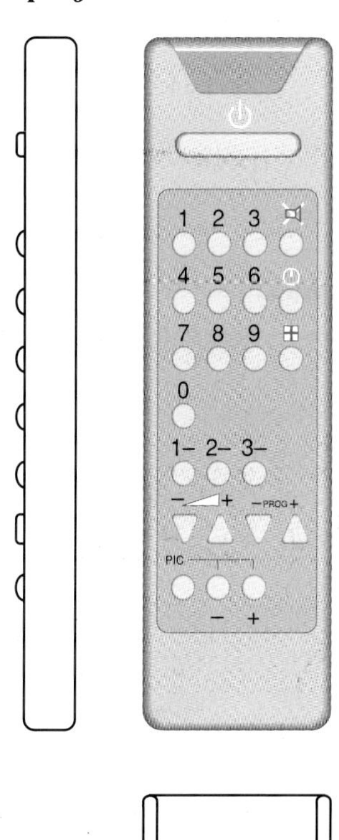

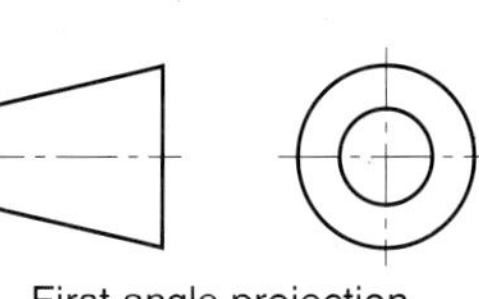

First angle projection

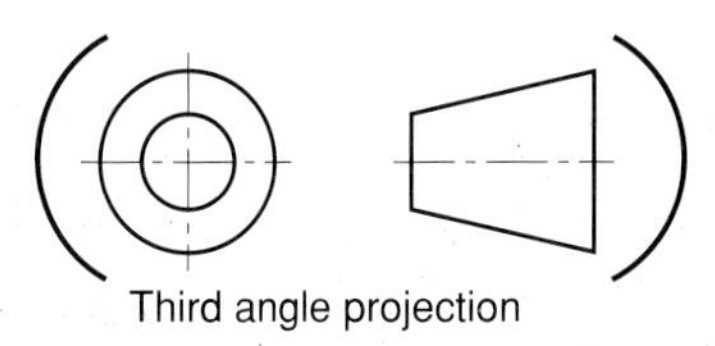

Third angle projection

Presentation models

An impressive way of showing the overall effect of your final design is through a presentation model. These are accurate three-dimensional models that are made to scale or actual size. They give a clear idea of space and proportion and help the client to imagine how a design will be used. You can make a presentation model from any material that is easy to work with and gives realistic results.

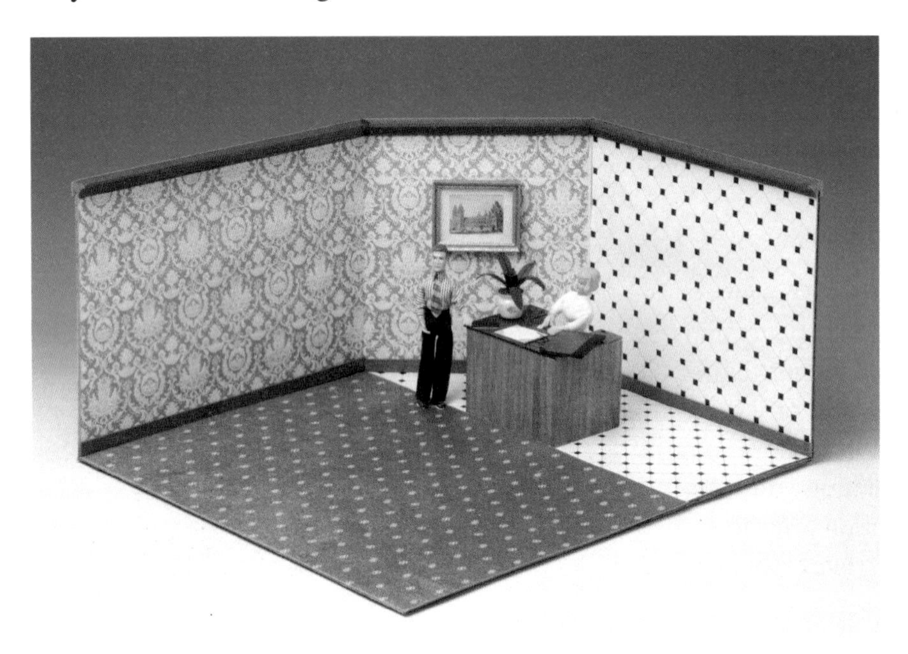

In a coloured model the patterns and textures are emphasized

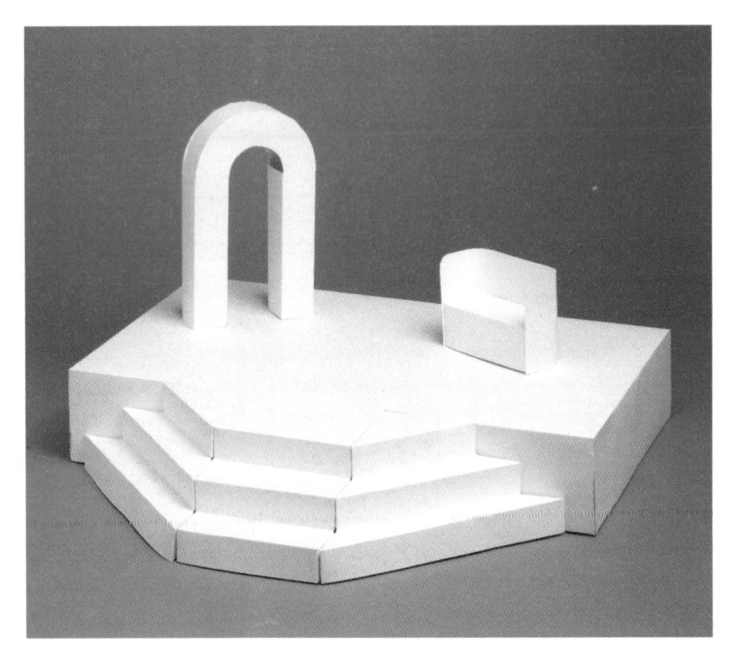

This completely white model of a stage set focuses attention on form and shapes in the design

Spray paint has been used to make this jelutong model resemble plastics. The detailed controls, raised graphics, and transfer symbols and lettering add to the realistic effect

Artwork for printing

When designing graphics for printing you will need to prepare accurate artwork showing all the information required by the printer. You can create artwork by hand or using computer software (see page 93).

Guide to hand produced artwork

- Draw artwork in black and white on **lineboard**. Text and illustrations can be pasted in position.
- Photographs should not be stuck down. Clearly mark their position on the board and include them separately.
- Draw the design full size or two or three times larger. Your drawing will look more accurate when it is reduced.
- The printer can add colour during production. You must specify the exact colour, with its reference number, from the printer's sample chart.
- Protect your artwork by taping an **overlay** of thin paper over the top.
- Write clear instructions to the printer on the overlay. Specify information about colour, backgrounds, borders, size and position of photographs, cutting edges and folds.

When your design involves more than one colour the printer may ask you to make **colour separated artwork**.

How to make a colour separation

- Carefully tape a plastic overlay (available from art shops) along the top edge of the baseboard.
- Draw in the second colour area. You can indicate the colour with a marker. Additional colours will need separate overlays.
- Use **registration marks** to ensure that the overlay lines up with the baseboard.

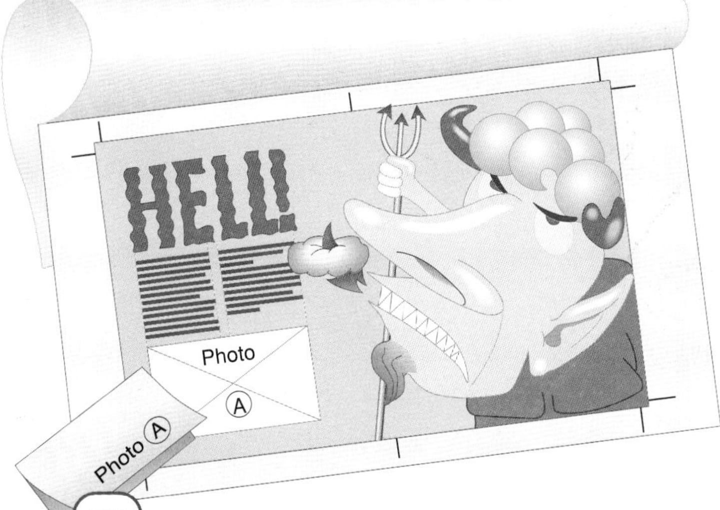

Scale drawing

A scale drawing is an accurate plan with elevations (side views) and sections (cut through views). Interiors are often drawn to a large scale such as 1:50, where one centimetre represents a half metre. This allows you to show details of furniture and fittings.

Floor plan

A floor plan usually shows a slice through the room at a height above floor level which enables you to show the position of furniture and windows. Symbols are used to represent doorways and windows. You will need to create your own simple symbols for furniture.

Wall elevation

This shows 'flat' views of the walls in the room and often includes the furniture and fittings that will be positioned on, or in front of the walls. Elevations are usually shown with the floor plan and should be drawn to the same scale.

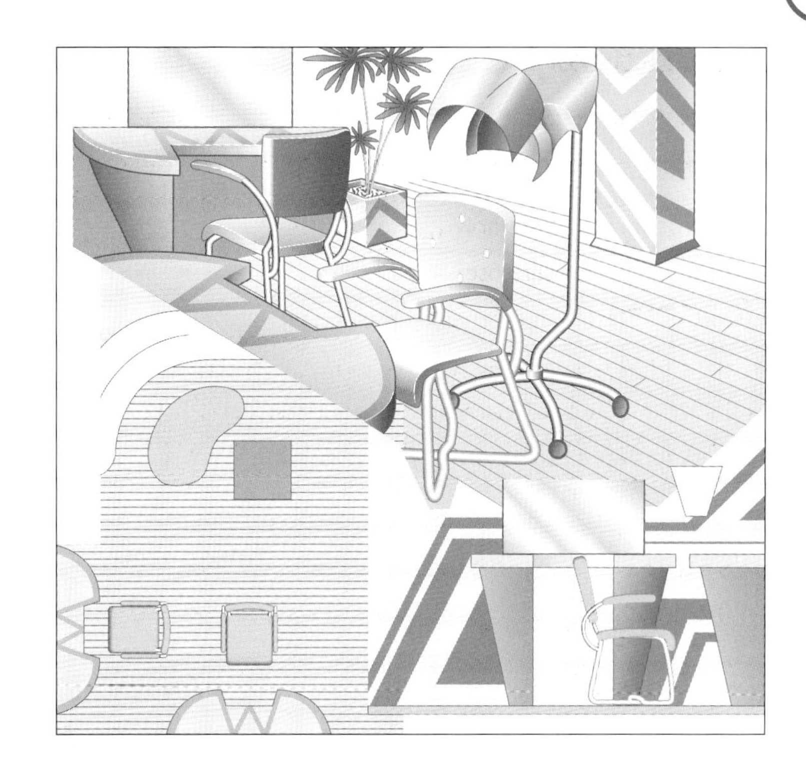

The illustration on the right shows different types of scale drawings a design drawing and a working drawing. The design drawing is used to show the appearance of the interior to a client. The working drawing shows constructional information for the manufacturer.

Hints for making a successful scale drawing

- The drawing should be well laid out and orderly. Lettering should be neat and kept horizontal. A dimension may be written vertically if it runs along a height line.
- Choose a scale that will allow you to show important details. Record the scale in the bottom right hand corner of the drawing.
- If the plan, elevations and sections are on one sheet, the plan should be at the bottom, with elevations above it and sections to the right.
- Use the plan as a guide to project lines for your elevation.
- The sides from which the elevations are viewed should be marked on the plan.
- Use pencil crayon or marker to add colour or texture.
- Grid paper can act as a useful guide. Mark the outlines in pencil to make sure everything will fit on the page. Then lay tracing paper over the top and mark the lines neatly in pen. Use different line thicknesses to make your drawing easier to understand.
- You can show the position of ceiling lights by making a tracing paper overlay that mirrors the floor plan.

User support

Many products include information to support the use of the product. This can include the following:

- instructions for assembly;
- instructions for safe use;
- instructions for maintenance and repair;
- information about insurance;
- information about associated products;
- how further information may be obtained.

Such pieces of information are graphic products in their own right. The panel below shows a range of user support materials.

Packaging

Why do we need packaging?

Packaging has several important functions:

- to contain and hold a product;
- to protect goods from damage;
- to inform the customer about the product;
- to promote a product and help it to sell;
- to make it convenient to carry, use and store the product.

Packaging is available in a vast range of shapes, sizes and materials

Choosing materials

The basic materials most often used in packaging design are paper, card, plastics, metal and glass. The material you decide to use will affect the design of the packaging.

Materials Chooser Chart

Material	Advantages	Disadvantages	Suggested material for dummy	Types of package
Paper and card	low density	easily affected by water	paper or card	cereals, washing powders
Thermoplastics	low density waterproof	easily affected by heat	two part vacuum-form moulding	soft drinks, toiletries
Metal	strong stiff waterproof	expensive high density	existing metal cans	soft drinks, tinned food
Glass	transparent waterproof	expensive shatters easily high density	existing bottles	upmarket drinks, coffees

Design guides – packaging

These questions will help you develop ideas for your packaging design.

- Who is the product for?

  Is it for: adults, children, teenagers, men, women or families? What ages are they? What appeals to the type of person for whom you are designing?
- What is the form of the product?

  Is it: powder, liquid, paste, granules, a solid block or small pieces?
- What are its physical properties?

  Is it: fragile, perishable, heavy, edible, sticky, smelly, frozen?
- How might the product be damaged?

  By: crushing, vibration, moisture, temperature changes, pests, insects, bacteria?
- What is the size and shape of the product?

  You will need to measure or work out how much room the product will take. Some packages have to hold several items. You will need to take this into account.
- How will you get it out of the packaging?

  Will it be poured, squeezed, spooned, dispensed one at a time?
- Where will it be stored and used?

  In the shop – will it be kept: on a shelf, in a display counter, hung on a rack?

  In the home – in a cupboard, in the fridge, in a handbag, on the dining table, by the sink?
- How much does the product cost?

  The materials and type of packaging used should be appropriate for the price of the product.
- What is the image of the product?

  Think about the kind of words that describe its character. Is it: firm, powerful, healthy, precious, exotic, old fashioned?

The panel below shows how these questions have been answered in the packaging for a box of after dinner mints.

- Who is it for?
  adults at dinner parties.
- What is the form of the product?
  small, thin pieces.
- What are its physical properties?
  fragile, perishable, edible.
- How might the product be damaged?
  crushing, vibration, moisture, temperature changes, pests, insects.

The Cellophane wrapper plus card box protects the product from crushing, moisture, pests and insects. The corrugated card insert and paper envelopes protect it from vibration. Temperature changes are dealt with by instructions to store at low temperature.

- How will you get it out of the package?
  dispensed one at a time.
  The paper envelope allows mints to be taken one at a time.
- Where will it be stored and used?
  in a sideboard drawer and on the dining table.
  The box is suitable for placing on the dining table.
- How much does the product cost?
  it is expensive.
  There is a lot of packaging; each mint is individually wrapped and placed in a box, indicating that it's a product worth protecting.
- What is the image of the product?
  slightly luxurious, a bit of a treat.
  The image of the box is one of stylish elegance in keeping with the product being a luxury rather than a necessity.

More about the user and using

It is important that you have a clear picture of the type of person who is likely to use the product. You will need to find out what attracts and appeals to this group of people. An image board can help you decide on the choice of colours and styles. You will need to consider ergonomics. The packaging must be comfortable to hold and easy to use. A narrow-necked bottle will let you pour out a liquid in a gentle stream, but if the neck is too wide, the liquid will flood out uncontrollably. A wide neck is more suitable for a paste that has to be scooped out, like peanut butter. Packaging that is difficult to open or use will irritate the user, who may not buy the product again.

Some examples of product image

The appearance of the packaging should suit the type of product that is inside. For example, washing powder packaging is usually bold and brash, giving the message that the powder is powerful, whereas the packaging of baby products looks delicate and kind to the baby.

Helping it to sell

On the supermarket shelf, your packaging must stand out from thousands of other products. You can do this by using a striking design and bold colours, or you can attract attention by making it unusual. A customer can even be persuaded to buy a more expensive item if the packaging gives it a feeling of quality. Unusual or fun-shaped packaging can make a product more desirable. Some packaging is far more exciting than the product inside. It will still have to fulfil all the requirements of protection, information and convenience, but its interesting shape may be its selling point.

Showing the product

Customers like to see what they are buying, so you should show what is inside. You can do this by:

- using transparent packaging, such as Cellophane, clear plastic blister pack or film wrap;
- putting a clear plastic window in the packaging;
- using a photograph or illustration (sometimes the goods inside are not very attractive so a picture can make them look more enticing);
- for products that aren't attractive or interesting to look at, the packaging often shows the results of using the product – sparkling clean glasses on dishwasher powder packaging and healthy animals on pet food packaging are examples.

Displaying the written information

The name of the product and the manufacturer may form the main part of your design. Choose a style of lettering that suits the character of your packaging, but is easy to read. Other details can be printed smaller, but should still be arranged attractively. Try not to use too many different lettering styles together, as this can look messy.

The best way to start planning the layout of the written information is to make a list of everything the user needs to know about the product. For example, food packaging should tell the user:

- the name and a description of the food;
- the name and address of the company that made it;
- the amount or weight of the contents;
- the ingredients that have been used to make it;
- nutritional information, such as the calories it contains, if it is high in fibre and so on;
- how the food should be prepared or cooked;
- how long it can be kept and in what conditions;
- the country of origin.

It may also display the maker's logo, a guarantee and the bar-code.

Point-of-sale displays

As the name suggests, point-of-sale (POS) displays are intended for use in shops and at points of direct sale to the public. They are designed to attract attention to a product, service or event and to highlight its positive qualities.

Answering the following questions will help you design your display.

- What is the display promoting?

  Find out about the product or event and decide how much information to display.
- Who is it aimed at?

  Identify the target group and the things that appeal to them.
- Where will it be used?

  Will it stand on a counter, on the floor or will it hang from a ceiling, window or wall? This information may also help you decide on a suitable display size.
- Is the display intended to hold anything?

  It may need to dispense leaflets or show samples of the product. You will need details about the size, weight and quantity of the items.
- Who will assemble the display?

  POS displays are transported as flatpacks. Do you intend the design to be assembled by a shop assistant or the sales representative?
- Does the client have special requirements?

  Your design may have to fit in with a company style or an existing advertising campaign.

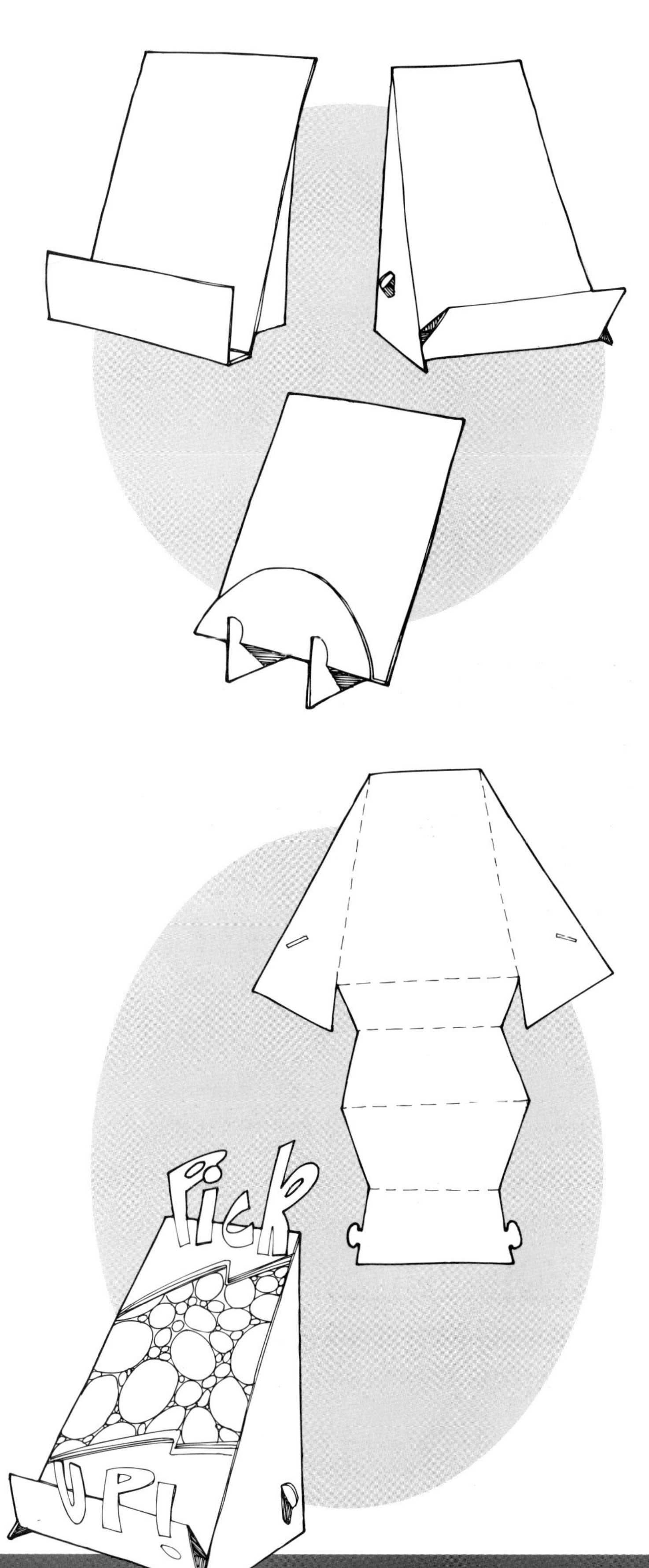

Designing the appearance

The display should have high-level impact to catch the attention of the public. You can achieve this by means of:

- exciting use of colour;
- attractive or unexpected images or shapes;
- clever wording of the message.

The graphic style will need to show the product to its best advantage and make it seem desirable. Make sure that the text is clear and easy to read and that your choice of lettering suits the style of the display. Look at the displays shown on page 122 and check how they meet these requirements.

Designing the construction

Once you have an idea for the image and shape of the display, you will need to think about the method of construction.

You can use the following questions as a design checklist.

- How will you make it stable?
- How will you stop it unfolding and collapsing?
- How will you make it last throughout the promotion?
- How will you make it easy to assemble?
- How will you make it economical and suitable for mass production?

POS displays are often developed from a single sheet of card and are assembled by clever folding and slotting of parts of the shape. You will find examples of card construction techniques on page 151.

Pop-up cards and books

Ingenious pop-up images bring graphics to life and always introduce an element of surprise. A successful pop-up design is the result of the image, message and mechanism all working together effectively.

Answering the following questions will help you get the balance right.

Who is it for?

Many pop-up cards and books are aimed at the younger age group, but a pop-up can provide an exciting way to convey information to adults.

You must be clear about the type of person you are designing for. An understanding of things they find appealing or amusing will help you decide on a style and theme for your design.

What will it look like?

Certain images have become clichéd and over-used. For example, an obvious idea for a Christmas card would feature a robin or Christmas tree. To help you devise an imaginative and original pop-up, it is important to research the theme and use brainstorming exercises to discover a richer source of images.

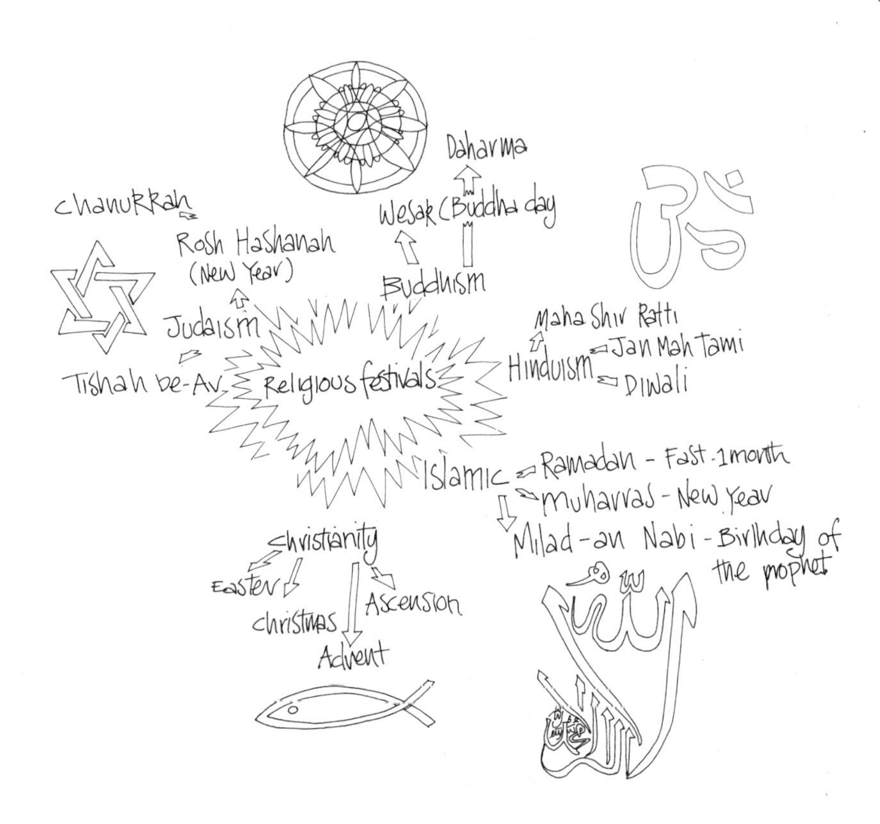

Give careful thought to the style of decoration of your design and the effect that you want to create. A pop-up storybook could use bright colours and an amusing cartoon style to encourage a child to learn to read, whereas a get well card for an elderly person would require a more gentle, cheerful style.

Remember that too much decoration may distract from the three-dimensional image. A pop-up can look impressive left quite plain.

You will need to consider the appearance of the message or text. The style of the lettering and the layout of the words should be attractive, but also suit the image of the pop-up design.

How will it work?

Pop-ups use a variety of different mechanisms. Some are very complicated, but even the most basic can have a lot of visual impact. It is useful to study pop-up books and cards and analyze how they are constructed. You can adapt a mechanism for your own design. You will find instructions for pop-up mechanisms on page 147.

Signs and signage

Looking at signs in a shopping centre

A shopping centre is full of signs. Here are some questions to help you make useful observations.

1 Where are they?
- up high rather than down low
- sometimes flat against the wall
- sometimes sticking out perpendicular to the wall
- sometimes they stand alone.

2 What do they tell you?
- the name of a shop
- what it sells
- directions to different places
- street names.

3 What is in them that conveys this information?
- letters and words
- numbers
- symbols
- images.

4 How do they manage to stand out from their surroundings?
- colours
- shape
- size
- illumination
- overall style.

5 How do they manage to fit in with their surroundings?
- colours
- shape
- size
- illumination
- overall style.

6 What is their style?
- Are they modern or traditional, serious or light-hearted, techno or natural, fancy or plain?

7 Is the sign part of a corporate image? If yes then is some or all of it be used elsewhere?
- on transport
- on uniforms
- on headed notepaper
- in advertising.

County Court
Cinema
Advice Centre
Job Centre
BURGER KING
OPTICIANS
Cashpoint
Information

Designing your own signs and signage

Answering the following questions will help you design signs and signage.

- What does the sign need to communicate?
- What visual devices might you use for this?
- Where will it be positioned?
- How will it be held in position?
- Who is it designed to attract – is it of universal appeal or aimed at a particular group?
- How will you ensure that it fits in/stands out?

Here is an example showing how the design of a restaurant sign answers these questions.

Choosing suitable materials

There are four criteria that you might use in choosing materials for your sign.

First, the overall style of the sign will affect your choice of material. Traditional signs are usually made from wood or metal (in the form of fancy iron work). A modern sign is more likely to be made from plastic or metal in the form of aluminium or chrome. It is possible to make traditional materials look modern by giving them high-gloss finishes.

Second, how hardwearing it needs to be. Most signs will need to be proofed against corrosion due to the action of the atmosphere or rotting due to the action of insects and fungus. You can find out more about the properties of materials from the Chooser Charts on pages 177–179.

Third, the colours and colourings that are available. Most plastics come in a wide range of colours and need no additional finishing. Some are translucent and let light shine through. Steel can be painted a wide range of colours or chromium plated to give a bright shine. Aluminium can be anodized to give a wide range of metallic sheens. Wood can be treated with stains, paints and preservatives to prevent rotting and give a wide range of colours and effects.

Fourth, you should consider the shaping and forming techniques available. You can shape wood by cutting out and wasting. You can shape metal strip and tube by simple bending techniques. You can shape plastic sheet by cutting and wasting. You can use hand-operated machine tools or computer-controlled routers. You can form thermoplastics by strip heating and vacuum forming.

Look at the signs shown in the panel below. Notice how different materials have been used to make the sign suitable for its situation and style.

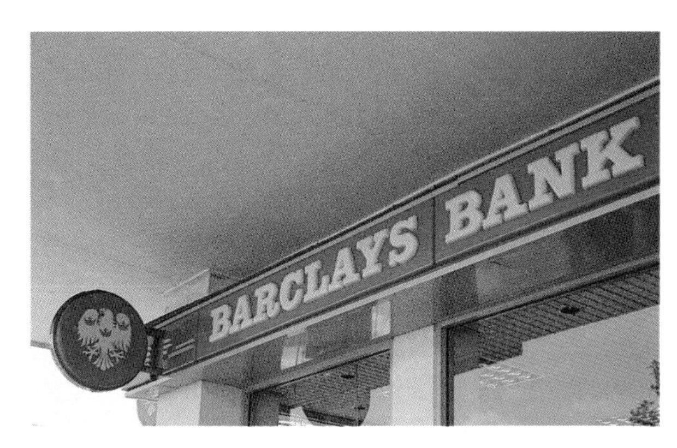

The Barclays Bank sign is made from toughened polystyrene

The MacDonald's sign is very modern. It is made from acrylic, illuminated from within

The pawnbroker's sign is a traditional sign made from brass and steel

User interfaces

Many modern products have to explain themselves to the user. The way they are to be used should be obvious from the appearance of the product. The more complicated the product, the more important it is that the user interface should be easy to understand. Here are some questions and discussion of them to help you think about the design of user interfaces.

What does the user need to know?

By asking this question you can find out if the user is a novice or an expert. Some user interfaces are designed for novices. The user interface at a cash point is a good example of this. All a user has to do is follow the instructions as they appear on the screen. The instructions are designed to be unambiguous and foolproof. The user interface of a modern single-lens reflex camera is designed for use by someone with expert knowledge. It is still designed to be simple and convenient to use, but the user has to know something about cameras and photography before using the camera.

What does the user see?

By asking this question you can begin to identify the visual elements that make up the user interface. Do they see letters making up words, numbers, geometric shapes, symbols or icons, indicator lights or dials? What form do the controls take – buttons, slides, switches, trackballs, joysticks? Do these visual elements always stay the same or do they change as on the screen in a video tape recorder? By identifying exactly what the user sees you prepare yourself for the next question.

What information does this provide?

Each visual element in the user interface should give a clear and unambiguous message to the user. If the visual element is a functional one, it should state clearly what it is for and it should be clear how to operate it. A good example here is the controls of a cassette player. There should be no confusion between play, stop, pause, rewind, fast forward and record.

Some parts of a user interface provide information that is needed to operate the product by using another part of the user interface. The key for the different washing and drying cycles on a washing machine is a good example of this. Each programme is described and linked to a number. By programming the machine with a particular number, the desired sequence of actions then takes place automatically. Without the key, the user would be unable to do this, so the information provided by the user interface should tell the user what to do in order to use the product.

How easy is it to carry out the required operations?

It is important that it is easy to do what is necessary. Buttons that are difficult to push in or so close together that the user cannot use them as required can make a user interface unsuccessful. In designing a user interface, you have to think about both the mental and physical operations of the user. The mental operations interpret the visual information and work out what has to be done, but it is hands and fingers that perform these physical operations. The controls should be chosen and positioned so that they can be used conveniently with as little physical effort as possible.

Here are two examples of product user interfaces. Answer the questions to help you think about the user interfaces that you design.

The Canon Sureshot camera

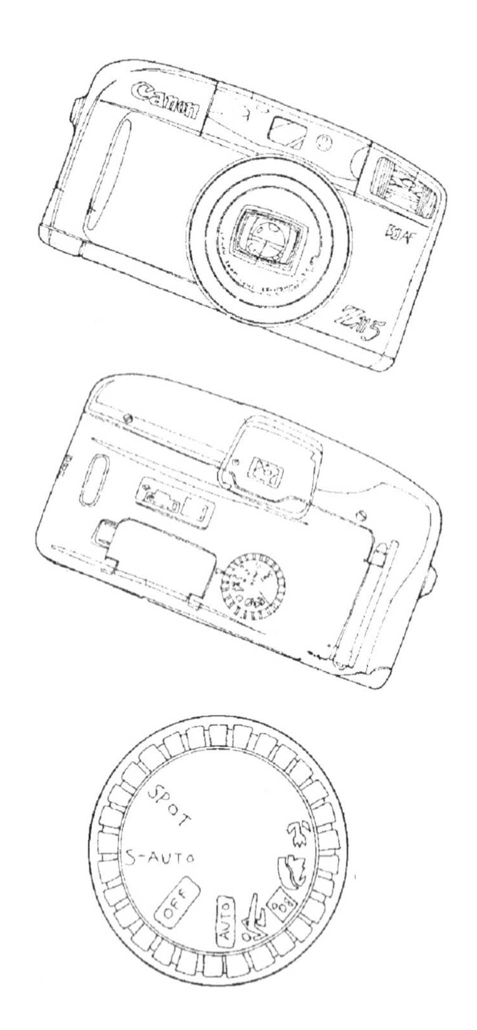

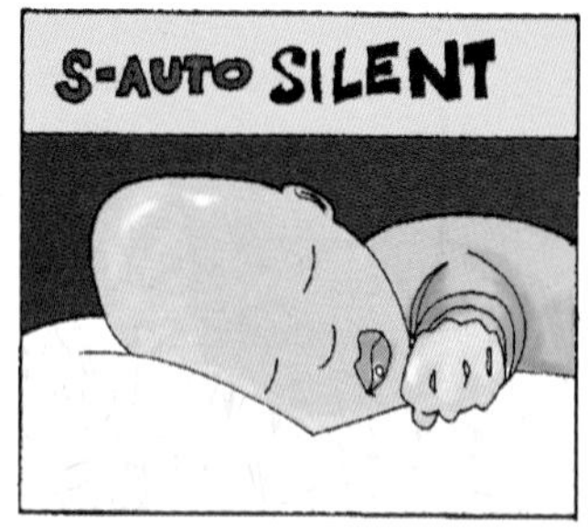

Questions

1. Are the icons self-explanatory?
2. Does the information presented make sense?
3. Can you think of any way to improve the user interface?

A personal CD player

Questions

1. Can you tell what the buttons are for?
2. Are the buttons a sensible distance apart?
3. Is the LCD screen easy to read?
4. Can you think of any way to improve the user interface?

Information

We are bombarded with information. Some of it comes in forms that are easy to understand and use, some of it is unclear and difficult. In designing information to be appealing and easy to comprehend, you will need to take three main features into account.

1 The methods you use to communicate the information

There will always be a choice of methods:

- images;
- words;
- numbers;
- symbols.

The exact nature of the information will govern which combination of methods is most appropriate.

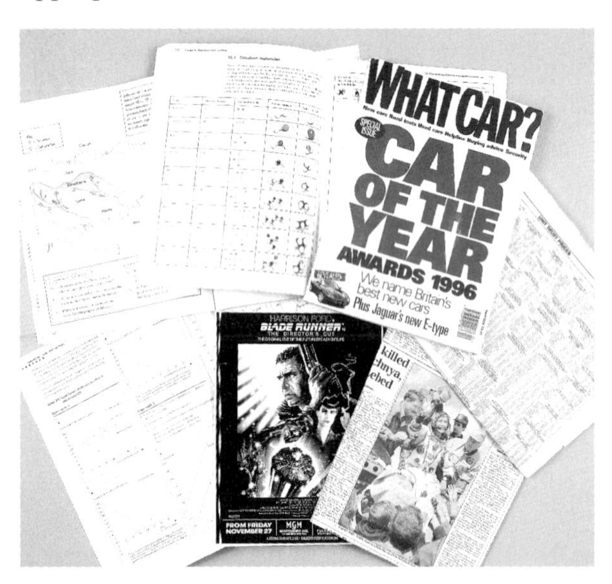

Different ways of communicating information

2 The intention of the information

There are many possibilities. Here are some of them.

- To provide information that leads to awareness, such as articles in newspapers about current affairs.
- To provide information that leads to understanding, such as textbooks.
- To provide information that leads to decision making, such as a menu for a take-away food shop.
- To provide instruction that leads to practical action, such as an assembly guide for flatpack furniture.
- To promote reflection that informs opinions, such as the editorial in a newspaper.
- To persuade, such as an advertisement in a magazine.
- To amuse, such as a strip cartoon in a newspaper.
- To intrigue, such as a picture taken from an unfamiliar angle.
- To evoke powerful feelings, such as a poster about famine relief.

Sometimes one intention will be used as part of another overall intention. For example, the pictures of Wayne and Maisie on page 102 in this book are amusing but are part of a piece with the overall intention of providing information about evaluation.

3 The audience

This will govern the level of sophistication and complexity with which you use the various methods and the sorts of intentions that are possible. Generally, the younger the audience, the less sophisticated or complicated the way the information is presented. However, it is also important to take into account the likely expertise of the audience. It is a mistake to assume that a young audience will always be naive. Some junior school children have extensive knowledge of their interests and would be insulted by information that was presented in a condescending way.

Here are some examples of information for you to consider. For each one, ask yourself the following questions.

- What methods are being used?
- What are the intentions of the information?
- What is the most likely audience for the information?

Here are some examples of information for you to consider. For each one ask yourself the following questions.

- What methods are being used?
- What is intended by the information?
- What is the most likely audience for the information?

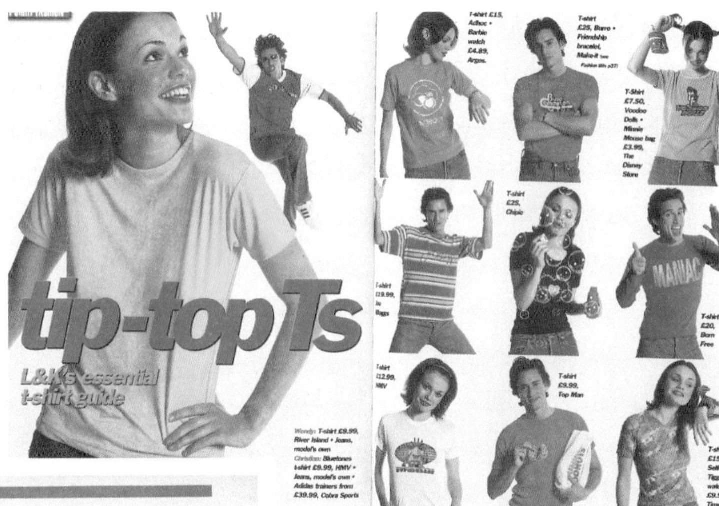

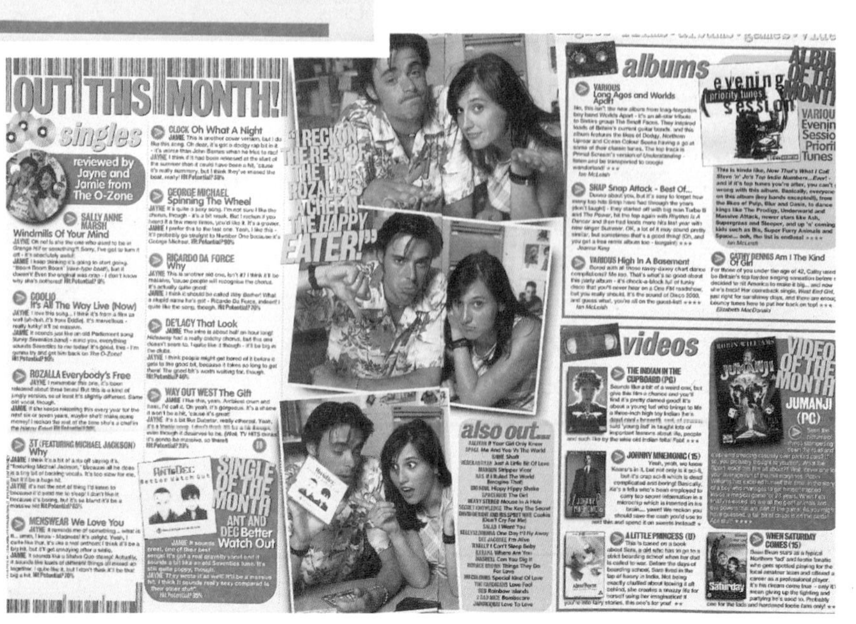

Board games

Board games have been played for many centuries. Some, like chess and draughts, rely purely on mental skill. Others, like shove ha'penny, rely on physical skill. Games like ludo rely entirely on luck. Yet others rely on a combination of skill *and* luck – Scrabble, for example.

Whatever the game, it will need to have some or all of the following features:

- a board – this sets the scene for the game and provides the framework in which it is played
- rules – these must state clearly how the game is played and what a player has to do in order to win
- ways of generating scores or moves – these can be a single dice or spinner or a combination of dice or a complicated spinning wheel (some dice have symbols rather than numbers)
- means of representing the players – these can be simple counters or complicated figures
- penalty or advantage possibilities – this adds to the excitement of the game and can be handled in different ways, so sometimes they are present as a fixed feature on the board, sometimes they are present as cards that are turned up on specific occasions
- a box – this holds the board, rule book, playing pieces and any other elements and is also what potential buyers will see on display in the shops, so its external appearance is particularly important as an exciting game in a dull-looking box is unlikely to be successful.

You can use the descriptions of the three games that follow to see how these features appear in different sorts of board games.

A simple board game – snakes and ladders

Notice the following features of this simple game, which can be used to teach small children to count:

- the cup and dice are suitable for small fingers
- the dice is simple spot numbered, though you can introduce two dice if you want to make the playing more difficult
- the counters representing each player are simple
- the rules are simple
- the number of squares you move is given by the number you get when you throw the dice
- if you throw a six (or a double six with two dice) you get an extra turn
- if you land on a snake, you have to follow it back to the bottom of its tail
- if you land on a ladder, you go up the ladder to its top
- the first player to reach the last square is the winner
- it can be played by up to four people
- the board is a simple grid that has a friendly appearance – the snakes don't look dangerous
- the box is simple and attractive to the children likely to be playing the game
- a single game probably takes only about 5–10 minutes to play.

A more complicated board game – Monopoly

Notice the following features that make it more complicated than snakes and ladders:

- the dice are smaller – making it more suitable for older players
- the pieces representing the players are more imaginative and there are other physical elements – Monopoly money, houses, hotels, Chance and Community Chest cards and cards representing deeds to properties
- the rules are complicated
- the aim of the game – being so successful that other players become bankrupt – involves a fair bit of skill and thought
- the Chance cards add an element of uncertainty and excitement
- the board layout is simple, but playing involves complicated activities
- someone has to act as a banker and control the money, property deeds and houses and hotels
- the box has a sophisticated look, which is attractive to the older children and adults likely to play the game
- a single game can take a long time to play.

An adventure game – Warhammer

Notice the following features:

- there are lots of different pieces representing different creatures – some human, some animal, some mythical – and they each have a particular strength, weaknesses and weaponry
- there is no board, but the pieces are arranged according to a set battle plan given in a guide book
- there is a set of complicated rules – set out in a 96-page rule book!
- there are cards summarizing the rules
- a player wins by destroying the opposing forces
- the dice are complicated, involving numbers and symbols
- there is another hobby linked to playing the game – collecting and painting the figures and this is supported by other publications (a painting guide and a 'bestiary')
- the box leaves you in no doubt about the nature of the game
- this is a complicated game for committed players who rapidly become experts – a game involving a complicated battle with lots of pieces can take several hours to set up and one or two days to play!

Interior design

This guide to interior design will help you use graphic products to make inside spaces attractive to look at and pleasant to use. You can use the following questions to find out what is required.

How many people will use the space?

In the design of any interior, there needs to be a balance between the amount of decoration and the amount of information on view. In a single person's study bedroom, it is likely that any graphic products will be used for decoration rather than information. In a large railway station, however, the display of information through graphic products becomes very important, although there will be some decorative features.

For a single person or small group, the graphic products can be designed to have individual appeal. They can relate quite specifically to the users as individuals – a block printing of the silhouettes of family members for a home dining room, for example. The graphic products for decorating places used by large groups or crowds need to have more universal appeal.

Is it a private place or a public space?

Private places, such as rooms at home or small offices, have to meet the needs of only a few individuals. Public places, on the other hand, have to meet the needs of a wide range of people, even though at any one time they might only be used by a few people or even a single person. The one-person toilet kiosks in some city centres is an example of this.

Many designers argue that the best way to prevent vandalism in such places is to make them attractive and pleasant to use as well as almost indestructable.

What sort of people will use the space?

The style of both the information and decoration provided by means of graphic products will vary according to the sort of people who use the space. Users could mainly come from one age group with perhaps one or two of a different age group acting as assistants or adult helpers, as in the case of a playgroup or primary school. Alternatively, the users might be a widely mixed group, as in the case of a department store.

What is the space used for?

The sorts of graphic products required by a space will depend on the detailed use of the space. A hostel and a bedroom are both used for sleeping, but they have very different graphic product requirements. Appropriate graphic products will help to make the space suitable for the detail of its use.

Here are some more contrasting examples:

- sleeping – bedroom or hostel
- studying – study bedroom or library
- socializing – familiy living room or local club
- dining – small restaurant or fast food outlet
- exhibiting – motoring organization booth or museum
- medical care – doctor's waiting room or hospital ward
- selling goods or services – clothes boutique or bank.

Using graphic products to organize a space

It is possible to use graphic products to help organize a space so that it is easier to use. Here are some examples:

- display screens in libraries to provide private reading areas;
- model photo boards in some clothes shops to divide up the shop and prevent large groups gathering;
- large overhead signs hanging above the aisles in supermarkets so that customers can find goods quickly.

Achieving organization by using graphic products

Appropriate lighting is important

Ensuring appropriate lighting

It is important to ensure that the lighting is right for an interior. Bright lighting is used in fast food outlets to ensure that customers do not linger. Subdued lighting is used in small restaurants to ensure that people *do* linger and order that extra bottle of wine. However, it is important that even where there is subdued lighting there is enough light for reading the menu! Signs that are poorly lit are either not read or misread, which leads to frustration.

So, while you may not be designing the lighting for an interior, if you are providing graphic products, you should specify the lighting conditions under which they should be used. In this way, the graphic products that you design will have maximum effect.

Here and over the page are some examples of different spaces. Look carefully at each one and answer the following questions.

- Is this a public or private place?
- Who will use this space?
- What will they use it for?
- What graphic products can you see in the space?
- Which are for decoration?
- Which are for information?

Again, ask yourself these questions.

- Is this a public or private place?
- Who will use this space?
- What will they use it for?
- What graphic products can you see in the space?
- Which are for decoration?
- Which are for information?

On the following pages you will find techniques to help you make card and paper mechanisms for pop-ups and packaging and constructions for POS (point-of-sale) displays. You can adapt these examples to create imaginative designs of your own.

Materials

Papers and card can be bought in a wide range of colours, textures, thicknesses and weights. This brief guide will help you decide on a suitable thickness of material. You will find more detailed information in the Chooser Chart on page 180.

For pop-up designs

The backing sheet on which the pop-up is built should be strong enough to open without buckling. For pop-ups that involve a lot of stresses and strains, use a rigid, heavy weight of card, such as mounting board. For the pop-up design, you can use thick paper, such as cartridge paper, or thin card. Card that is too thick will be too bulky to fold flat and thin paper will not keep its shape when the page is opened.

For packaging and carton design

The card must be strong enough to keep its shape and protect the product inside, yet it must be flexible enough to fold without cracking. Choose card from 350 microns up to 640 microns thick. Anything thinner will not have enough stiffness, while anything thicker will not fold properly.

For point-of-sale displays

Displays tend to be fabricated from heavy weights of card or even corrugated board. This is necessary if they are designed to be self-supporting or are intended to hold a product. They also need to resist knocks and damage from use in the store.

Decoration

Take care when using water-based paints to colour your design. Too much moisture will wrinkle the surface of paper and cause thin card to warp. You can achieve effective results with markers, pencil crayon and pastels, or use a colour photocopy of your original artwork.

Scoring and folding

Scoring makes it easier to produce a neat fold. Using a metal ruler as a guide, run the tip of a scalpel along the line of the fold. Only the surface of the card should be cut (do not cut too deeply or the card will break). The card is then folded away from the score line so that it can open slightly along the cut. You will find that the card bends and folds accurately. Remember that paper and card will fold more smoothly with the direction of the grain.

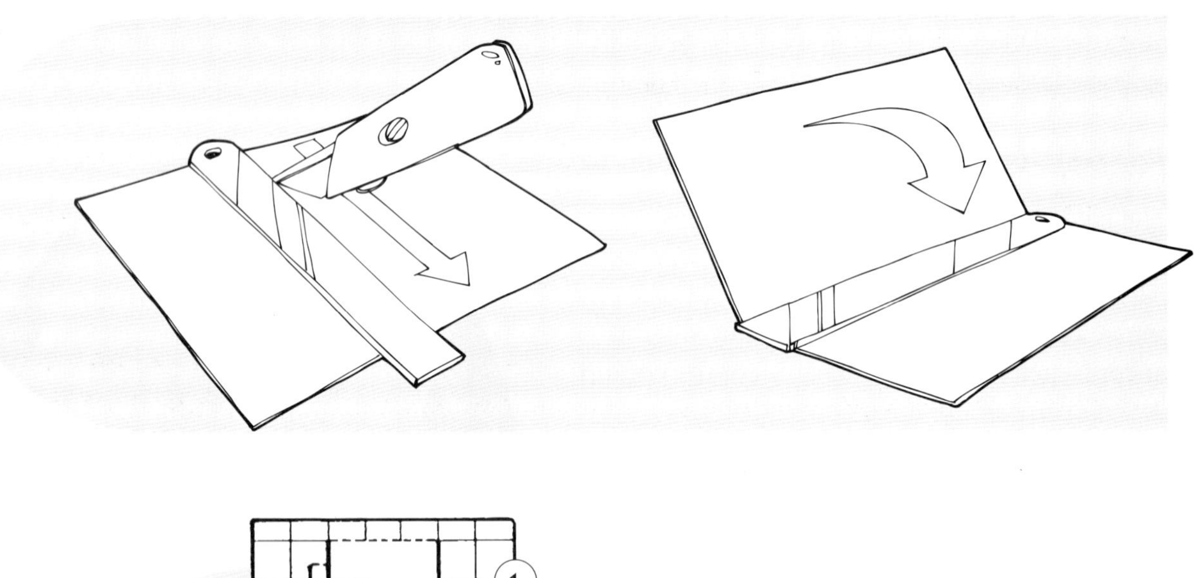

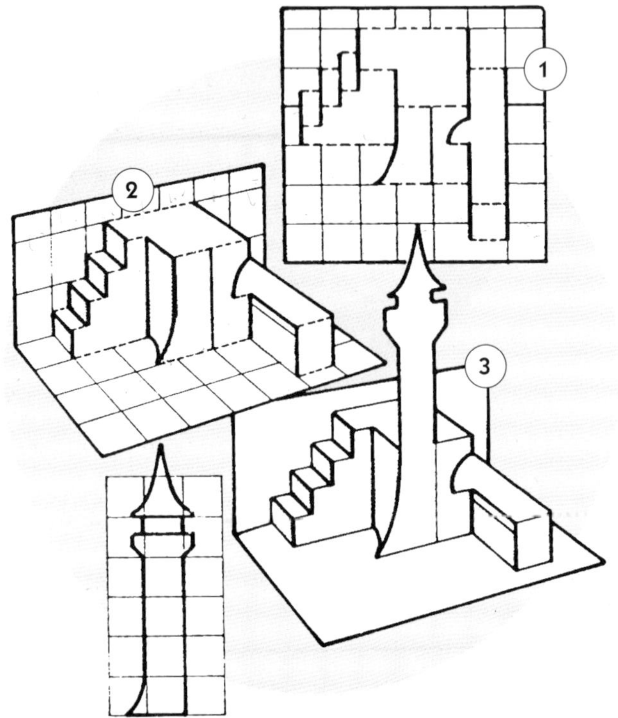

1. A pop-up design with scoring lines (- - -) and cutting lines (——)
2. Just fold and the castle 'pops up'
3. Adding extra detail. Can you explain why the tower can't be included in the original piece?

Remember – when using a sharp knife or scalpel with paper or card take great care!

Pop-up mechanisms

The V fold

This is a simple but versatile mechanism. The pop-up images are attached to the page by means of V-shaped flaps or an inverted V shape, depending on the effect that you wish to create.

1 Apply glue to the undersides of the tabs and attach them to the backing sheet so that the point of the V touches the central foldline.

2 If the angle of the V is 90 degrees, the pop-up will stand vertically when the card is open. If the angle of the V is less than 90 degrees, it will lean backwards, but if it is more than 90 degrees, it will lean forwards.

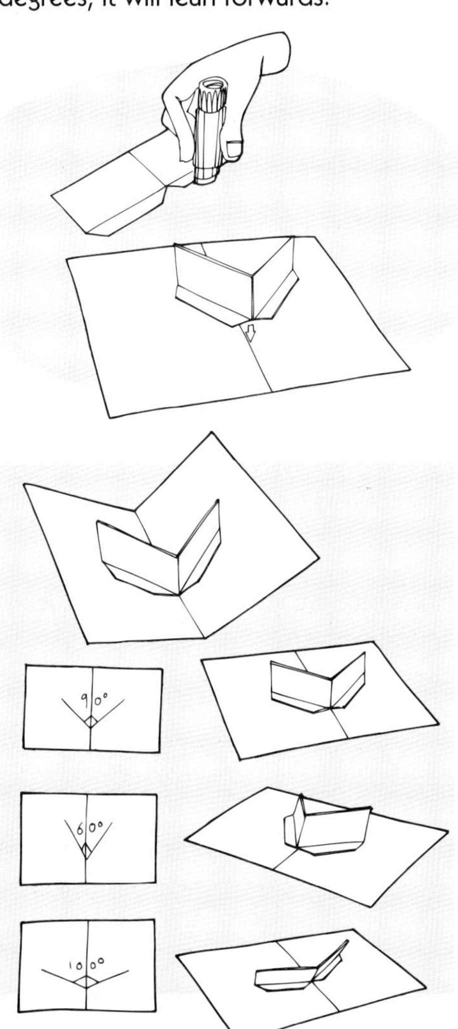

The pop-up box

This design is based on the V-fold mechanism. The hollow box shape can be modified to create all sorts of objects.

1 Scale up the diagram to the required size. Cut it out and score along the foldlines.

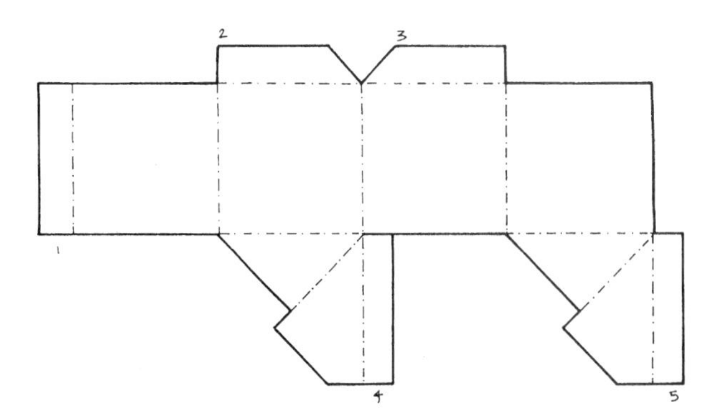

2 Apply glue to the end tab and fold to join the sides of the box, making a square 'tube'.

3 Apply glue to the lid tabs. These will look neater if they are attached to the inside of the box – but will have more strength if they are glued to the outside. You will have to decide which is more suitable for your design.

4 Fold back the base tabs inwards and glue these to the backing sheet using the V-fold technique.

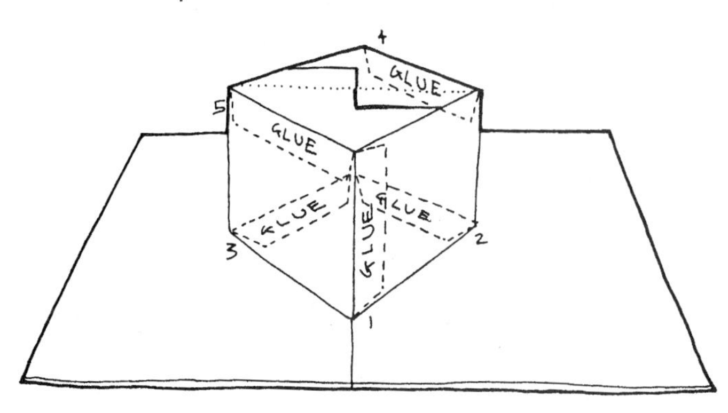

Layer mechanisms

This mechanism is based on parallelograms and involves accurate measuring, but, again, is quite simple to make.

The single layer

1. Cut a strip of card, allowing for glue tabs and fold as shown checking that the pop-up will not protrude outside of the card when it is closed.
2. Find the correct position by holding the strip in place with paper-clips. All parts should be parallel to one page or the other. Mark the position for gluing with a pencil.
3. Glue tabs in place. The pop-up design can be glued onto the moving layer.

Multiple layers

1. Cut two or three strips of card of different lengths. The length will depend on the size of your card. Allow for glue tabs.
2. Hold in position with paper-clips. Check that the layers are parallel and that the pop-up will not show when the card is closed. Mark the correct positions with a pencil.
3. Glue the tabs in position. Glue the pop-up designs onto the individual layer mechanisms.

Floating layers

This mechanism uses a similar construction technique to multiple-layer pop-ups. The layers are positioned to support a design that spans the page, increasing the impression of depth.

Incized mechanisms

Using this mechanism, you can create quite complicated designs from one piece of card with no gluing.

1. Mark in pencil the central foldline on the backing sheet.
2. Draw the layer mechanism at 90 degrees to the central fold.
3. Position as shown in the diagram. Rub out the pencil central foldline on the layer.
4. Measure AB (the distance between the short end and the central fold).
5. Mark the same distance at the other end. This line will be formed into a fold on the finished mechanism.
6. Now cut and fold your drawing to create a layer mechanism from one sheet of card.

This technique can be used to produce a multiple-layer effect or to create the whole pop-up design.

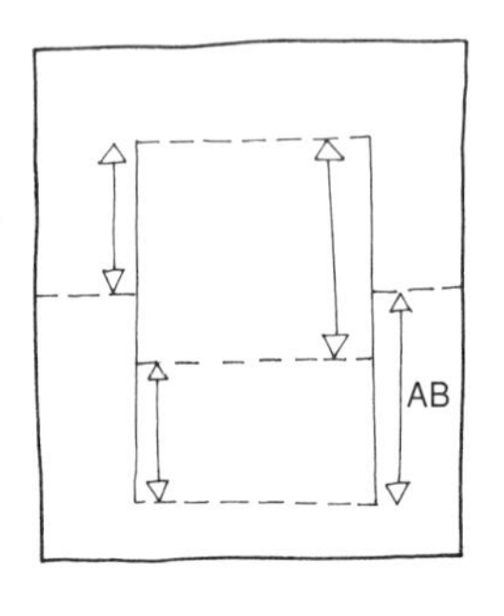

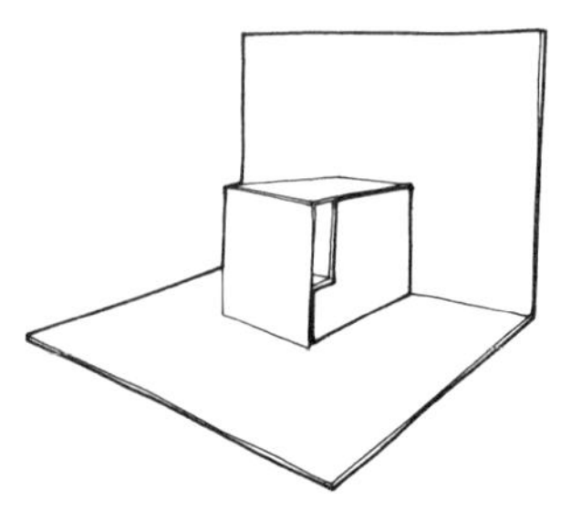

Mechanisms that produce movement

The sliding mechanism

Linear movement can be produced using a sliding mechanism.

1. Cut a slot in the card backing sheet, in the direction of the required movement.
2. Fold two small pieces of card in half and pass these through the slot – as shown.
3. Cut a strip of stiff card as a pull tab. The length will depend on the size of your card.
4. Glue this to the back of the two smaller pieces.
5. Near the edge of the card, attach a guide for the pull tab.
6. The image that is required to move can now be glued to the front of the two small pieces of card.

The rotary mechanism

This mechanism will give a circular or rotating motion.

1. Cut a 10 mm hole in the backing card at the centre of the circular movement.
2. Use another piece of card and cut a 30 mm diameter circle. This can be cut to act as gluing tabs. Mark out and cut as shown in the diagram.
3. Stick the centre circle of the tabs to the image that is required to move.
4. Now cut a circle of card that is large enough to protrude beyond the backing card. Push the tabs through the hole and glue them to the centre of the disc. This will provide a wheel to turn the image on the front of the card.

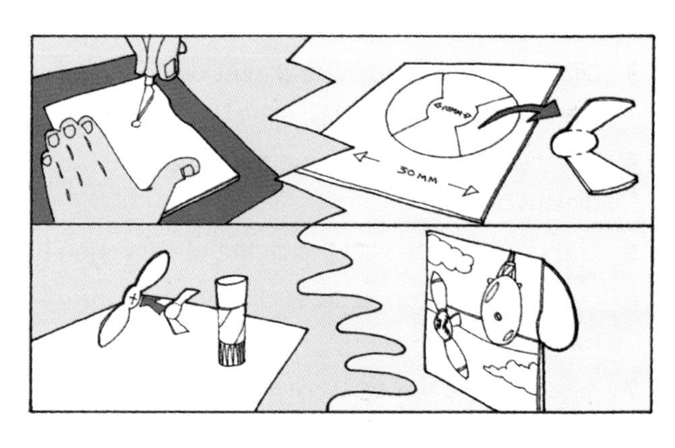

The crash lock base for packaging

You can adapt a net for a rectangular carton to make this closing mechanism for the base. It is stronger and will hold a heavier product than the standard 'tuck in' base.

1. Draw the net of the carton body and lid to the required size and add the base as shown in the diagram. The card grain should run widthways.
2. A equals half of dimensions B.

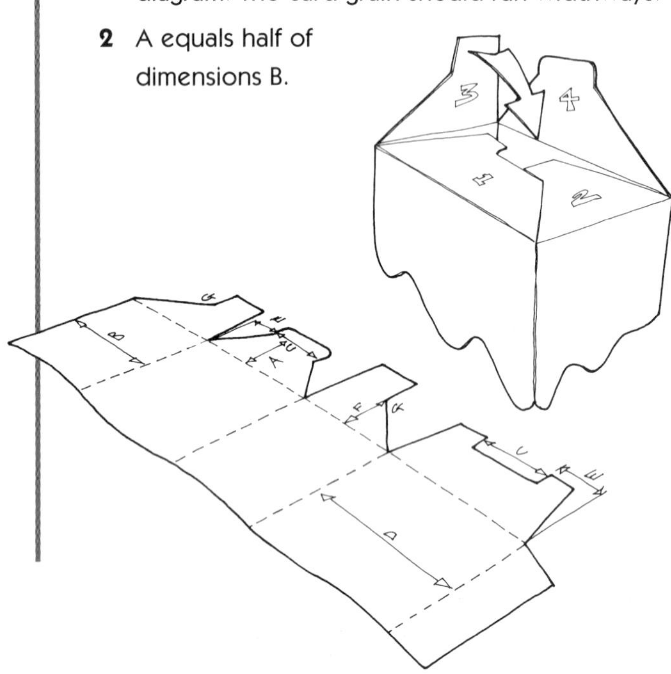

3. Dimensions C are equal, and must be no longer than dimension D.
4. Dimensions E are equal, and the same as dimension F.
5. Corners G line up with the centre of dimension B.
6. Cut out the carton, score and bend along the foldlines.
7. Assemble the box by sticking the front panel in place with double-sided tape.
8. To close the base of the carton, fold in flaps in the order shown in the diagram.

Pop-up carton lid

In this design, the lid pops up automatically. It is stronger and gives a more professional finish than the usual lid with 'tuck in' flaps.

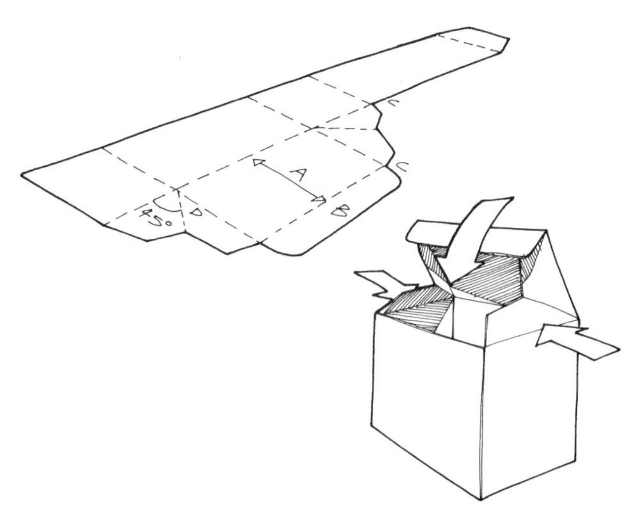

1. Draw the net of the carton body and base to the required size and add the lid, as shown in the diagram. The grain of the card should run widthways.
2. Draw the centre panel of the lid A first. This should be 1 mm shorter than the width of the sides of the carton. This allows room for flap B to be tucked in when the carton is closed.
3. Flap B must be at least 15 mm deep to prevent it from slipping out of the carton. Notice that only the flap corners are rounded. The straight sides grip the inside of the carton when it is closed.
4. Cut out the carton and score along foldlines.
5. Make perforations marked D, by making small cuts (3 mm or 4 mm) with the tip of a scalpel. Start near the base and work towards the outside edge. Make sure that the last cut is not too near the edge or it is liable to tear in use.
6. Fold all score lines and perforations and assemble by gluing the carton front in place.
7. Push the lid down. As it closes, the side panels will bend inwards along the perforations. As the lid is opened, the side panels pop up.

Point-of-sale construction

A display stand for flat items

This display stand is made from one piece of stiff card and does not require gluing. It can be folded flat for transportation.

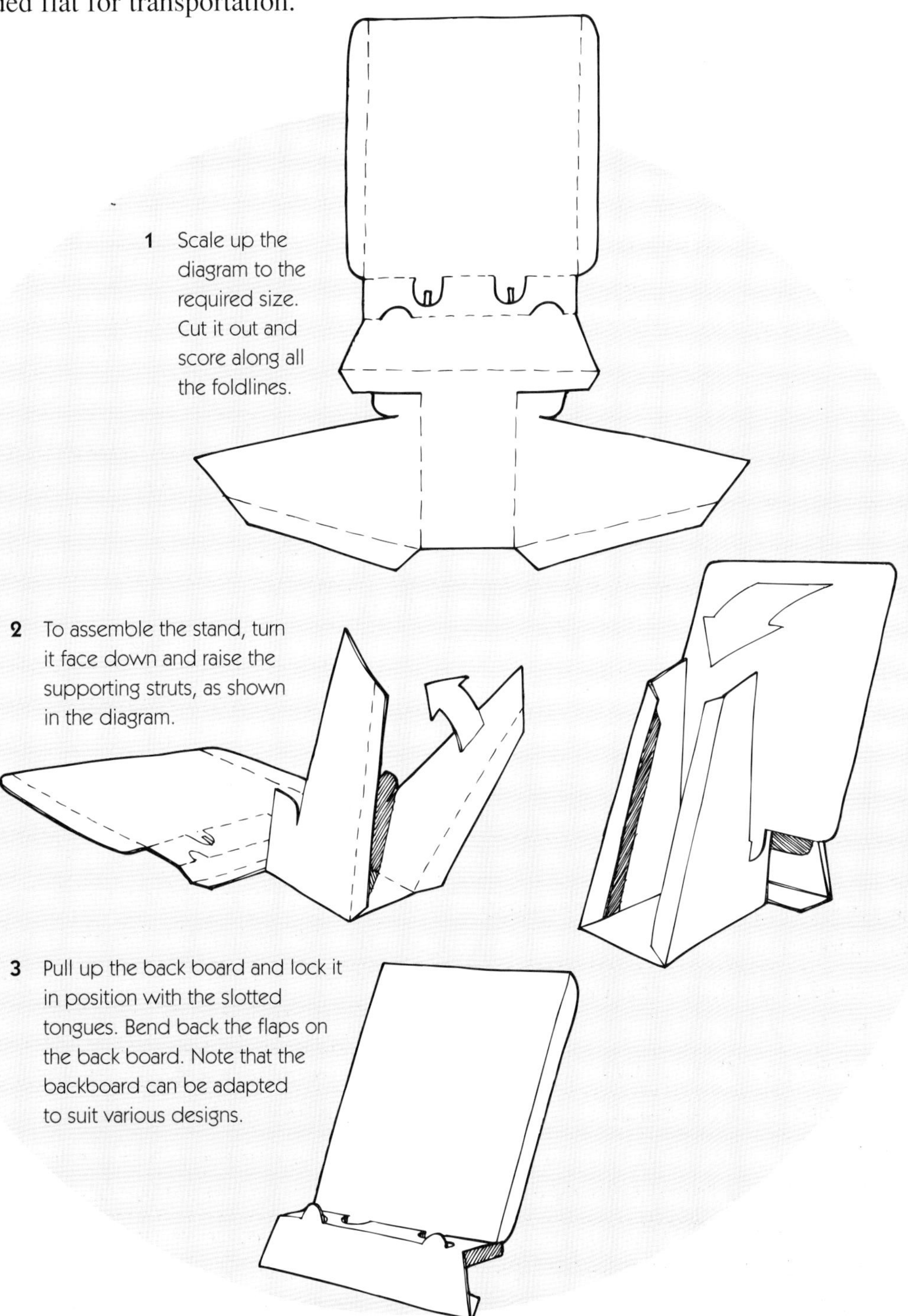

1 Scale up the diagram to the required size. Cut it out and score along all the foldlines.

2 To assemble the stand, turn it face down and raise the supporting struts, as shown in the diagram.

3 Pull up the back board and lock it in position with the slotted tongues. Bend back the flaps on the back board. Note that the backboard can be adapted to suit various designs.

A display stand with a wide octagonal base

This stand is cut from two pieces of thick card and involves gluing.

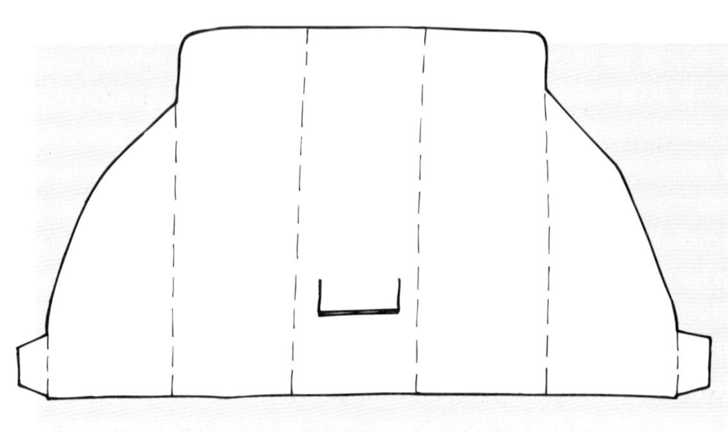

1 Scale up the diagrams to the required size. Cut them out and score along all fold lines.

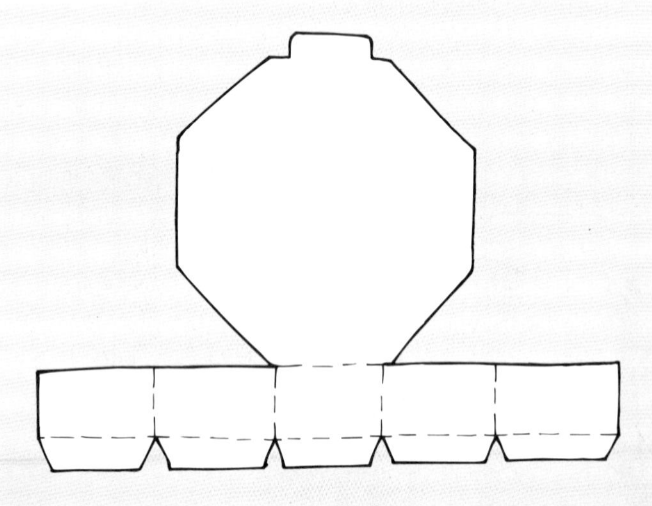

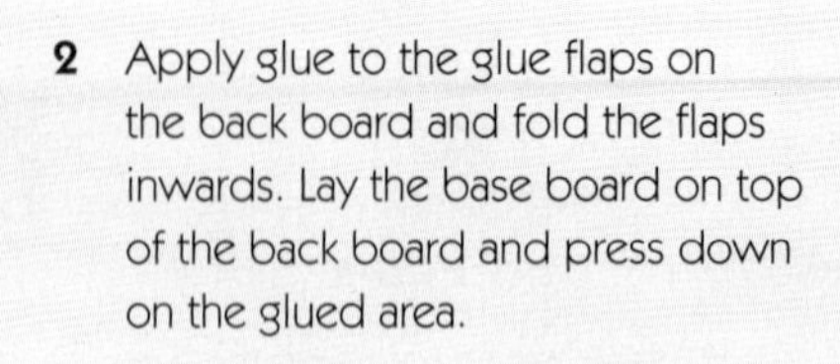

2 Apply glue to the glue flaps on the back board and fold the flaps inwards. Lay the base board on top of the back board and press down on the glued area.

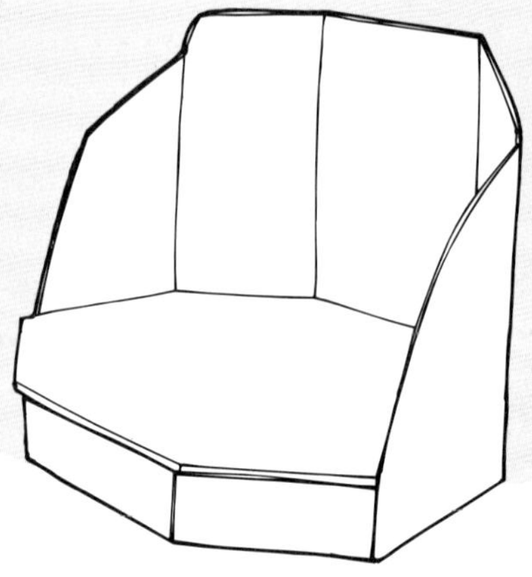

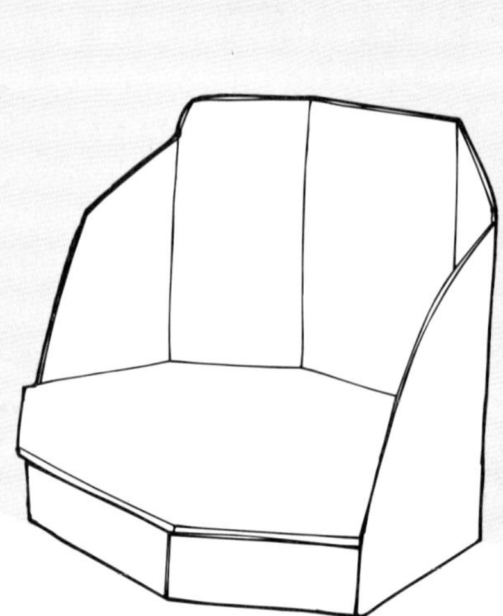

3 Stand the whole thing up and push down the platform section in the base until the tongue clicks into the slot in the back board. Fold the three base flaps under to complete the stand.

Layout and typography 8

Whenever you are designing printed materials, you will need to make decisions at different levels of detail. To begin with, you will need to decide on the key features of the overall layout. Once you are satisfied that this is correct, you can begin to think about features like the use of headings and, later still, design features for the main text. Then you need to decide on which style of lettering would be best to use. At this stage, you have decided on all the important features of the design and you can set these up within desktop publishing software as a style guide, which automatically produces the layout in line with your design decisions.

The main features of the layout

At the very beginning, you need to make decisions about the number of columns of text on each page, the size, number and position of illustrations on each page and the amount of white space. You might find it useful to think about these in terms of double-page spreads. You can work out the main features by exploring different numbers of columns, different illustration arrangements and different amounts of white space through rough sketches as shown.

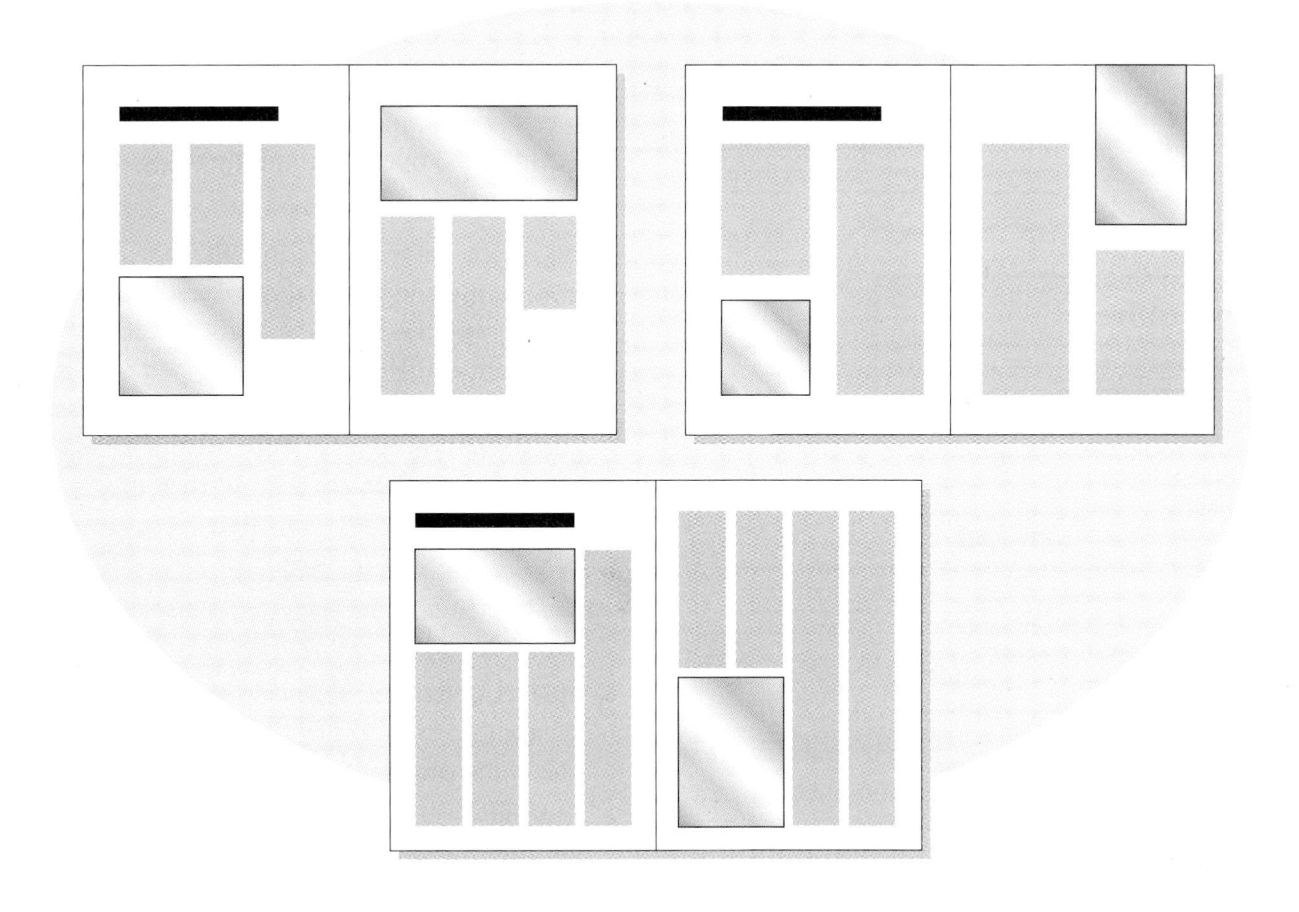

Use of headings and subheadings

You can draw attention to the content of a page by providing a main heading. This is usually in large, bold letters. You can also make it easy to scan the text for points of interest by including subheadings. You can use the following devices to indicate subheadings:

- coloured letters;
- coloured stripes;
- bullet points;
- underlining.

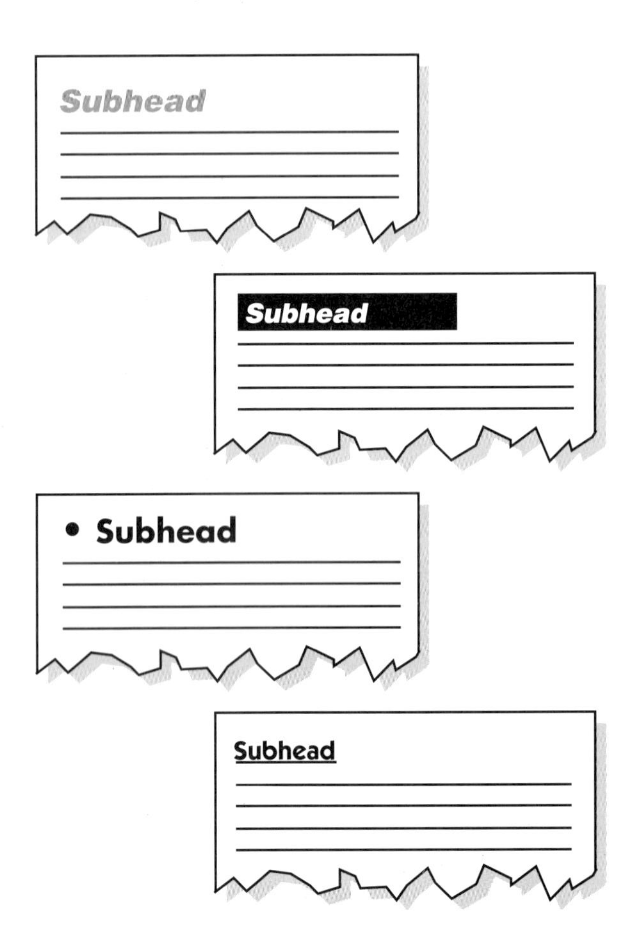

Too many subheadings, though, make the text both look and read in a disjointed way.

If you design your layout on a computer screen, it is easy to compare different versions so that you get the effect you want.

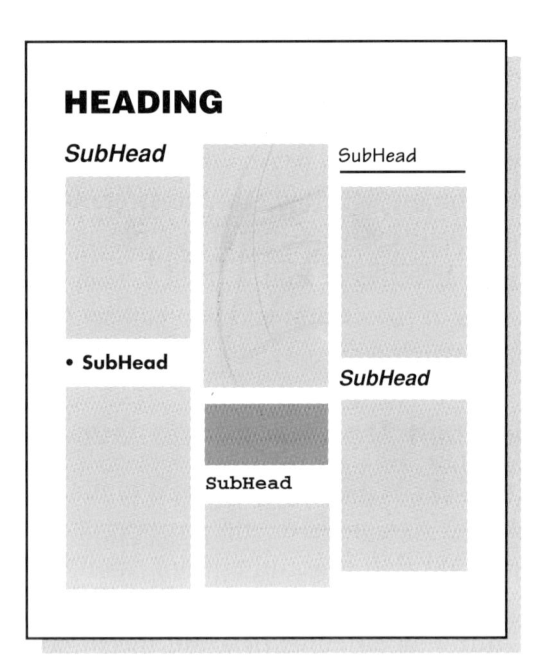

Designs like this do not help!

The body text

You can control the appearance of the body text within the overall layout by using the following devices.

- Alignment – alignment to the left gives a ragged edge at the end of a line; alignment to the right gives a ragged edge at the start of a line; alignment at the centre gives a ragged edge at both the start and end of a line; justifying gives straight vertical edges at both ends of a line by squeezing or stretching the text to fit the paragraph width.
- Drop capitals – at the beginning of an article the first letter of the first word is made larger and dropped.
- Indents – often the beginning of a paragraph is indicated by indenting the text at the first line of the paragraph.
- Spacing – you can vary the spacing between lines and between paragraphs.
- Listings – you can use numbers, letters, bullets or small icons to add emphasis.

Page 170 of this book, shown below, is a clearly laid out page that makes use of some of these devices.

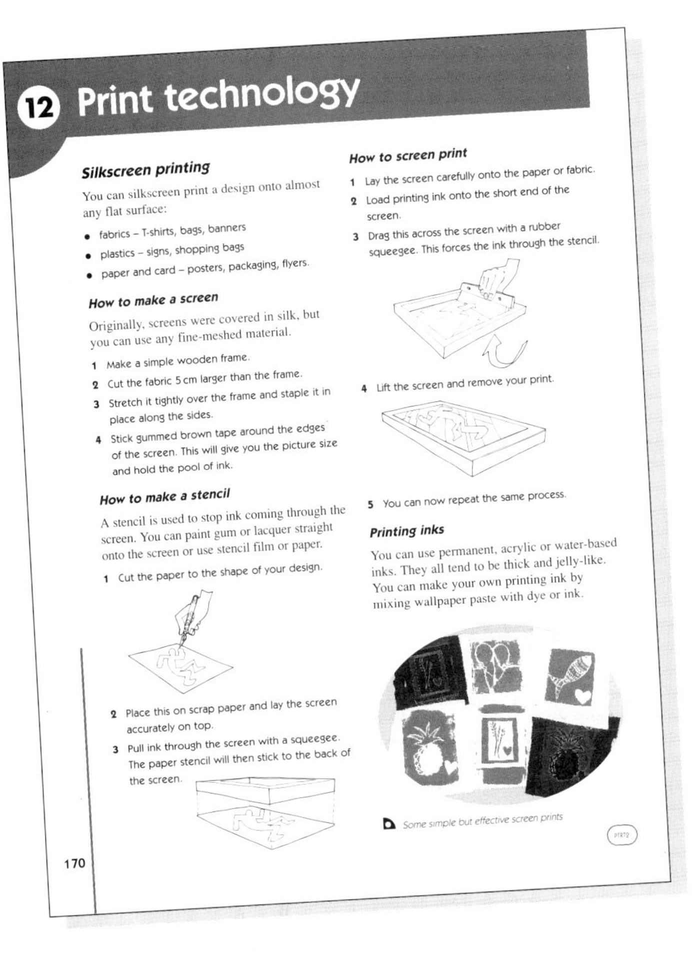

12 Print technology

Silkscreen printing

You can silkscreen print a design onto almost any flat surface:

- fabrics – T-shirts, bags, banners
- plastics – signs, shopping bags
- paper and card – posters, packaging, flyers.

How to make a screen

Originally, screens were covered in silk, but you can use any fine-meshed material.

1. Make a simple wooden frame.
2. Cut the fabric 5 cm larger than the frame.
3. Stretch it tightly over the frame and staple it in place along the sides.
4. Stick gummed brown tape around the edges of the screen. This will give you the picture size and hold the pool of ink.

How to make a stencil

A stencil is used to stop ink coming through the screen. You can paint gum or lacquer straight onto the screen or use stencil film or paper.

1. Cut the paper to the shape of your design.
2. Place this on scrap paper and lay the screen accurately on top.
3. Pull ink through the screen with a squeegee. The paper stencil will then stick to the back of the screen.

How to screen print

1. Lay the screen carefully onto the paper or fabric.
2. Load printing ink onto the short end of the screen.
3. Drag this across the screen with a rubber squeegee. This forces the ink through the stencil.
4. Lift the screen and remove your print.
5. You can now repeat the same process.

Printing inks

You can use permanent, acrylic or water-based inks. They all tend to be thick and jelly-like. You can make your own printing ink by mixing wallpaper paste with dye or ink.

Some simple but effective screen prints

PTRT2

170

Notice that the page does not use all of the devices – this would make it 'over busy'.

Choice of font and type size

The style of lettering you choose is important. This is called the font. Some fonts are associated with certain sorts of information or certain sorts of reader. Here are some examples.

Avante Garde	Courier
Chicago	Garamond
Geneva	Helvetica
M Bembo	Monaco
Palatino	Times

Can you match these fonts to information or readers?

The most important criteria is legibility. If the size of the lettering is too small or the background tint makes it difficult to read, it does not matter how attractive the overall layout is because readers will get frustrated, tired and annoyed and stop reading. Here are some examples of a short sentence in the same font but in different type sizes.

Smaller than this and I can't read it (14 point).

Smaller than this and I can't read it (12 point).

Smaller than this and I can't read it (10 point).

Smaller than this and I can't read it (9 point).

Smaller than this and I can't read it (7 point).

You can also change the style of the font so that it can appear as follows:

bold	*italic*	outline
shadow	reversed out	

or in a combination of effects, for example:

italic outline.

Using a style guide

At this stage, you have decided on all the important features of the design and you can set these up within desktop publishing software as a style guide that automatically produces the layout in line with your design decisions.

This book was designed using a style guide. Here the graphic designer has annotated a page with instructions according to the style guide instructions.

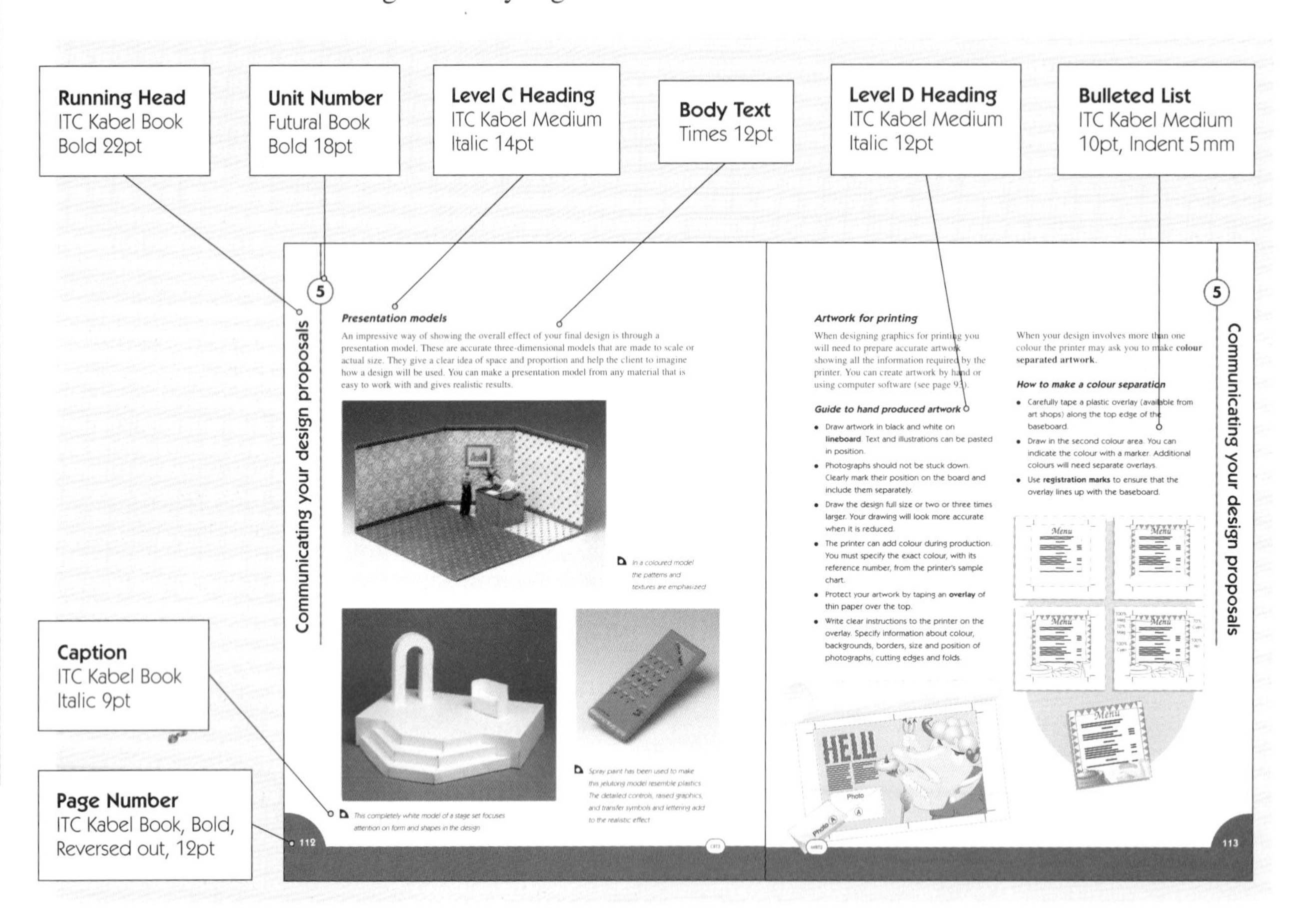

Achieving impact

By skilfully combining appropriate aspects of typography and layout, you can make your work have real power. Here is an example of innovative modern graphic design. It incorporates photos picked out in black, wide use of large, bold type, key words emphasized, all superimposed on the aggressive image of the handcuffs.

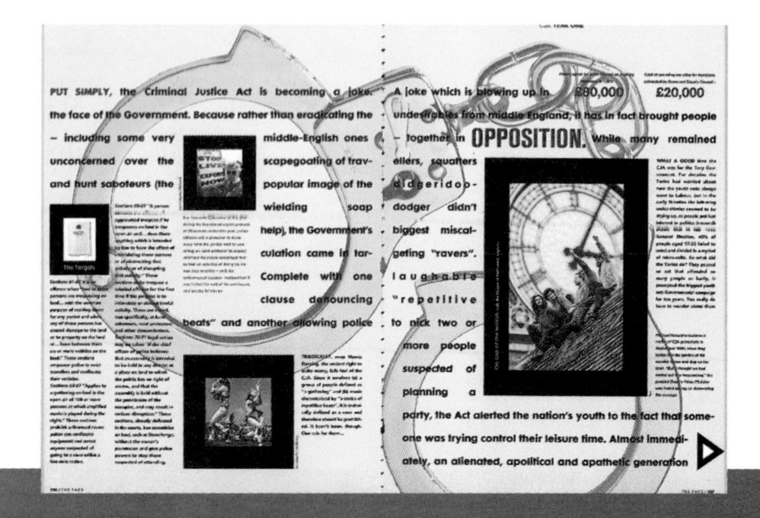

Showing spaces 9

In your work on interior design, signs, information and games and puzzles, you may find that you need to show spaces. Here is a reminder of some graphic techniques that you may have used already.

Oblique views

This form of drawing starts with a front or side view. You can add the third dimension very quickly by drawing in lines at an angle of 45 degrees as shown. Notice that these are not drawn 'true' to the length or scale of the starting shape, but drawn roughly half as long. This avoids the risk of a distorted appearance.

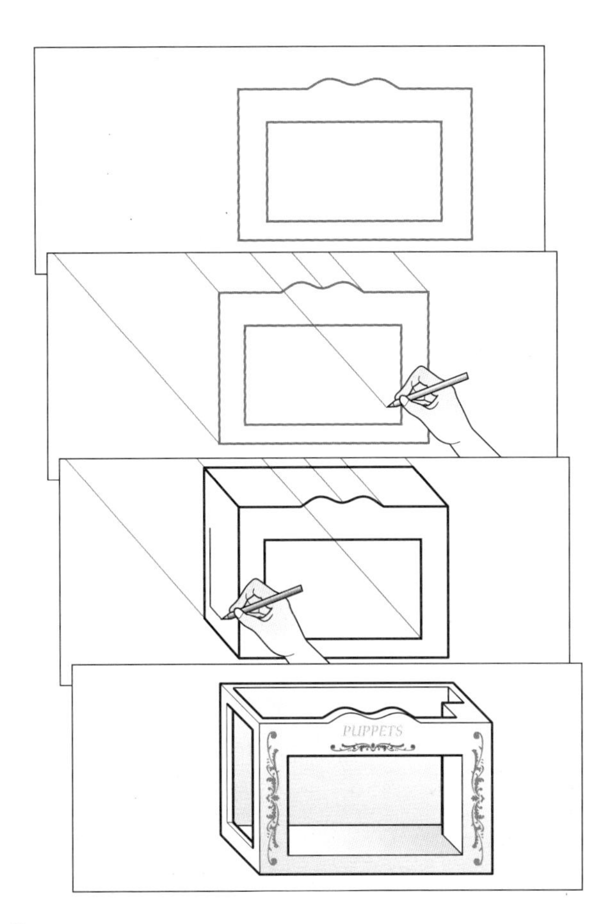

Drawing an oblique view from a front view

Isometric views

This form of drawing is more realistic than oblique projection. Vertical lines are drawn upright, but horizontal lines are drawn at an angle of 30 degrees as shown. You can use isometric grid paper as an underlay for rapid working. Notice that all lines along the isometric axes are true lengths, but lines not on these axes are distorted. A square appears as a rhombus because the 90 degrees angles become angles of 120 degrees and 60 degrees, so, while the lengths of the sides can be drawn to their true length, the diagonals cannot; one will be longer than true length and the other will be shorter than true length. Similarly, circles become ellipses, with one long and one short 'diameter'.

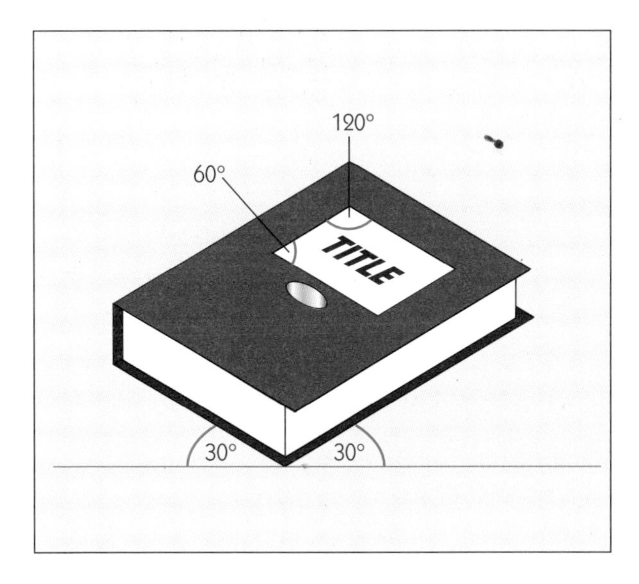

Drawing an isometric view of a book

Perspective views

This form of drawing is even more realistic than isometric drawing as it gives an accurate impression of depth as well as height and width. Perspective drawing uses the ideas of vanishing points and a horizon line to create a realistic view. A vanishing point is the point at which certain lines converge. The horizon line is drawn as though it is at eye level above the base line.

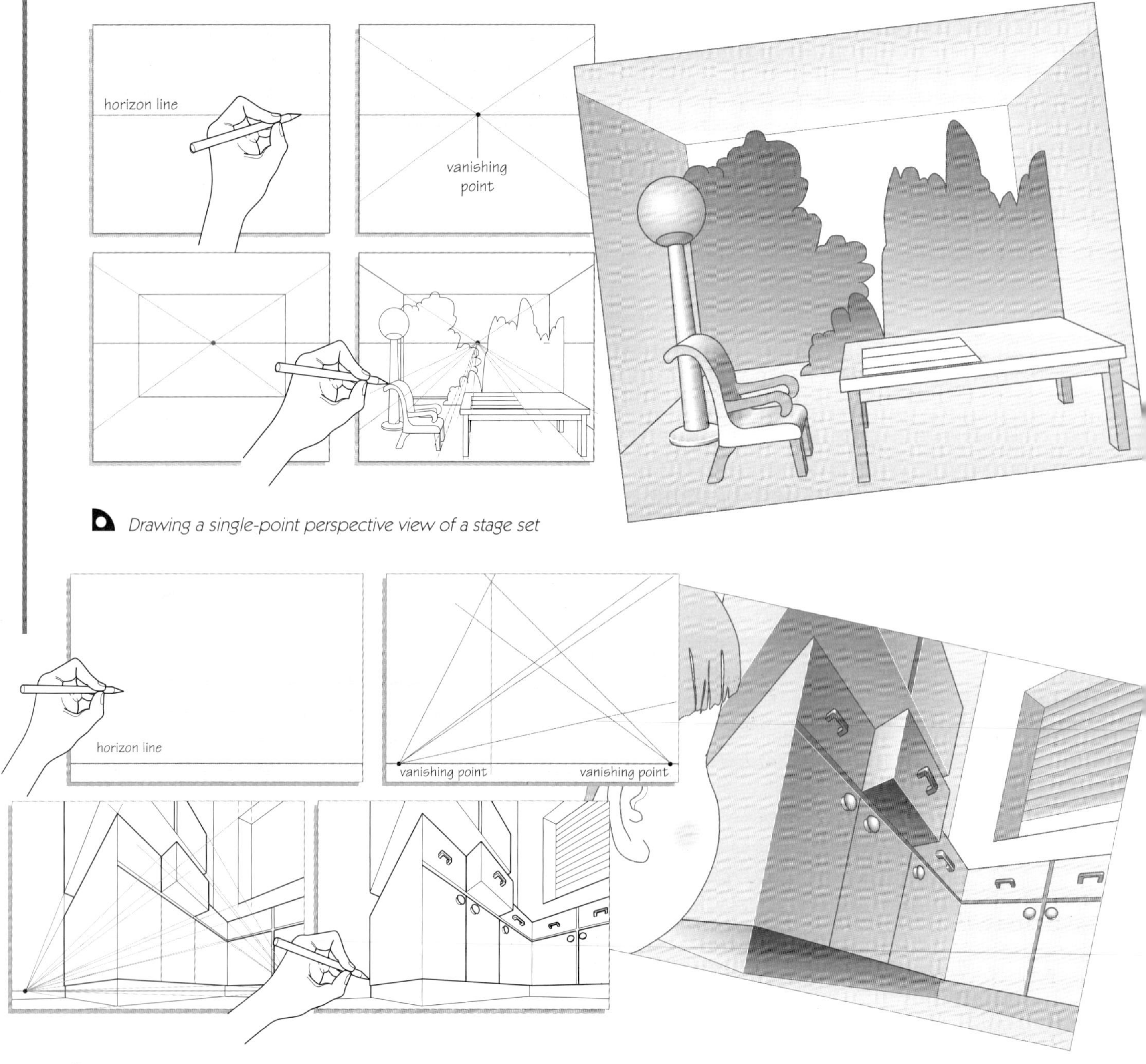

Drawing a single-point perspective view of a stage set

Showing an interior from a small child's point of view – the horizon line is low

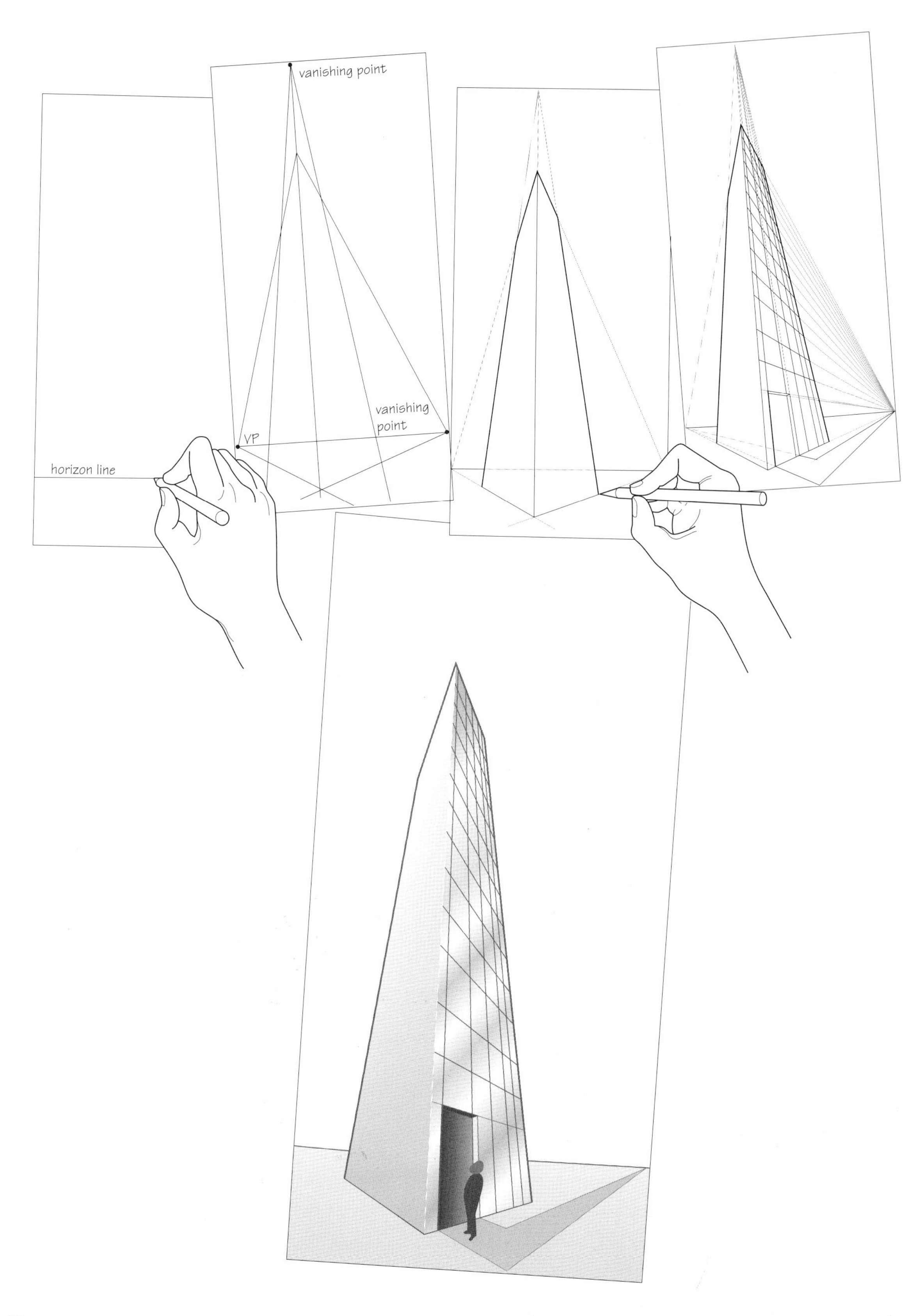

Giving a sense of size using three-point perspective

Making a site model

Sometimes to be able to show the location of a building (or buildings) in its environment, you will need to build a site model that reflects the way the land rises and falls. You can base the model on a contour map as shown here. You can use a range of 'found' materials to represent trees and foliage – steel wool, sponge, table tennis balls, crumpled paper, wood shavings and twigs – all of which can be sprayed. They can be supported on panel pins. You can use simple plain blocks and simple nets to represent buildings.

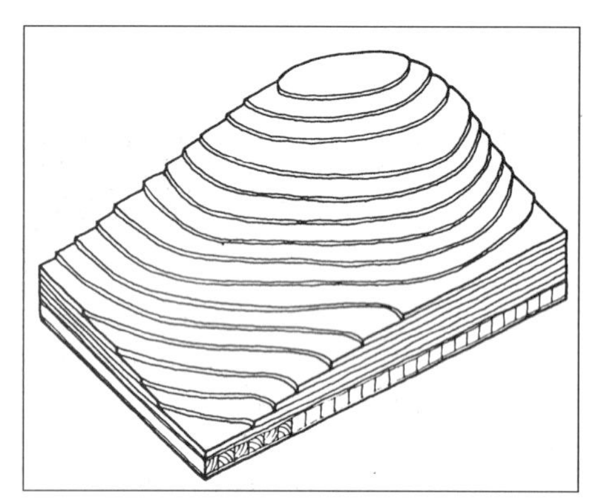

Build site models on a rigid base such as chipboard or blockboard. Contours can be assembled from glued layers of coloured card, Styrofoam, cork, or Masonite.

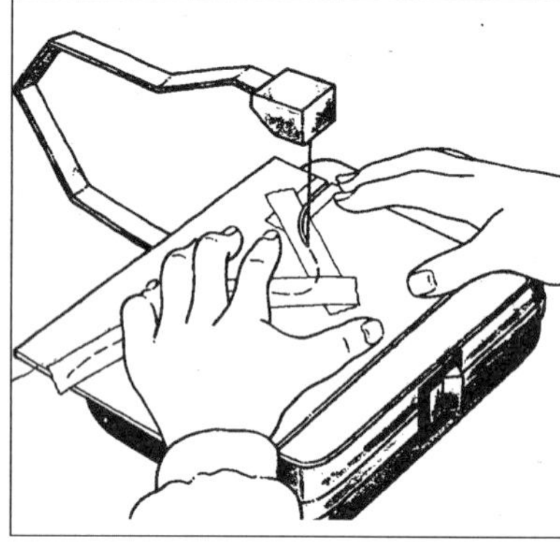

Cut contours with a vibro saw.

For realism, finished surfaces can be painted or sprayed, or coated with glue to receive "powdered grass". Coloured particles can be mixed from tempera, sawdust, wallpaper paste, and water (mix, allow to dry, then apply).

If required, contours can be softened with a thin coat of emulsion paint or smoothed off with plaster of paris or a water-based crack-filler medium.

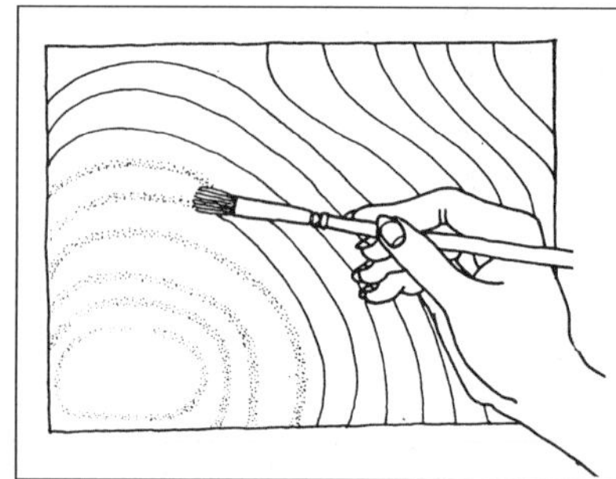

Using a computer

The latest computer software is capable of providing clear views of spaces at different levels of detail and from different viewpoints. It allows the user to 'walk through' the space in real time, looking around, up and down during the journey. Once the details of a space have been fed into the computer, you can use the software to evaluate the design of a space. If there are features of the space that you want to change, then you can do this quite easily. And you can test out the effect of your changes immediately. Of course you can use such software to design spaces from scratch. It is likely that this type of virtual reality software will become a standard tool of architects and town planners. The examples here show designs for a water treatment works.

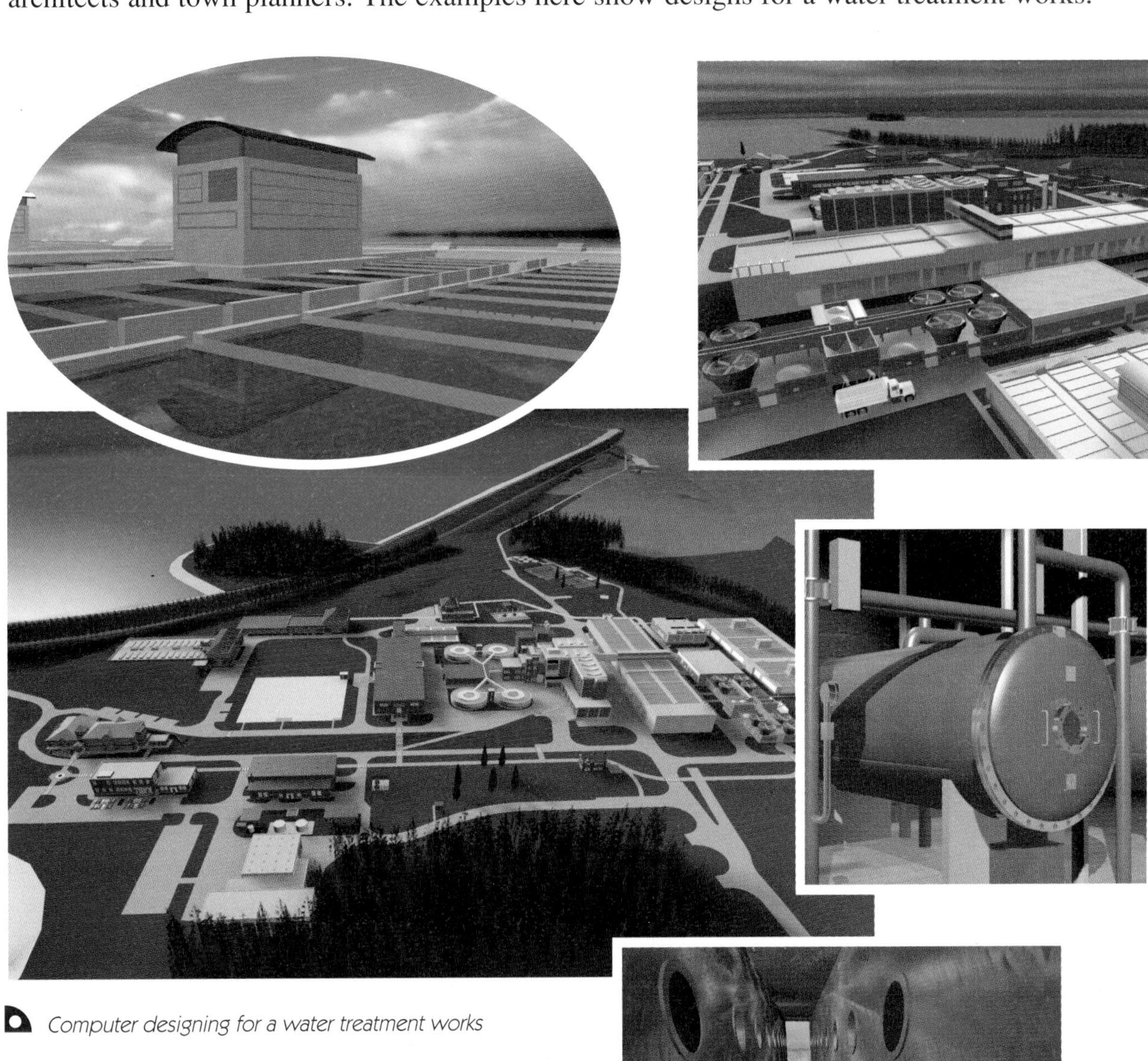

Computer designing for a water treatment works

Planometric views

Many people find it difficult to interpret plans. Strangely, they often find planometric drawing, which begins by drawing plans, much easier to understand. You start by drawing the plan and then generate a three-dimensional view by drawing in vertical lines as shown here.

Planometric is frequently used in connection with maps and guides because the accuracy of the plan is retained while an improved impression of the scene is provided to allow better visualization of the surroundings. At first glance, it looks the same as an isometric drawing – but look closer. You will see that all the horizontal components of the view – the floor, ceiling, roof and so on – are in true shape with rectangular corners remaining at 90 degrees and circles staying circular.

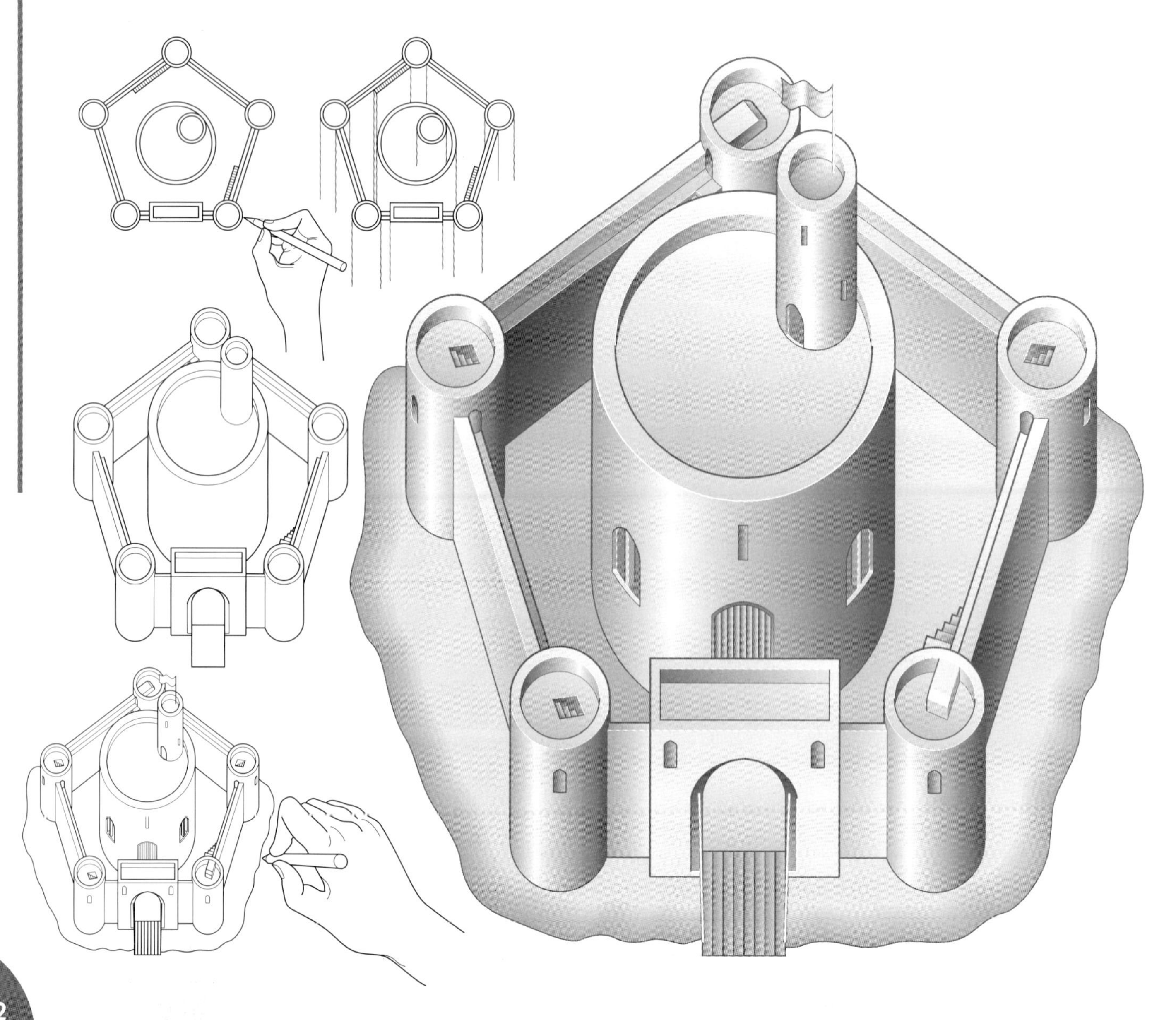

Scaling

When you are drawing something very large, you will need to draw it to a scale so that each line on your drawing is only a fraction of the true length. This is called drawing to scale and is used by architects when they draw plans. Architects use scale rulers, which are marked out in scaled measure.

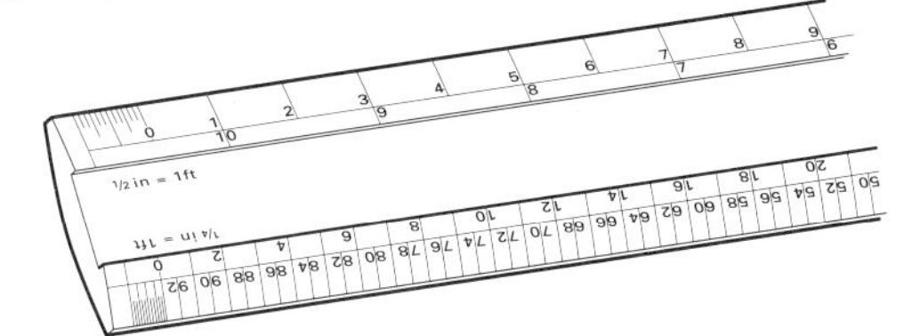

Enlarging and reducing

By drawing

There will be occasions when you need to enlarge or reduce a drawing. This is sometimes called scaling. You can do this using the grid method as shown below.

You can also enlarge a drawing using proportion and construction as shown opposite.

Using equipment

You can use the following equipment for enlarging and reducing.

- Overhead projector (enlarging only) – copy the drawing onto transparent film and then project onto paper mounted on a flat wall. Then simply trace over the enlarged version. Large increases in size are possible using this method.
- Photographic enlarger (enlarging only) – the original must be in the form of a slide or negative. Large increases in size are possible.
- Photocopier (enlarging and reducing) – limited to A3 size, unless the image is enlarged in sections and then they are fitted together like tiles.
- Computer software (enlarging and reducing) – the original must be on disk and you are limited to A3 as the maximum size.

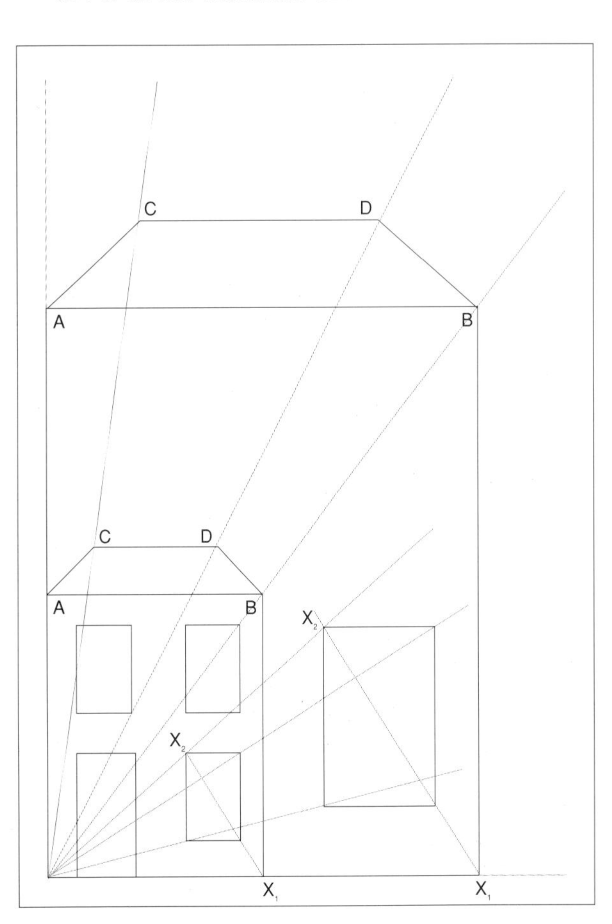

10 Technical drawing

Flowcharts

By using the set of symbols shown here you can draw flow charts which use a systems approach to describe a process in terms of input, output, and feedback. Here is an example showing how to play snakes and ladders.

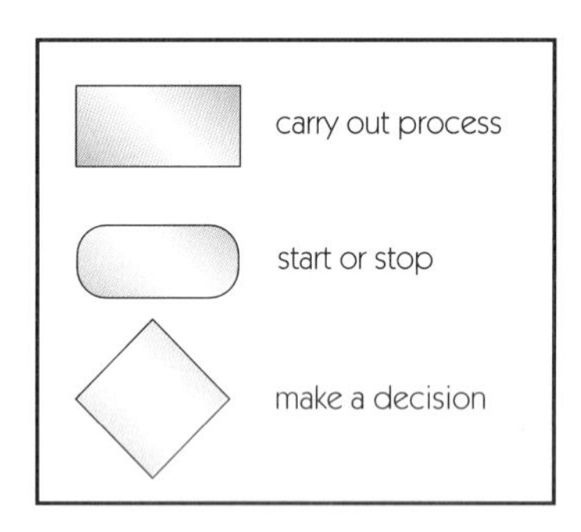

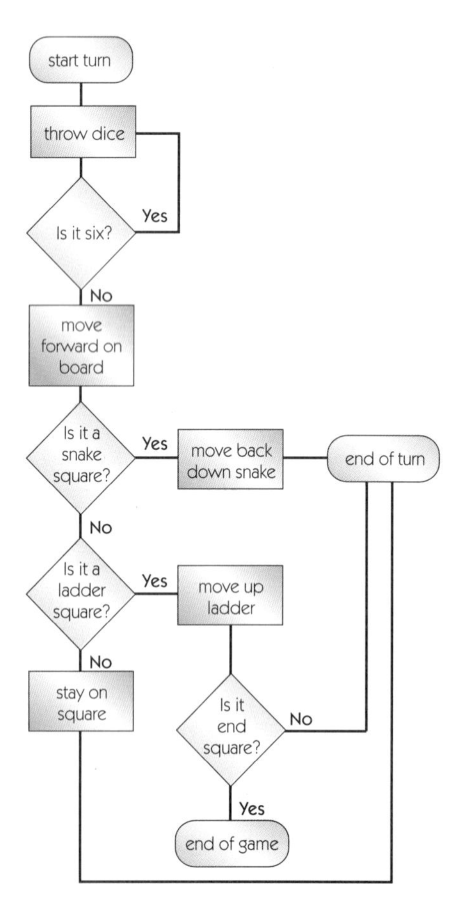

Drawing plane figures

By using a compass, T square, set square and a ruler you can draw plane (flat) geometrical shapes very accurately. You may need to do this when you are constructing nets for packaging. Here are some examples.

To construct a scalene triangle given its side lengths

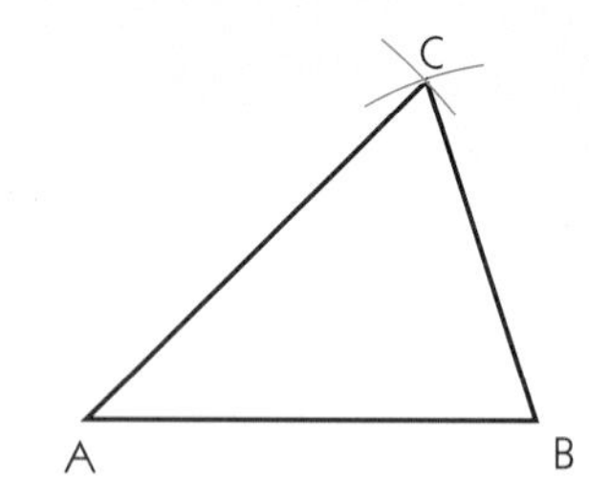

AB=80mm, BC=62mm, CA=84mm

Draw AB 80mm long
With compasses set to 62mm and centre B draw an arc
With compasses set to 84mm and with centre A strike an arc crossing the first arc A to C
Join AB and BC

To construct a regular hexagon given side length

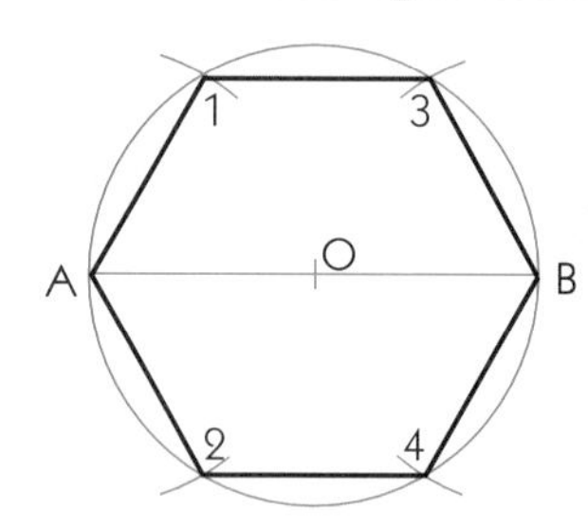

Side length = 40mm
With compasses set to 40mm draw a circle of centre O
Draw diameter AOB
With compasses still set at 40mm and centre first at A, then at B, draw arcs on the circle at 1, 2, 3 and 4
Complete the hexagon as shown

To construct a regular pentagon given side length

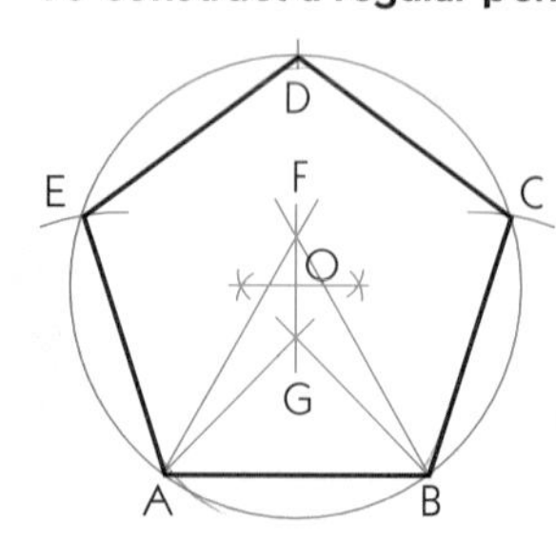

Side length = 60mm
Draw AB 60mm long
Both at A and B draw angles of 60° and 45° to meet at F and G
Join FG and bisect at O
With centre O and radius OA draw a circle
With compasses set to AB draw from A and B arc to get E and C
Produce GF to meet the circle at D
Join BC, CD, DE and EA

Auxiliary circles method of constructing an ellipse

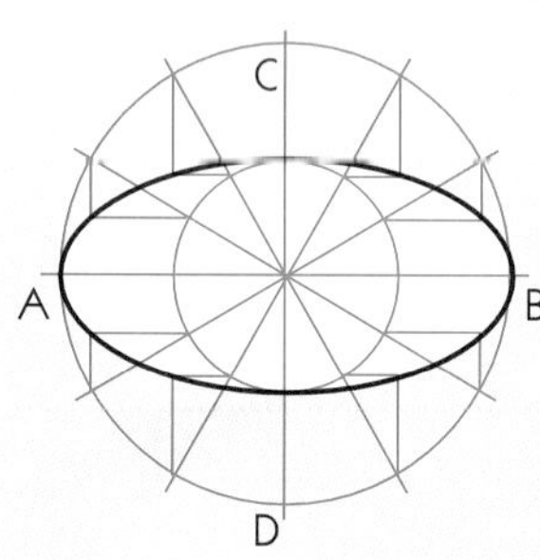

Major axis AB = 100mm
minor axis CD = 50mm
Draw two concentric circles, one 100mm diameter, one 50mm
Draw a number of diameters across both circles. Where each diameter touches the larger circle draw verticals. Where each diameter touches the smaller circle draw horizontals. The right angle corners formed by this process are points on the curve of the ellipse. Draw a smooth curve.

Drawing how parts move

You may find that you need to see exactly how a part might move for an animated point-of-sale display. You can plot the path (or locus) of the movement as shown in this example of a four bar linkage. Note that although the end of the crank is moving in a circle the point on the connecting rod is not. This will make for a more interesting display than simple rotation.

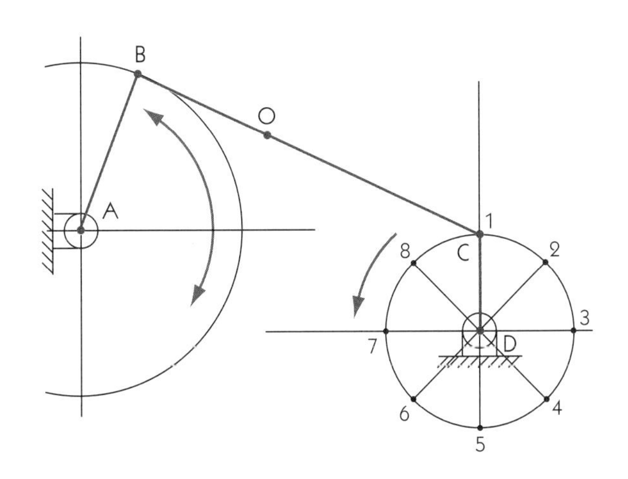

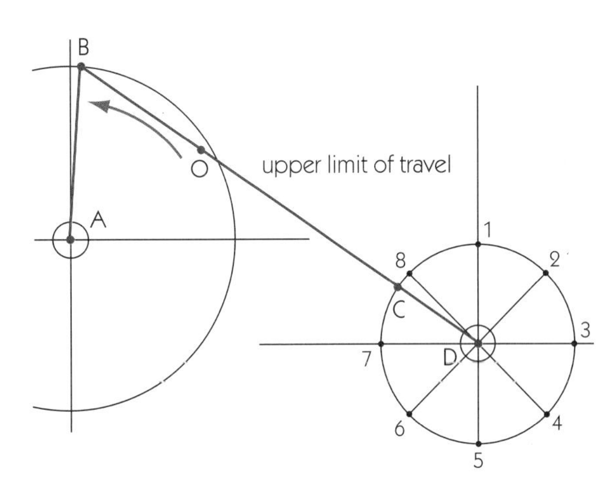

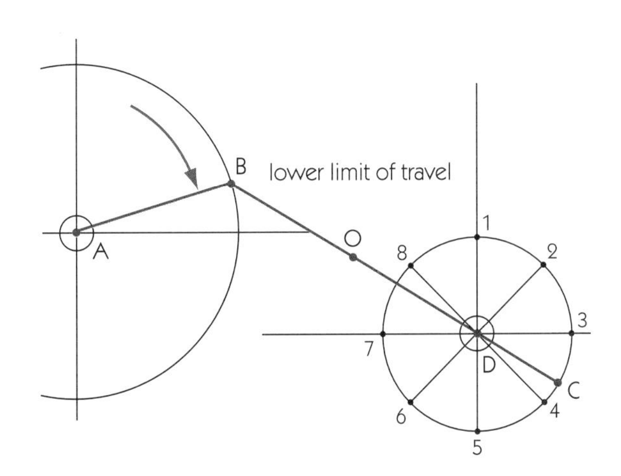

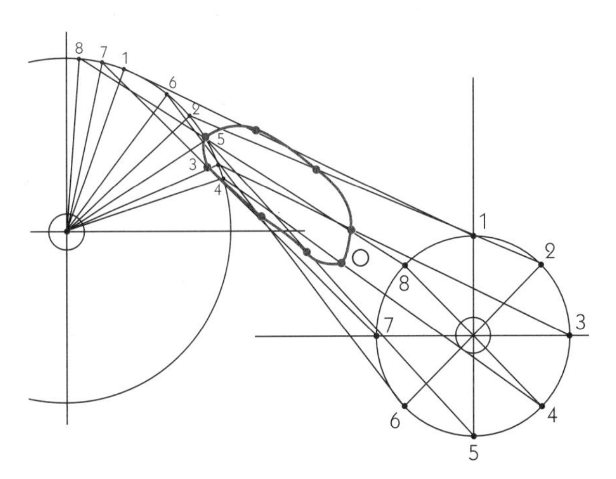

AB = follower
CD = crank
BC = connecting rod
O = point on connecting rod

11 Visual language of images

Images are used within graphic products to make them appealing and sell products when they are advertised. Our senses and imagination respond to these images in a variety of ways. Just as words are made up of different letters, images are made up of colours, shapes, patterns and textures. You can use this silent language to reinforce the message in your design and make it appeal directly to a particular target group.

Colour

The right combination of colours can give the impact needed to attract and hold the interest of the viewer. It is also mainly colour that communicates the mood of a design – a colour scheme of contrasting blues, yellows and pinks can look exciting and youthful, while rich browns and gentle greens suggest a natural, earthy quality. Many colours have meanings that are understood internationally to indicate various actions, products or warnings. Traffic lights all over the world use red as a code for stop and green for go, for example.

Different shades and intensities of colour can change our understanding of the meaning. Red is associated with fire and is seen as a hot colour, strong and full of energy, and so it is often used to symbolize danger. If red is diluted with white to make pink, it becomes much quieter and gentler.

Some of our responses to colour work on a deep emotional level. One colour experiment showed that people in a blue room set the thermostat higher than when they were in a red room because they believed it was colder – even though the two rooms were the same temperature!

When choosing a colour scheme for a design, you should consider the connections that it can awaken – is it warm or cool, is its volume loud or quiet and is its market image stylish or cheap, traditional or modern?

Shape

From our earliest attempts at drawing, we use shapes to communicate feelings and emotions. An upwardly turned curve is a symbol for a happy, smiling mouth, but a downward curve means sadness, and we all recognize the jagged flash shape used in cartoons as standing for an explosion. Designers use the shapes that we connect with certain feelings in more subtle ways to create a message or mood. A shape with a narrow base can be used to make the viewer feel uncomfortable because it seems unstable and about to topple over. A rounded shape with soft edges gives an impression of being friendly and kind. Your choice of shapes within a design can be used to reinforce the message created by the colours you use – or even contradict them.

Pattern and texture

The arrangement of shapes to form a pattern can give a very different message to that of a block of plain colour. Bright green printed as a circle and given a high-gloss finish will look sharp and dynamic. The same green used with an intricate leaf-like pattern, and printed on a matt surface will suggest a natural, fresh quality.

Some patterns and textures have such strong associations that they are totally unsuitable in certain design situations. For example, a lacy pattern is unlikely to be successful on a product sold specifically to men. Equally, designers can use strong associations successfully, such as using traditional patterns to evoke a period of design or a foreign culture, creating nostalgic or exotic atmospheres.

Typefaces and lettering styles

There are so many different styles and typefaces available that deciding on just the right one can seem bewildering. The easiest way to approach this problem is to regard the lettering in a design as similar to the level and tone of voice you would use to give the message. Large, bold lettering communicates in a loud, confident voice, whereas delicate, curving letters may suggest a seductive whisper.

Every typeface has its own character and associations. Boxes of luxury chocolates usually adopt a flowing style of lettering that has long thin stems to create an image of elegance and sophistication. Newspaper headlines use solid, strong typefaces that are clear and matter-of-fact.

Look at the lettering in magazines, on packaging and posters and try to work out why that particular style has been used and how it affects the mood of the design.

Look at the visual language in both the products and the advertising

Using images in your designing

To begin with, you need to decide on the main mood you want to communicate. Here are some contrasting options: traditional v modern, feminine v masculine, cool v warm, luxurious v budget. Once you have decided on the main mood of your design, you can use the following chart to select the appropriate visual language for it.

Contrasting moods	Colours	Shapes	Pattern and texture	Lettering	Graphic medium and material
Traditional old-fashioned, nostalgic, reliable, handmade, rustic	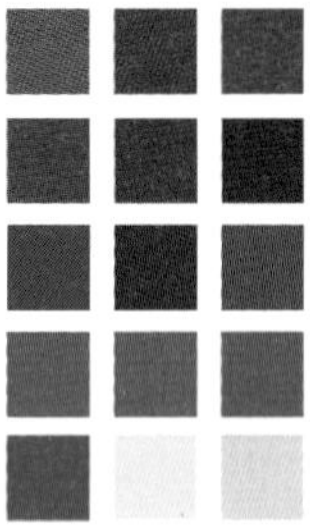		highly-patterned traditional motifs – paisley, tartan, marbling, hessian, basket weave, leather	serifs, rounded letters, hand lettering	pencil crayon water colour pen and ink textured wood cut printing handmade papers vellum or fabric
Modern lively, contemporary, fresh, exciting, new, fashionable, young	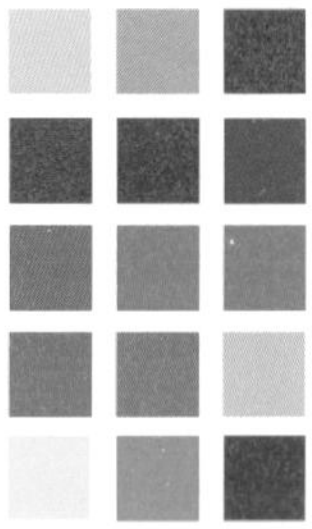		whimsical or geometrical, simple and mostly unpatterned, plain and unfussy, uncluttered smooth, glossy texture	sans serif small letters – open or wide spacing, overprinting or the unexpected, breaking conventions	computer generated, airbrush or markers, undecorated materials such as steel, acrylic or brown paper
Gentle delicate, graceful, kind, soft, pure, sensitive			light natural or lacy patterns, leaves, flowers, soft clouds, water whirls and wisps. Silky, satin, velvet or soft finishes	serifs, light, flowing, delicate, graceful, slim, intricate	pencil crayon, pastels, water colour, handmade papers or tissue paper
Strong bold, tough, powerful, aggressive, confident, hard			blocks of contrasting patterns; bold, strong and solid with lines, stripes or machine like outlines or abstract tough and plain	sans serif, bold, hard edged, angular, plain	markers, pen and ink, acrylic paint, coloured papers, print, metallic spray paints

Contrasting moods	Colours	Shapes	Pattern and texture	Lettering	Graphic medium and material
Cool fresh, chilled, crisp, quiet, hygienic, clinical, remote		sharp, spiky, crisp, angular, jagged, slim, hard, teardrops and water swirls	sharp angular patterns, triangles and snow flakes, narrow stripes, geometric and jagged, metallic, glassy, glossy, shiny and frosted surfaces	sans serif, light, crisp, spiky, tall, slim, angular	airbrush, marker, computer generated, flat colour and glossy metallic, shiny or frosted
Warm comforting, friendly, inviting, summery, cosy, happy, energetic		rounded, soft, curved, open, sensuous, large and 'blobby'	irregular, fluffy, rounded, matte, eggshell, natural materials, wood, fabric and ceramics	serifs and italics, hand lettering, open and generous, rounded and curved	water colour, pastels, pencil crayon, handmade papers, fabric, matte card and textured surfaces
Luxurious sophisticated, expensive, rare, quality, classical, conservative, upmarket		elegant ellipses and columns, balanced geometric forms, rectangles, circles, hand produced with details (tags, seals, buttons and labels)	restrained, elegant or traditional, cultural patterns, textures, natural leather, linen, velvet, silk, metal and wood	serifs, slim, delicate, light graceful, classical italics or hand written, individualistic	water colour, pen and ink, pencil crayon, embossing, handmade and Japanese papers, fabric, wood, gold and silver
Budget everyday, inexpensive, popular, brash, honest, downmarket		simple bold shapes, cartoon look with black outlines and crisp edges or over decoration	bright lively hectic patterns, spots, lines, glossy, shiny textures, plastics and metal foils	sans serif, chunky, bold, large, broad, easily read	markers, felt tips, printing, computer generated, plastics, gloss finishes

12 Print technology

Silkscreen printing

You can silkscreen print a design onto almost any flat surface:

- fabrics – T-shirts, bags, banners
- plastics – signs, shopping bags
- paper and card – posters, packaging, flyers.

How to make a screen

Originally, screens were covered in silk, but you can use any fine-meshed material.

1. Make a simple wooden frame.
2. Cut the fabric 5 cm larger than the frame.
3. Stretch it tightly over the frame and staple it in place along the sides.
4. Stick gummed brown tape around the edges of the screen. This will give you the picture size and hold the pool of ink.

How to make a stencil

A stencil is used to stop ink coming through the screen. You can paint gum or lacquer straight onto the screen or use stencil film or paper.

1. Cut the paper to the shape of your design.

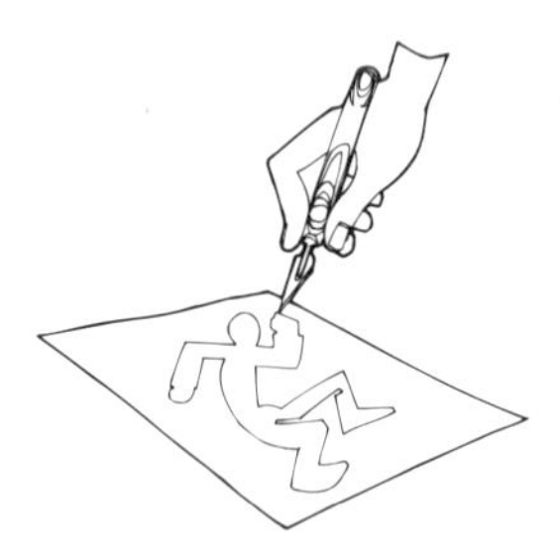

2. Place this on scrap paper and lay the screen accurately on top.
3. Pull ink through the screen with a squeegee. The paper stencil will then stick to the back of the screen.

How to screen print

1. Lay the screen carefully onto the paper or fabric.
2. Load printing ink onto the short end of the screen.
3. Drag this across the screen with a rubber squeegee. This forces the ink through the stencil.

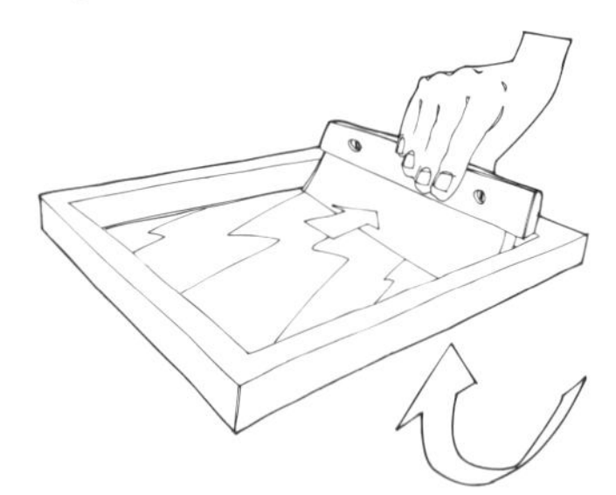

4. Lift the screen and remove your print.

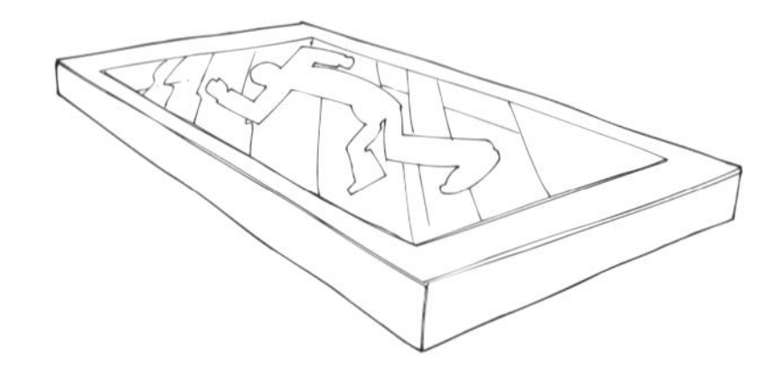

5. You can now repeat the same process.

Printing inks

You can use permanent, acrylic or water-based inks. They all tend to be thick and jelly-like. You can make your own printing ink by mixing wallpaper paste with dye or ink.

Some simple but effective screen prints

Block printing

Block printing, or relief printing, is the quickest and least expensive form of printing. A print is made by transferring ink from the raised part of a block. Potato-cut printing is a simple example of block printing.

How to make a lino cut

1 Glue the lino onto a block of plywood so that it is easy to handle. Draw the outline of your design onto the surface. Remember that it will print as a reversed image.

2 Cut the outline with a fine V-shaped gouge or scalpel. Use a U-shaped gouge or craft knife for broad areas. The part of your design that will be coloured should be left as a raised surface. All areas that are white can be carved away. ***Always* use the gouge *away* from the body and your other hand.**

3 Put printing ink onto a foam pad on a plate and press the lino block onto this. When the block is covered in ink, you are ready to print. Try to press the block against the paper with even pressure.

4 Alternatively, cover the roller with ink on an inking pad, apply the ink evenly to the lino block. Put the paper on the block and rub over the design with the back of a spoon. You can then carefully remove the paper.

5 You can glue string, card shapes or even leaves onto a board to print from.

Simple, effective block printing

Transfer printing

You can use this process to print 'one off' images onto paper, card and fabric. For best results:

- print onto white backgrounds
- avoid words and numbers as the process reverses the image
- always pre-wash the fabric.

Some simple but effective screen prints

How to transfer colour magazine photographs onto paper

This is a simple way of adding figures and backgrounds to visuals.

1. Select an image that fits the scale of your drawing. Place it face down onto clean paper and coat it with a solvent, such as white spirit or nail varnish remover.
2. Position the photograph face down on your drawing and burnish the area that you want to transfer.
3. Peel away the magazine paper to reveal the transferred image.

How to transfer photocopies onto fabric

Transfer colour or black and white photocopies of your designs onto T-shirts and bags using a special transfer paste available from art shops.

1. Spread a layer of paste over the front of the image and press it onto the fabric. Leave to dry.

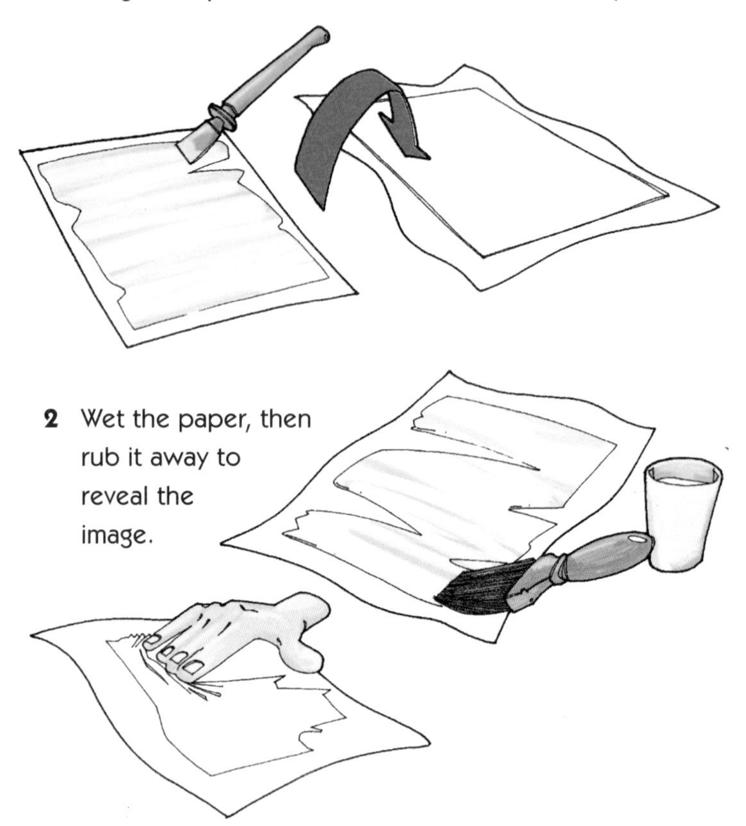

2. Wet the paper, then rub it away to reveal the image.

3. Seal the transferred design with a thin layer of paste

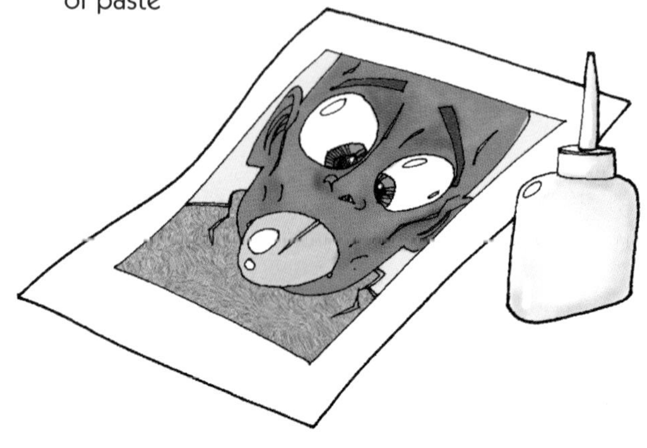

Spray techniques

You can use spray techniques to create interesting colouring effects on all types of materials and graphic work.

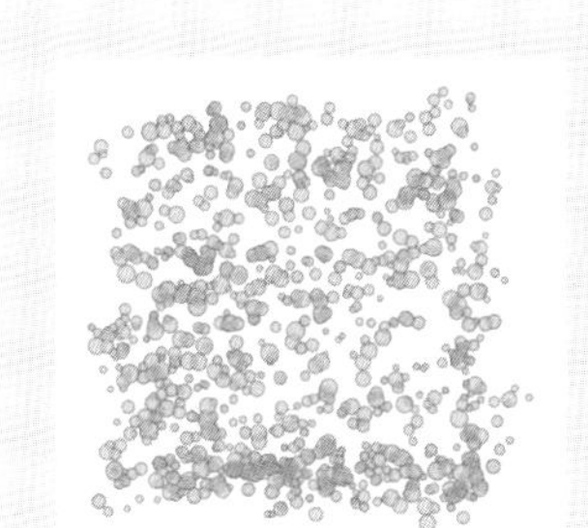

Spatter
This is a simple way of producing a speckled effect. Dip a toothbrush in paint, ink or fabric paints and scrape a knife across the bristles to spatter droplets on to a surface.

Diffusers and sprays
Use a plant spray or perfume atomizer to spray ink and thin paint. A diffuser gives similar results but is operated by blowing.

Airbrushes
These are small spray guns that are operated by compressed air. They are expensive, but give a controlled spray and can produce impressive results on detailed visuals and models.

Aerosol sprays
You can buy aerosol sprays for all types of surfaces. They provide the best method for covering large areas. Build up the colour in thin layers. Always work in a well-ventilated place.

Remember – if possible carry out spray techniques in a spray booth with extraction

Masks

All forms of spraying involves the use of masks. They act as a stencil and control the area to be sprayed. You can cut masks from adhesive masking film, thin card or newspaper and masking tape.

How to use a mask

1 Draw the outline of the design and plan the order of colouring.
2 Mask off the whole area, exposing only the section to be sprayed with the first colour. You can build up a darker tone by giving this several coats of spray.
3 Afterwards this should be re-covered and another area exposed to receive a different colour.

Using professional technology

There is a wide range of professional print technologies available in most schools. You can use the information in the table below to decide when to use them.

Black and white photocopier

Run length	Materials	Size	Unit cost	Typical applications
• up to 500	• paper • overhead transparency	• A4 • A3	• low	• reproduction of information, handouts, brochures and booklets

Colour photocopier

Run length	Materials	Size	Unit cost	Typical applications
• one-off	• paper • overhead transparency • heat transfer paper	• A4 • A3	• high	• visuals for dummy packaging • transfer of designs to fabric

Plotter

Run length	Materials	Size	Unit cost	Typical applications
• one-off	• paper • card	• A4 • A3 • and larger	• low	• interior design plans • nets for packaging • nets for card engineering • outlines for signs

Laser printer

Run length	Materials	Size	Unit cost	Typical applications
• one-off	• paper • thin card • overhead transparency	• usually A4	• low for black and white • high for colour	• text panels for dummy packaging • originals for information handouts, brochures and booklets

Offset lithography

Run length	Materials	Size	Unit cost	Typical applications
• over 500	• paper • thin card	• A4 • A3	• low	• reproduction of information handouts, brochures and booklets

Black and white photocopiers

Key features of most school machines include the following:

- automatic feed
- automatic backing
- automatic collating
- automatic stapling.

This makes the machine a useful tool for medium-length print runs of information handouts, brochures and booklets, providing illustration is limited to line drawings. Shades of grey do not reproduce well and large amounts of solid black often streak and rapidly use up the toner cartridge. In addition, most machines can produce reduced or enlarged versions of line drawings. This is useful in developing designs when you need to explore the effect of size. Also, you can use photocopiers to produce multiple copies of the same image, which can then be used to explore patterns or colourways.

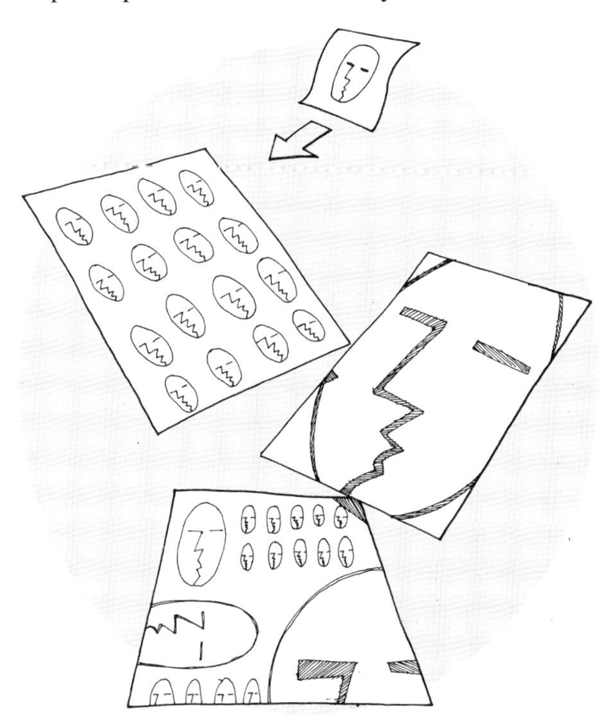

Pattern design made easy!

Your school may have a photocopier like this

Colour photocopiers

Your school may not have this facility, but most 'print shops' can do them for you. The colour reproduction is usually excellent, but it is expensive and you are unlikely to be able to afford to make lots of copies. They usually have magnification and reduction functions.

Plotters

These are X-Y plotters. The pen moves backwards and forwards along one axis while the paper moves backwards and forwards along the other axis. In this way any straight line or curve can be drawn. The plotter takes data from a computer, usually developed via CAD (computer-aided design) software and controls the movement of both the paper and the pen to make the drawing. If you need more than one copy of the drawing, it is quicker to photocopy from the original than to plot each one separately.

Drawing this by hand would take forever!

Laser printers

A laser printer takes data from a computer, usually developed via CAD software, and prints it onto paper. In your school, this is likely to be A4 size but A3 versions are available. They operate on a 'wysiwyg' principle, which stands for 'what you see is what you get'. So, whatever you have designed on screen will be faithfully reproduced. This includes shades of grey and solid areas of black. Colour laser printers are available, but only a few schools have them.

You can get reasonable-quality colour images from ink jet printers. You can find out more about how to generate images on a computer on page 93.

High quality at low cost for short runs

Offset lithography

This printing process requires the production of a printing plate. The quality of the printed material depends on the quality of the original from which the printing plate is made. High-quality laser-printed originals give high-quality printing plates.

Offset lithography printing machines work at a much faster rate than photocopiers. They are really only useful if you require a large number of copies. Many schools have this facility, but it is only a cost-effective solution if you require a long print run and using such a printing machine requires specialist training.

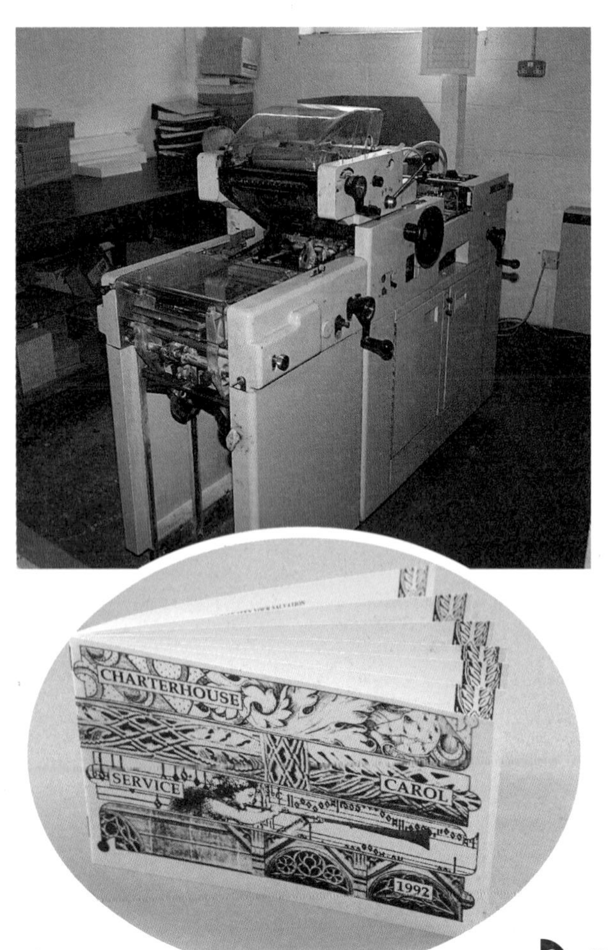

Offset lithography is for that really long print run

Natural timber

Natural timber has a grain direction that affects its working characteristics. For example, timber will split *along* the grain but not *across* it, but shrinks or expands *across* the grain rather than along the length. Timber should be treated with preservative to protect it from the effects of moisture, rot and insect attack.

Use the Chooser Chart below to help you choose which timber is best for your design.

Timber Chooser Chart

Material	Description	Properties and making tips	Uses for graphics products	Cost
Pine (red deal) (1)	cream and pale brown. straight grained but knotty.	quite strong. fairly easy to cut, trim, shape and join. rots quickly unless protected.	frameworks for 3D structures. stage sets and exhibitions. block models.	low
Jelutong (2)	cream, light. beige straight-grained. no knots.	more durable than pine. easy to trim, cut, shape and join.	block models for product designs, mock-ups of bottle shapes, etc. moulds for vacuum forming.	medium
Balsa (3)	whitish pink. very light in weight.	easy to break. very easy to cut and trim or shape. join with balsa cement.	lightweight small structures. rapid model making. small-scale models.	high
Willow and cane (4) (5)	cream or pale greenish. slender stems.	very pliable. easy to bend, cut and trim.	lightweight frameworks. curved structures.	low

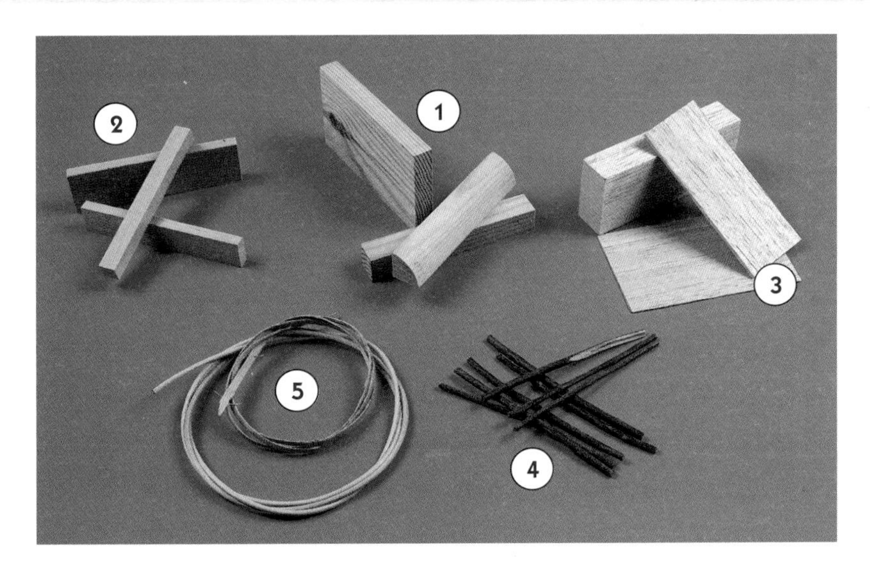

Manufactured boards

Natural timber can be cut into thin sheets or strips, or broken down into chippings or fibres that are glued and pressed to make boards. These have many properties that are different to those of the original timber. Manufactured boards have two main characteristics:

- they are available in large, flat sheets of various thicknesses
- they do not expand, shrink or warp under reasonable conditions.

Use this Chooser Chart to help you choose which manufactured board is best for your design.

Manufactured Board Chooser Chart

Material	Description	Properties and making tips	Uses for graphics products	Cost
Plywood (1)	thin layers of veneer running at right angles to the grain of its neighbour. various colours.	tough. does not warp. exterior plywood is waterproof. can split when cut.	flat cut-outs for signs and displays. sides of containers and crates.	high
Hardboard (2)	dark reddish brown. textured on one side, smooth on the other.	brittle. tears easily. difficult to finish edges. goes soggy in water.	covering panels for stage sets etc.	low
Medium-density fibreboard (MDF) (3)	beige colour. smooth surfaced. dense. quite heavy.	easy to shape. drills well. keeps edges well. finishes well. blunts tools. goes soggy in water.	flat cut-outs for murals and displays. block models for product design and packaging. vacuum forming moulds.	medium
Chipboard (4)	coarse particles, sometimes sandwiched between veneers of plastic or timber.	brittle. edges are easily damaged. difficult to shape. finishes poorly. blunts tools. goes soggy in water.	large bases and plinths for stage sets or exhibitions.	low

Notice that most sheets are sold in a standard size – 2440 x 1220 mm

Plastics

You can use this Chooser Chart to help you choose which plastic material is best for your design.

Plastics Chooser Chart

Material	Properties	Making tips	Uses for graphics products	Cost
Acrylic (available as sheet, rod and tube)	stiff and strong but not tough. scratches easily. wide range of colours available. thermoplastic.	good for strip heating. finishes well. join using Tensol cement.	flat cut out shapes for signs. small 2D and 3D forms for games.	medium
Polyvinyl chloride (PVC) solid sheet	stiff, strong and tough. more scratch-resistant than acrylic. thermoplastic.	join using liquid solvent (sold as plumbers' material).	small 2D and 3D forms for games.	medium
Polyvinyl chloride (PVC) high-density foam sheet	stiff, strong, tough and light. wide range of colours available. thermoplastic.	good for machining cuts easily and well.	flat cut out shapes for signs. small 2D and 3D forms for games.	medium
Polystyrene sheet	not tough. wide range of colours available. thermoplastic.	good for vacuum forming. join using liquid polystyrene cement.	shell forms for packaging and point of sale.	low
Polypropylene corrugated sheet (Corriflute)	stiff but not strong. lightweight. wide range of colours available.	can be joined with special rivets for quick assembly.	point of sale sheet structures.	low
Acrylonitrile butadienestyrene (ABS) – sheets, rods and tables	stiff, strong and tough. scratches easily. wide range of colours available. thermoplastic.	tubes can be joined with special components to form structures.	point-of-sale structures.	medium
Polyester resin	liquid, sets to a hard solid. wide range of colours. thermosetting plastic.	important to use the correct amount of catalyst for hardening.	solid castings for games.	medium
Expanded polystyrene block	light. impact absorbing.	cuts, shapes and finishes well.	packaging. block models.	low
Card-backed foam board	light and stiff. not strong.	cuts easily and well.	architectural models.	high
Melamine-formaldehyde (Formica)	stiff but not strong. very scratch resistant. thermosetting plastic.	cuts cleanly. can be engraved. usually glued to a thicker board.	small signs.	medium

Paper and card

You can use this Chooser Chart to help you choose paper and card for your various projects.

Paper and Card Chooser Chart

Material	Source	Uses for graphics products	Cost
Lining paper (1)	DIY stores	for large, exploratory work with pencils and markers for large templates	low
Layout paper (2)	art/graphics suppliers	visualizing new ideas rapid overlay development	medium
Tracing paper (3)	art/graphics suppliers	detailed overlay development	high
Cartridge paper (4)	art/graphics suppliers	presentation visuals simple pop-ups	medium
Watercolour paper	art/graphics suppliers	presentation visuals	medium
Tissue paper	department and other stores	interior design models	low
Crêpe paper (5)	department and other stores	interior design models	low
Corrugated card (6)	specialist suppliers discarded packaging	point-of-sale displays	low
Thin card (< 300 microns)	art/graphics suppliers	pop-ups	low
Medium card (350 to 640 microns)	art/graphics suppliers	cartons and packaging	medium
Thick card (> 650 microns)	art/graphics suppliers	point-of-sale displays	medium
Mounting board	art/graphics suppliers	architectural models	high

Prototype products

Books

You can assemble a prototype book in the following ways.

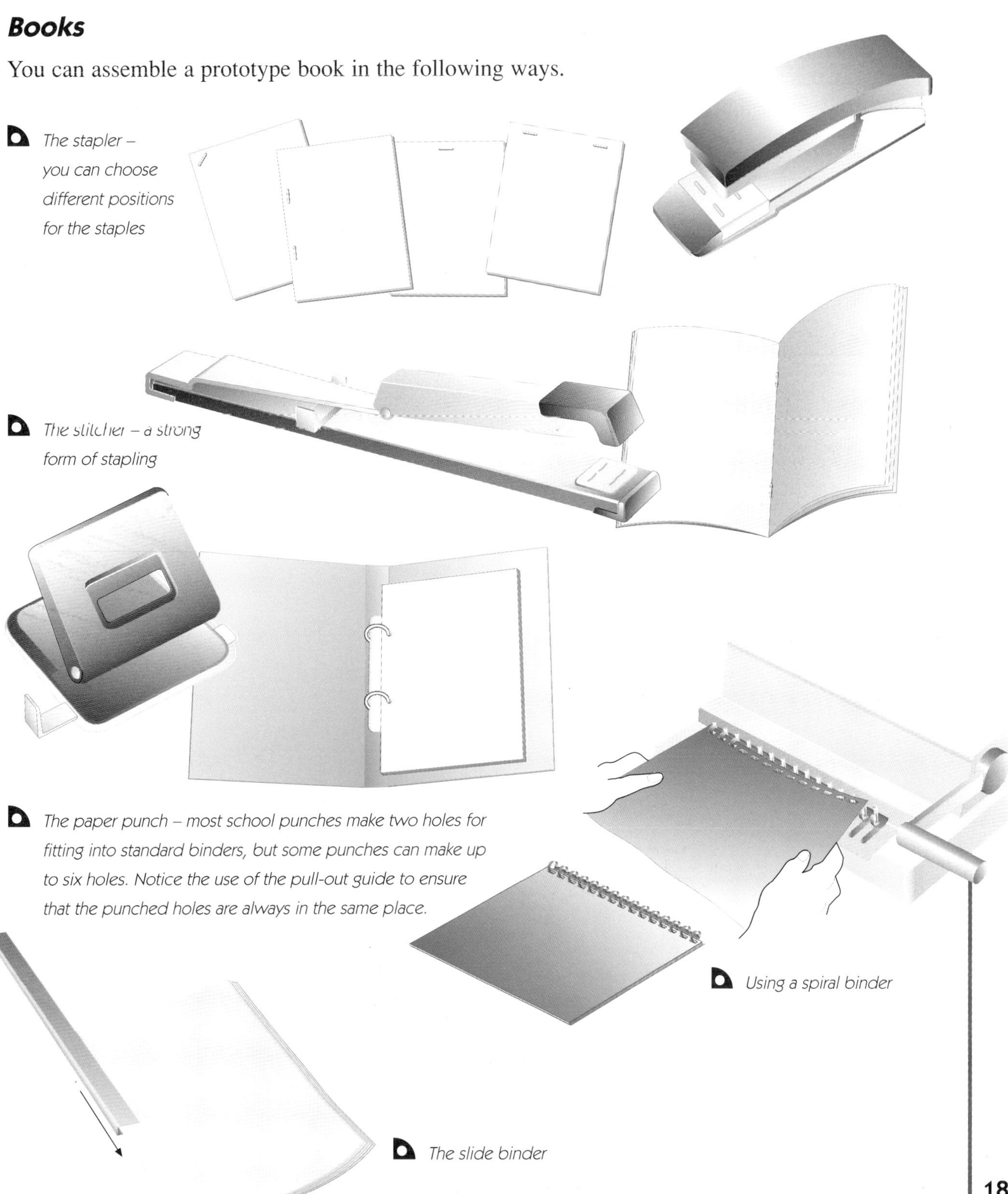

The stapler – you can choose different positions for the staples

The stitcher – a strong form of stapling

The paper punch – most school punches make two holes for fitting into standard binders, but some punches can make up to six holes. Notice the use of the pull-out guide to ensure that the punched holes are always in the same place.

Using a spiral binder

The slide binder

Some of these methods are also used in industrial assembly. The difference between mass-produced ring-bound publications and those made in school is that while you would clip your prototype into the folder, mass-produced folder publications come shrink wrapped and loose inside the folder. This is because the publishers would have to pay someone specially to insert the pages. This is an economic consideration when something is mass produced.

A shrink-wrapped insert

The most commonly used method of binding a mass-produced publication is by gluing. The pages are compiled in batches and glued by a machine.

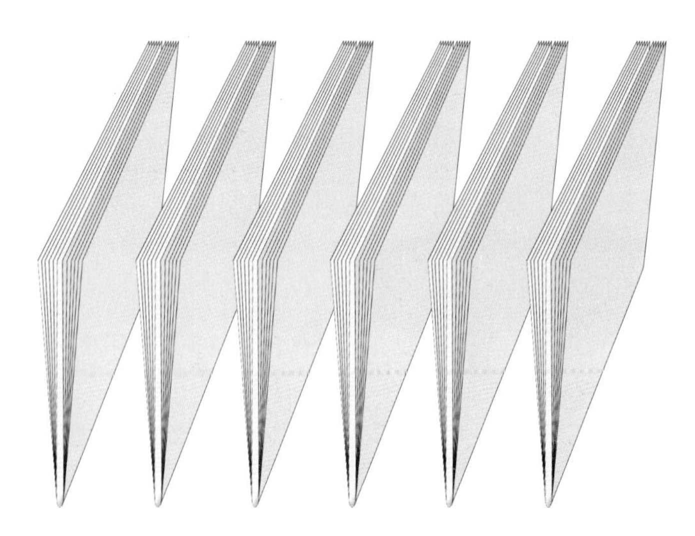

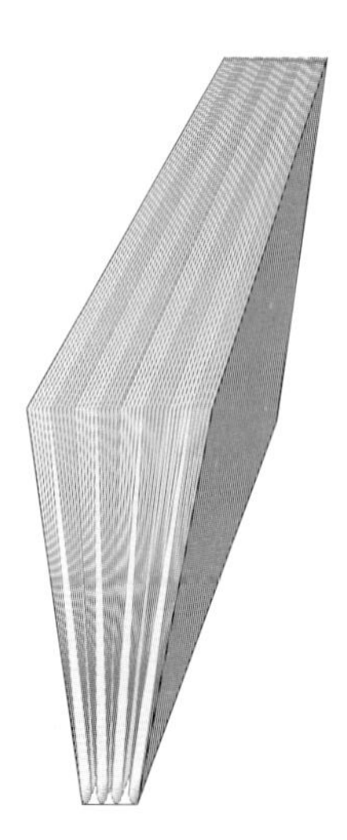

Signatures (left) are combined to produce a book

Book covers

You can produce covers in a variety of ways, as shown on this page.

Laminating makes covers more durable. The process is suitable for paper and lightweight card.

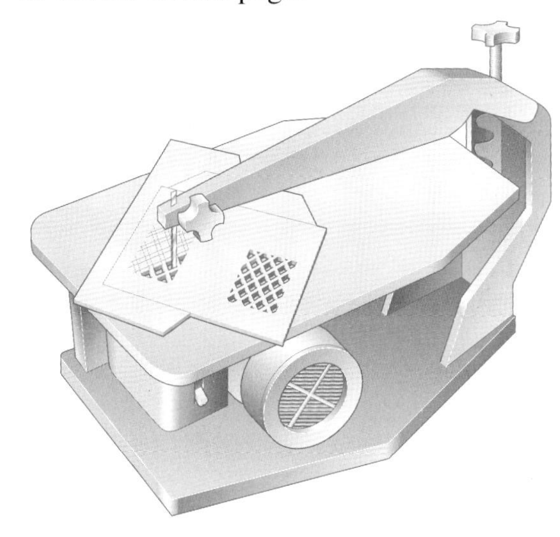

Cutting a shaped card cover using a jig saw; suitable for stiff card. Note that for internal holes the card is drilled and the saw blade threaded through the hole

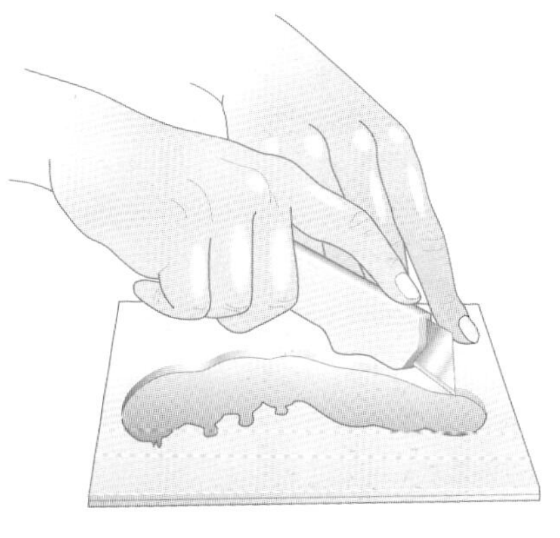

Cutting a shaped cover by hand; suitable for stiff card.

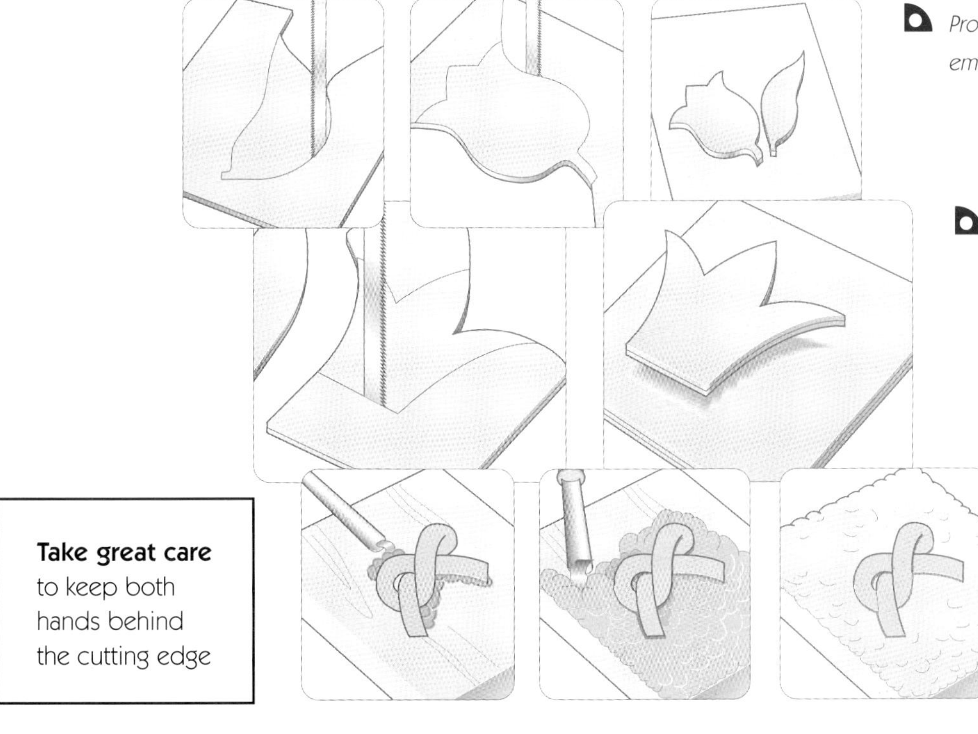

Production of card embossing tool

Production of plywood embossing tool

Production of wooden block embossing tool

Take great care to keep both hands behind the cutting edge

Using nets

There will be times when you need to create a three-dimensional form from a flat sheet. To do this, you will need to draw the net (sometimes called the surface development). This flat shape can be cut out and folded to give a three-dimensional form, as shown here.

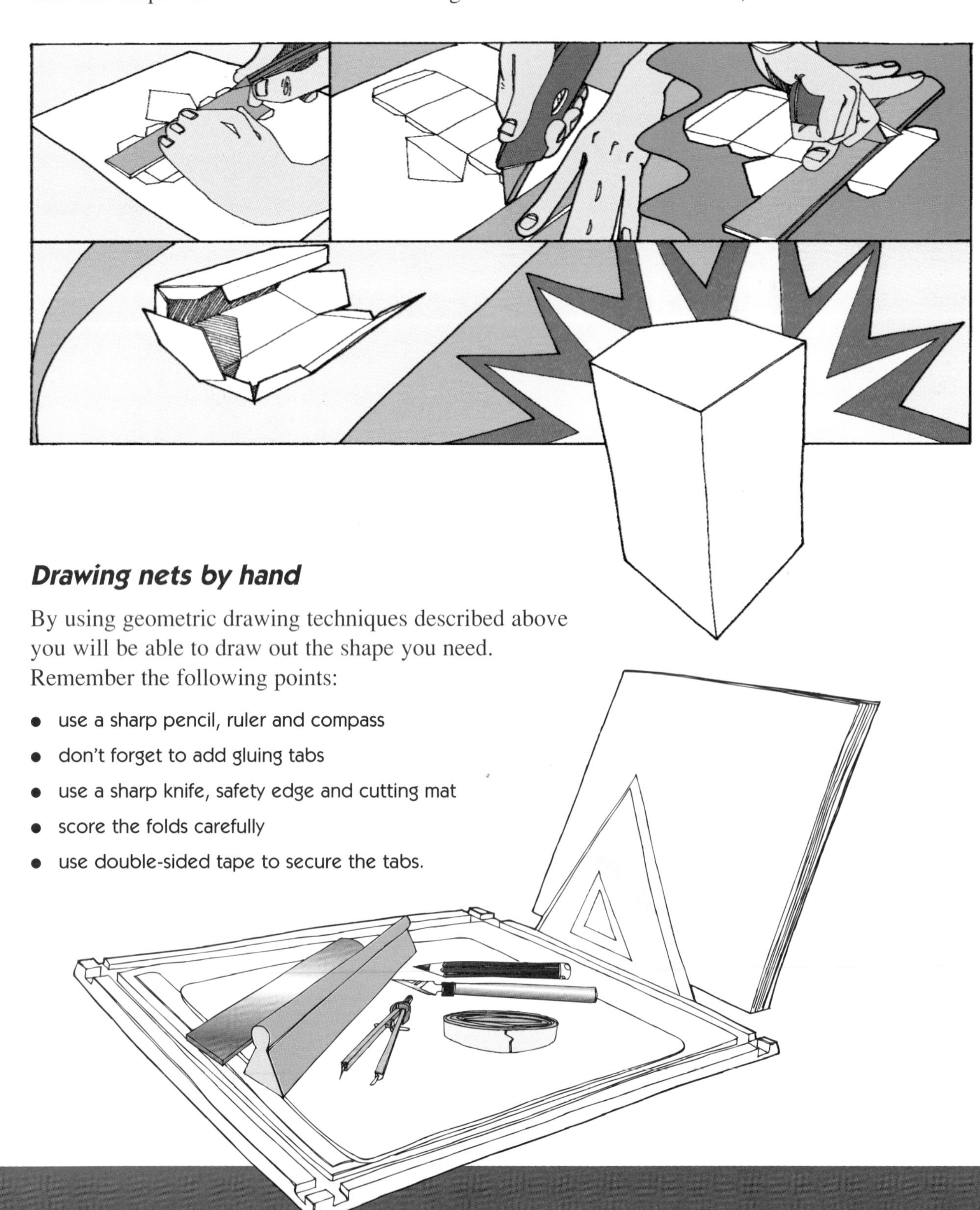

Drawing nets by hand

By using geometric drawing techniques described above you will be able to draw out the shape you need. Remember the following points:

- use a sharp pencil, ruler and compass
- don't forget to add gluing tabs
- use a sharp knife, safety edge and cutting mat
- score the folds carefully
- use double-sided tape to secure the tabs.

Drawing nets with a computer

The sequence below shows how graphics software can be used to create the net for a truncated hexagonal pyramid. Each operation only takes a few seconds, so this is a very rapid and efficient way of drawing a net. You can print out the net using a laser printer or draw it out on a plotter. You can fit some plotters with scoring and cutting blades so that the entire process is carried out via computer. All you have to do is add any surface decoration and stick it together!

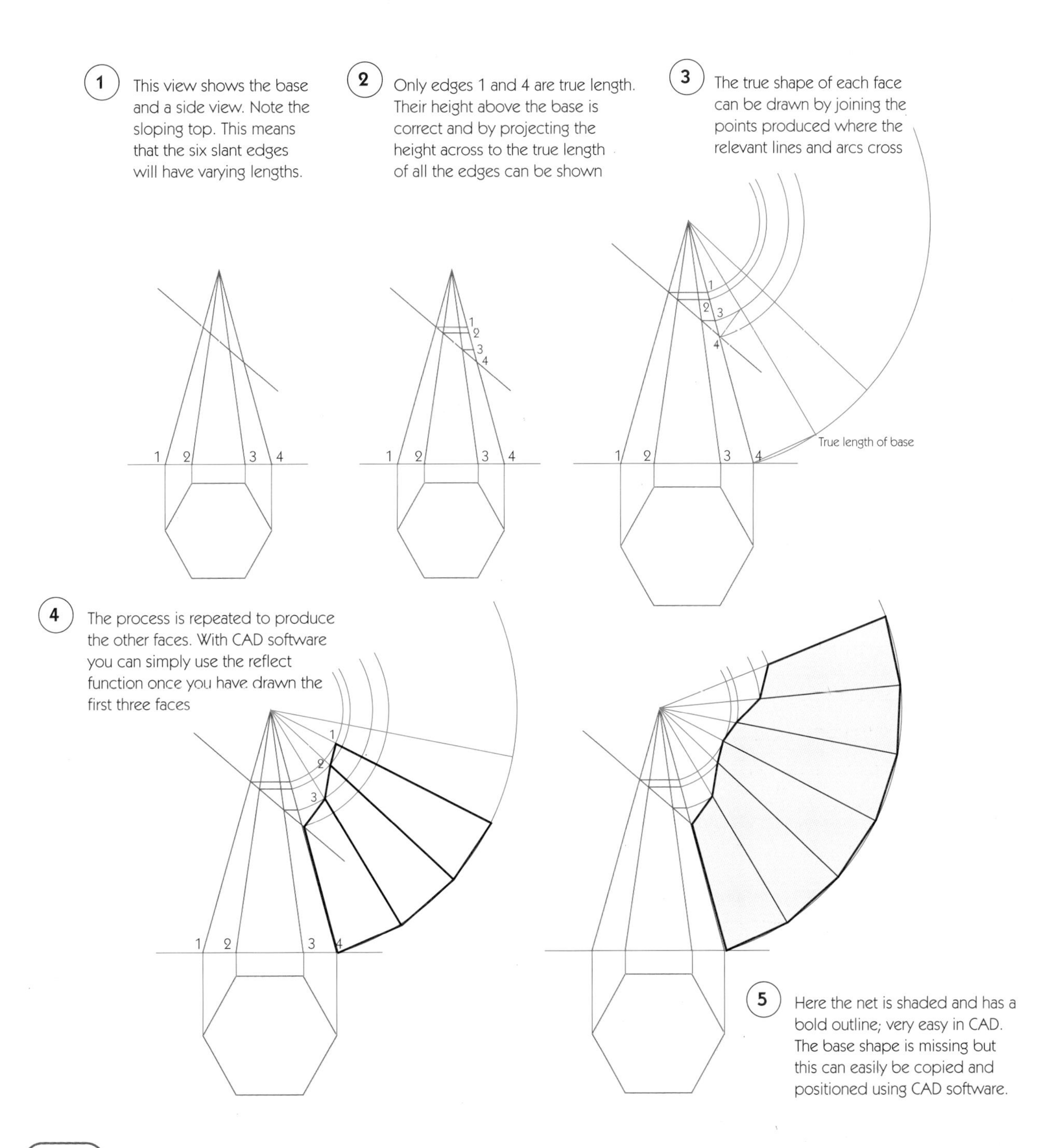

Using resistant materials

Here is a guide to the various making techniques that you can use to produce your product from resistant materials. You can use the information in this section to choose the techniques that you need to make your design. You will need to get detailed advice and guidance from your teacher on the safest way to carry out the techniques.

Cutting shapes from sheet material

	Manufactured board	Thermoplastic sheet	Manufactured board and thermoplastic sheet
Straight lines and flat surfaces	for cutting to length for cutting sheet for trimming	for cutting to length for trimming	N/A
Curved lines	for cutting for trimming	for cutting for fine work for trimming	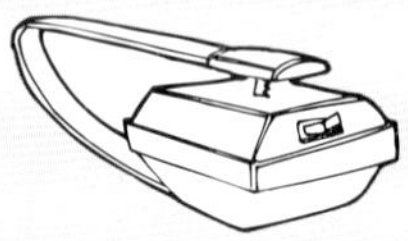
Curved surfaces	for cutting for trimming	for cutting to approx shape for trimming	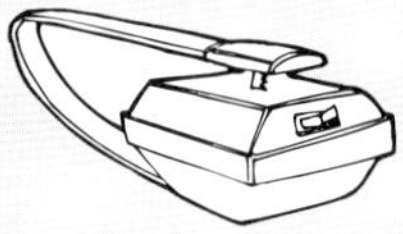
Round holes	for marking for holes up to 6 mm for larger holes	for marking for holes up to 6 mm	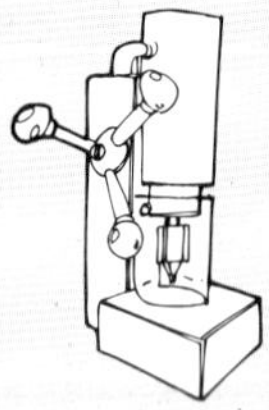
Square holes	for through holes in thin material for flat-bottomed holes	Drill 3 mm hole inside required shape and use coping saw as for wood.	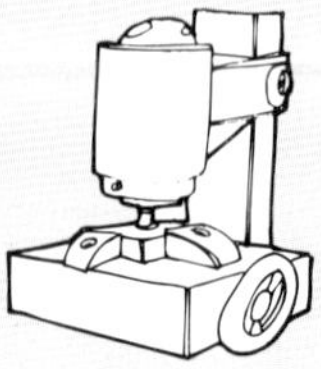
Irregular-shaped holes			
Grooves		Use a milling machine.	
Slots		for chain drilling for trimming	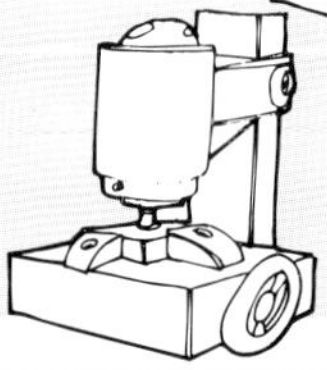

Producing three-dimensional forms from sheet plastic

Using a strip heater

1 Heat until soft enough to bend.
2 Use bending jig to get the required angle.

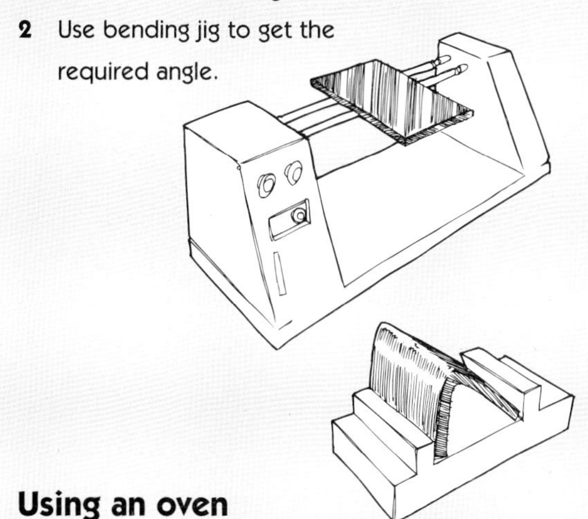

Using an oven

1 Heat in an oven.
2 Drape softened acrylic over a former.

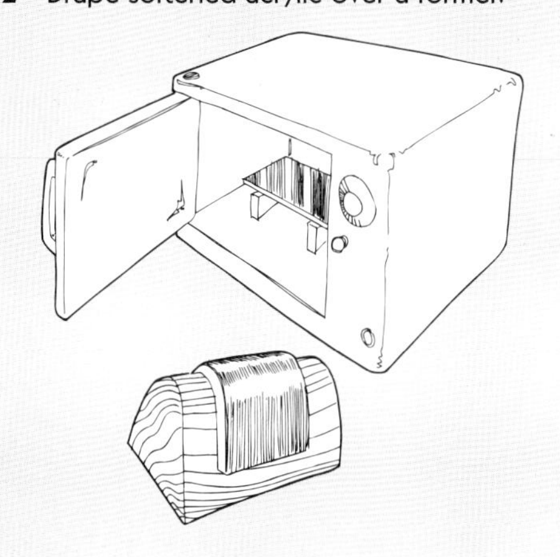

Forming thermoplastics

You can form thermoplastic sheet in two ways:

- plug-and-yoke forming;
- vacuum forming.

Plug-and-yoke forming

1 Cut out plug shape from mdf.
2 Glue yoke onto a basepiece.
3 Place hot, soft plastic sheet over yoke.
4 Press plug into yoke.
5 When cool remove formed plastic sheet.
6 For thicker sheet use a smaller tapered plug and clamps to apply pressure.

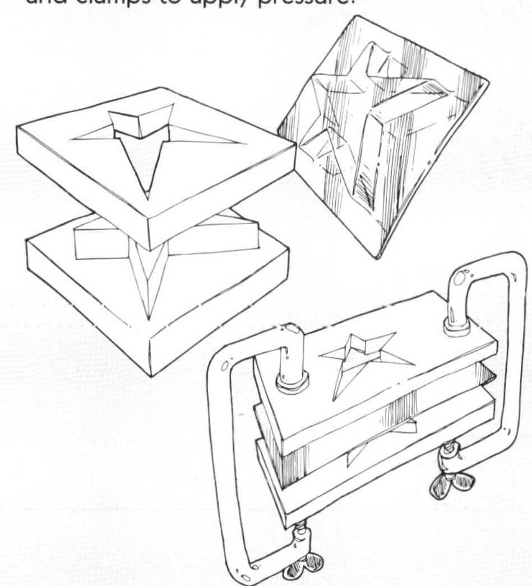

Vacuum forming

1 Clamp thermoplastic sheet into position and heat until soft.
2 Place it over the former and switch on the vacuum pump.
3 Removing the air causes atmospheric pressure to force the soft plastic over the former.

Note: you can use card and string formers for low-relief forms.

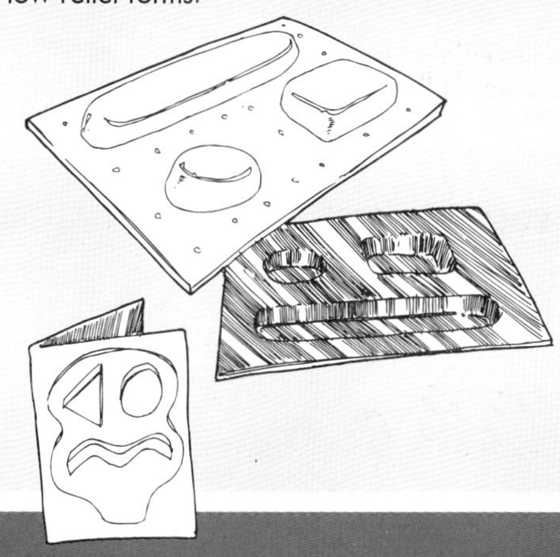

CRT2, LIRT1, LIRT8

Producing block models

You can use the equipment listed in the table below to produce block models.

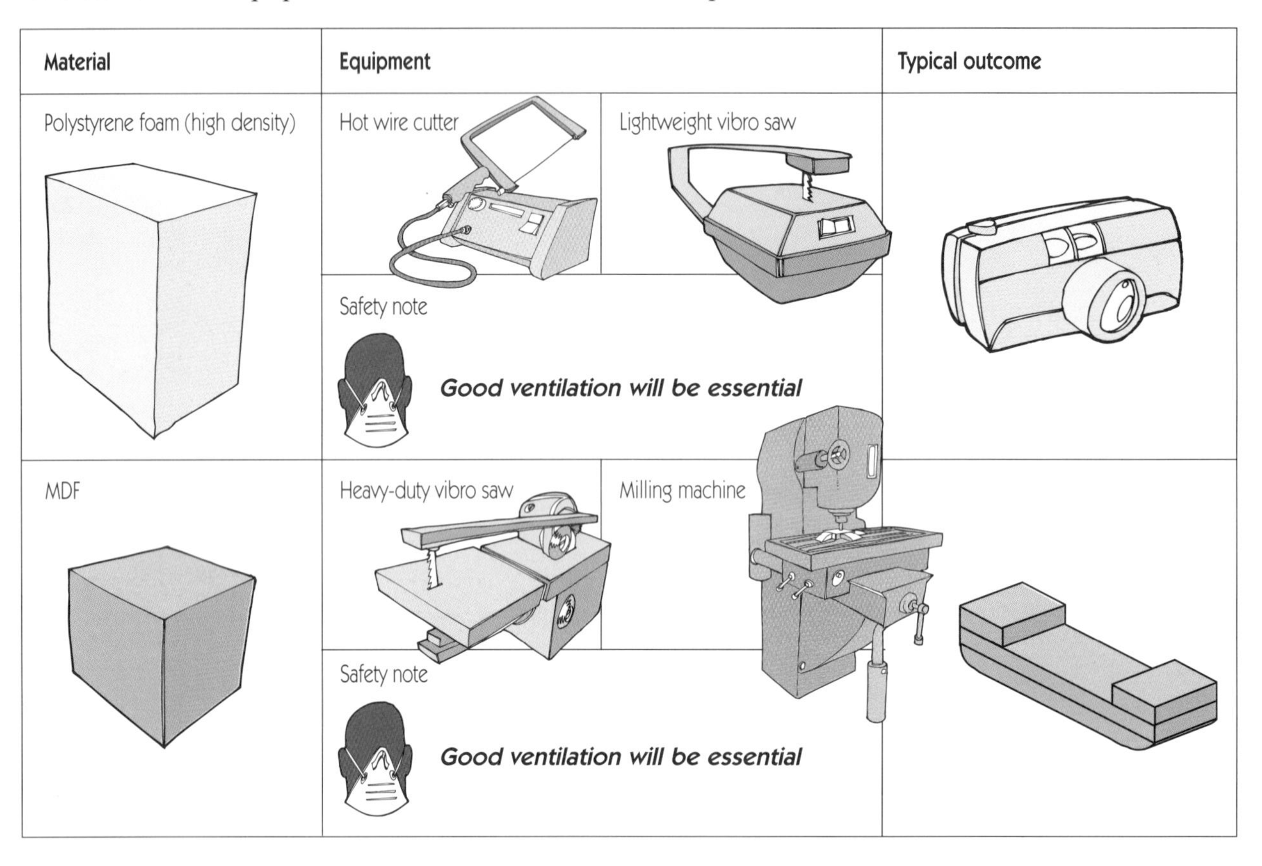

Material	Equipment		Typical outcome
Polystyrene foam (high density)	Hot wire cutter	Lightweight vibro saw	
	Safety note: *Good ventilation will be essential*		
MDF	Heavy-duty vibro saw	Milling machine	
	Safety note: *Good ventilation will be essential*		

Producing architectural models from plans

You can build architectural models of buildings by using a plan as a starting point. Simply cut out card pieces to represent the walls and glue in the correct places over the plan. The building takes shape in front of your eyes. You can use the floor plans for each separate floor and assemble the whole into a complete structure.

CRT1

Finishing

Finishing plastic

A quality finish on plastic depends on the surface being as smooth as possible so that it can be polished. Scrapes, scratches and glue spots are impossible to hide.

Finishing wood

Often in graphic products it is necessary to finish manufactured boards so that they look like plastic. To achieve this, the material needs to be as smooth as possible and spray painted with an undercoat and several layers of top coat.

Finishing and safety

There are many hazards in finishing processes. The following list gives guidance as to how best to control the risks.

- Sanding – protect your eyes with goggles. Protect your nose and lungs with a mask and extraction system.
- Painting and varnishing – use adequate ventilation or a fume cupboard. Protect your nose and lungs with a mask.
- Brushes and rags – clean them immediately after use or dispose of them safely.
- Sensitive skin – some finishes may cause rashes or allergic reactions. Wear gloves or use a barrier cream.

Is this wood or plastic?

Simple electrical circuits

Circuit and wiring diagrams

The picture below shows a drawing of a point-of-sale unit with integral lighting.

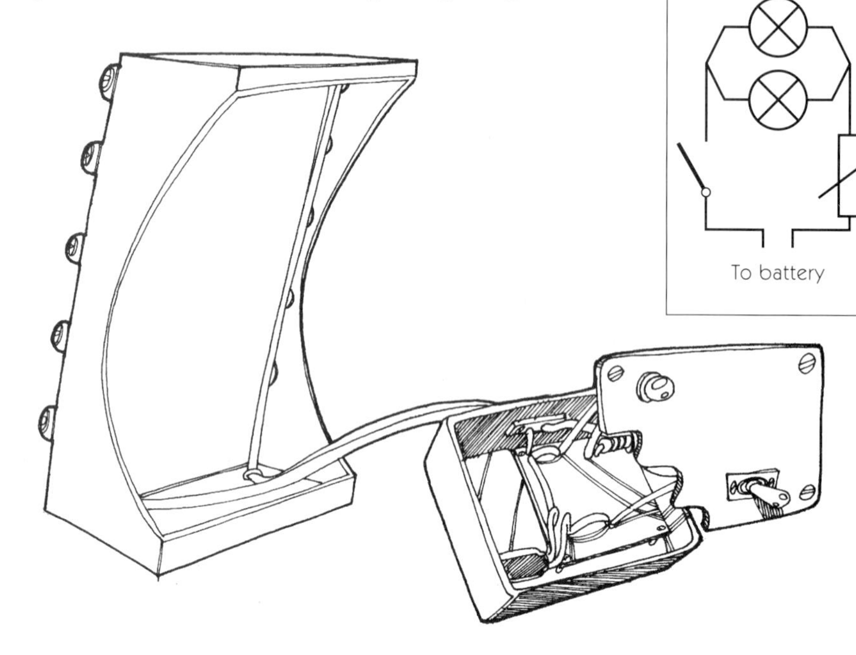

Each shelf in the unit has two bulbs in a reflector to cast light over the contents of the shelf. The unit is made from shelving modules that stack on top of each other. Each pair of bulbs is controlled by a single switch (for on and off) and a variable resistor (for brightness). The bulbs are arranged in parallel to give the required brightness and also to ensure that if one bulb blows the other bulb will stay on. If the arrangement was in series then, in the event of a blown lamp, the sales assistant would have to test all the bulbs to find the faulty one. The arrangement is powered by a 12V rechargeable battery, so that the unit may be used where there is no easy access to mains electricity – at a car boot sale or at an 'on the street' demonstration. There is in overall on and off switch that uses an LED connected in series to a protecting resistor to show when the power is on.

The circuit diagram for the arrangement is shown with the wiring diagram. Note the following features of the wiring arrangement:

- the battery is connected to a plug unit suitable for up to four shelving modules;
- the wiring for each shelf is enclosed in flexible conduit;
- the switch and variable resistor are at the back of each shelf;
- the way to connect an LED;
- the switch used is a simple on and off toggle switch.

Notice also how the order of connecting the components in the wiring diagram is identical to that in the circuit diagram, although at first sight it looks very different.

Making connections

Remember that to make an electrical connection, you have to strip the plastic insulation from the connecting wire.

You can make temporary connections using these components:

- crocodile clips
- connecting blocks
- jack plugs and sockets.

You can make permanent connections using solder as shown below.

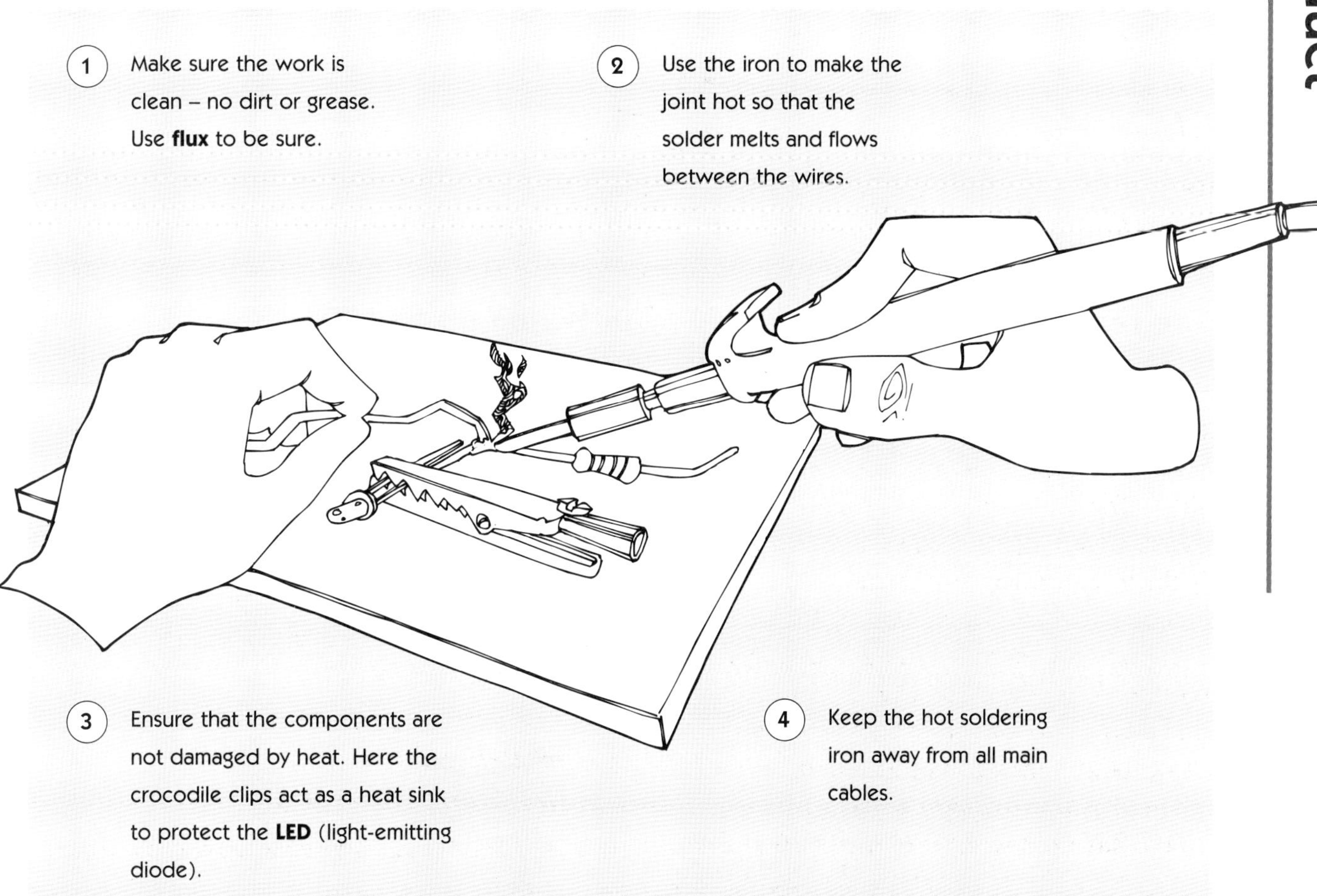

Types of switches

There are different switches for different applications, as shown in the panel below.

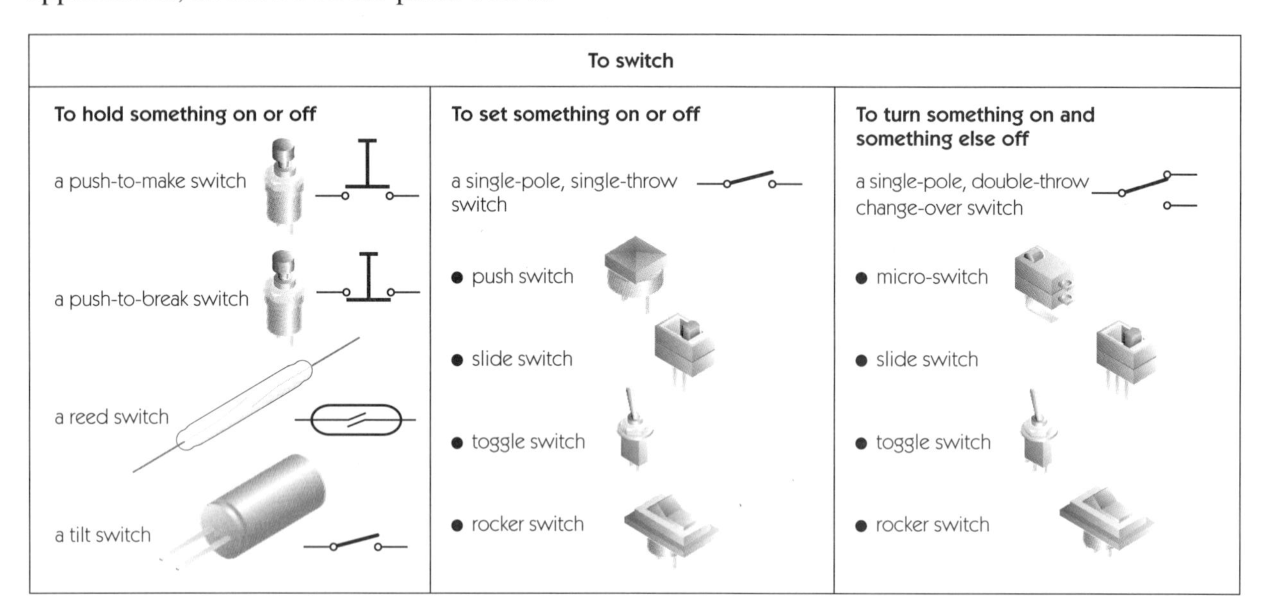

The resistor colour code

Resistors control the size of an electric current. They restrict the flow of current by providing a resistance to it. The value of resistance of a resistor is measured in ohms (Ω). Four coloured bands on the resistor show the value of the resistance provided. The first three bands give the value, while the fourth – usually silver or gold – gives the accuracy to which it has been made (the tolerance).

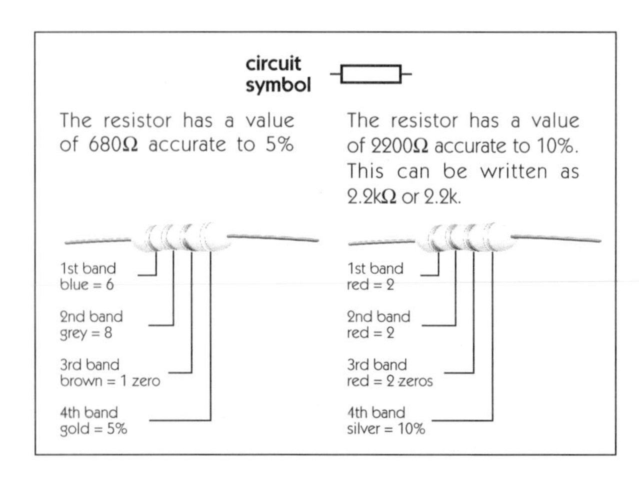

Wiring up an LED

An LED conducts electricity in one direction only, so it has to be placed in the circuit the correct way round, as shown below.

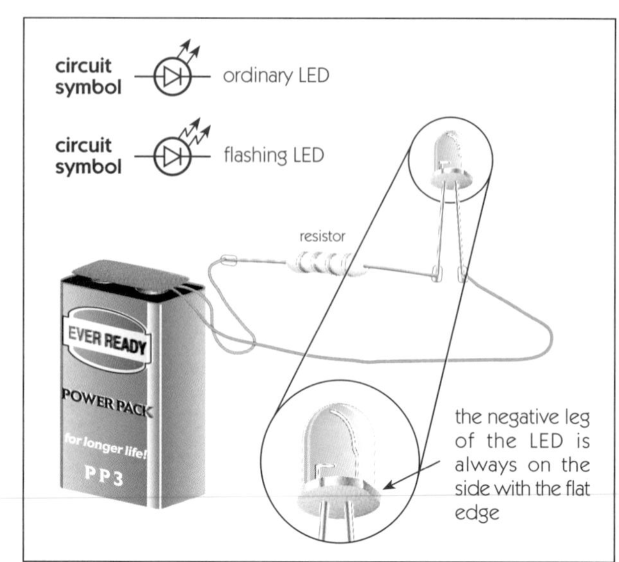

Mechanisms in graphic products

There will be occasions when you will need to use a mechanism to achieve a certain sort of movement – in a point of sale display, in a moving sign or in a complex board game perhaps. You can use the chart below to choose a mechanism that will give the required movement from a rotating input.

Mechanisms Chooser Chart

For this mechanical function	You can use
from rotating to linear	wheel and axle, rack and pinion, screw thread, rope and pullet, chain and sprocket
from rotating to reciprocal	crank, link and slider (4 bar linkage), cam and slide follower
from rotating to oscillating	crank, link and slider (4 bar linkage), cam and lever follower, peg and slot
from rotating to intermittent rotating	Geneva wheels (a cam plus a peg and slot)
increased rotational speed	gear train
decreased rotational speed	gear train
reverse direction of rotation	gear train
change axis of rotation	bevel gear, worm and wheel

You can use hand power, a battery plus an electric motor, or a wind-up clockwork motor for the rotating input. These means of input are compared in the table below.

Input	Turning force	Turning speed	Power source	Cost
hand turning	medium	low	human muscle	very low
clockwork motor	low/medium	low	human muscle work stored in spring	medium
electric motor	low	high	battery	low

Photography

There will be many occasions when you need to take photographs. It may be to provide stimulus materials for your designing. It may be to capture situations in which new products might be needed. It might be to capture images that will be included in information. Whatever the reason, you will be successful if you use the equipment and techniques described here.

What sort of camera?

It is best to use a single-lens reflex (SLR) camera. What you see through the viewfinder has reached your eyes through the lens of the camera, so you can be sure about the image you will capture. A camera takes a picture by focusing an image onto a photographic film. You focus the image by rotating the lens. As you look through the viewfinder, you will see the image go in and out of focus as you do this. You simply adjust the amount of turning until the image is sharp.

The quality of the image also depends on the amount of light hitting the film. You can control this in two ways. First, by changing the size of the aperture through which the light enters the camera. If this is open wide, then lots of light gets through, but if it is closed down, only a little light gets through. Second, by altering the length of time the shutter is open. If it is open for a long time, this lets in a lot of light, but if it is only open for a short time, less light is let in. Most single-lens reflex cameras have built in metering and signal clearly when the aperture and shutter speeds set on the camera will give a satisfactory photograph.

A basic single-lens reflex camera kit might include the following:

- a single SLR body with a built-in flash
- three lenses of fixed focal length – standard; moderate wide-angle; moderate telephoto
- one or two zoom lenses to cover a similar range.

You will probably need a tripod to hold your camera steady. A cable release is also useful as it reduces vibration and can be locked for long exposures.

Which film?

You have to ask yourself the following questions.

- *Do I want prints for a display or slides for a show?*
  Buy the sort of film that will give you the end product you want.
- *Do I want colour?*
  You can get colour slide film, colour print film and black and white film, plus some specialist films, like infra-red. You can get colour slide and print film processed much more quickly than black and white or specialist films, but you can process black and white film yourself.
- *What film speed do I need?*
  The sensitivity of film is talked about in terms of its speed. Medium speed film is for most natural lighting. The ISO (International Standards Organisation) number system is universal:
  - slow films are between ISO 25 and 32
  - medium films between ISO 100 and 125
  - fast films are ISO 400.

  Fast films are usually more convenient than the other two to use in almost any situation. However, slow films are better for high contrast or a lot of detail. The effects of film speed are shown in the photographs. The photograph on the top was taken with a slow film, the one on the bottom with a fast film. The graininess of the fast film is clear.

Can you see the difference caused by the speed of the film?

Filters

Filters are the best way to control the colour and tone of your images. They fit over the camera lens and there are different types.

- Polarizing filters help cut out reflections from anything except metal. They are most useful with water and glass.
- Graduated filters give gradual shading from dark to clear.
- Diffusing filters break up the definition of the image slightly and conceal detail.
- Fog filters cut both colour saturation and contrast and can give a more 'natural' look.

Flash

The usual way to light a subject for photographing is by using electronic flash. The easiest way is to use a flash that is built-in or 'dedicated' to a particular camera.

Some cameras have a pulse button, which helps stop the flash light being reflected directly back from the retina of the subject (which causes red eye in the finished photograph). Another way round this is to avoid taking direct eye-on shots when using flash.

Some effects of using filters

Using colour

It is important to plan out what you want in your finished image in terms of colour. Here are some approaches.

Would this be as effective in natural colours?

- Use filters on the camera to block out colours you don't want to be strong.
- Use coloured filters (or shades) on lights (just like you do on the stage, in a club or even at home) to shed different colours on the subject.
- If you want strong contrasts in colour, look for subjects that clash in this way. Opposites on the colour-wheel give this effect.
- Some colours have a particular meaning. For example greens, browns and ochres are often associated with the country or rural life. You might use *just* these colours to convey this message directly or you might contrast them in a startling way against colours from another situation – such as graffiti pinks/purples.
- Shooting collections of objects or scenes involving similar colours can help create a mood. For example, using all pinks/reds will give a warmer feel than would a collection of greens. Such groupings can also often give a sense of the unity in a setting such as a kitchen or bedroom in a furnishings catalogue.
- If you want a bold colour image, using a subject that is in primary colours will achieve this.
- If you want a more subdued effect, choose a subject without any strong colours.

Creating a rural mood

Photographing outdoors

Lighting outdoors

There is a wonderful variety to natural light. It is almost impossible to control, but should be planned for when photographing outdoors. The factors that control the quality of daylight most are:

- the position of the sun
- the amount of diffusion by clouds, mist or haze.

The positioning of the subject and the camera with regard to the position of the sun can give widely different effects.

- Shooting into the sun creates silhouettes.
- Shooting sideways to the sun gives good contrast to detail and texture.
- Front lighting (with the sun behind the camera) is useful if you want very rich colours.

Using flash outdoors

Back-lit subjects outdoors are likely to be recorded as a silhouette. This is because the metering system in the camera will usually record the bright sky as the main light source. By using a flash, you can 'fill in' the details of the foreground subject that would otherwise be lost in the shadow.

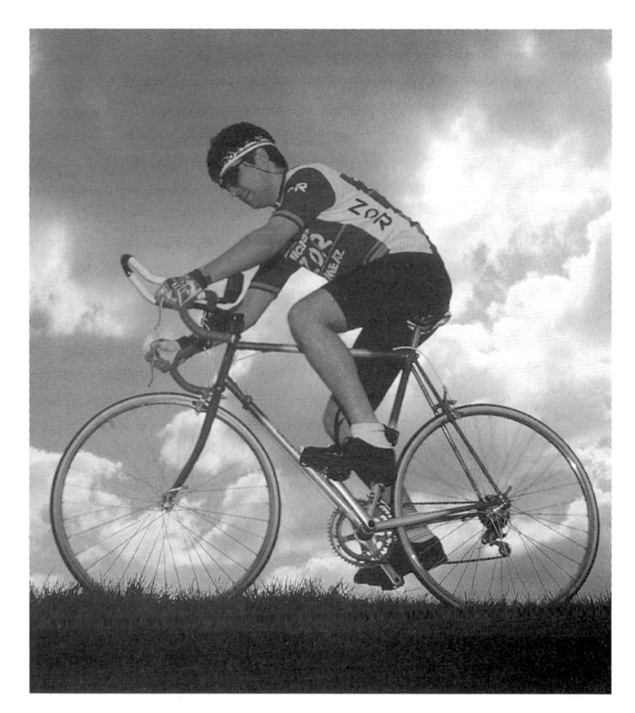

The use of flash outdoors on a bright day gave improved detail

Photographing in the studio

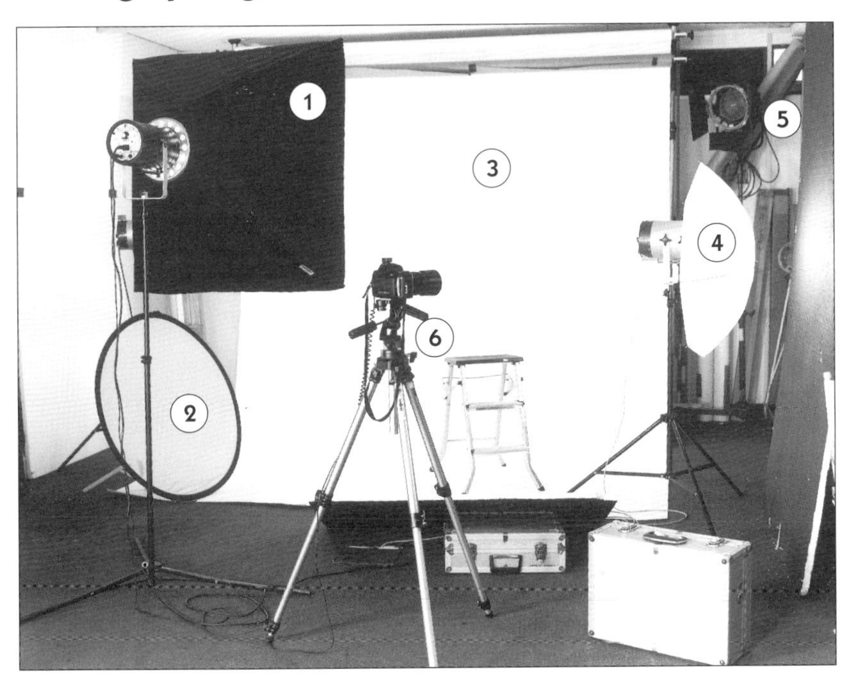

1. soft box – a construction on the front of a normal light containing two diffusers; gives a big, soft, broad light
2. foldable gold reflector
3. white reflector
4. light and diffusing umbrella
5. tungsten spotlight
6. SLR on tripod

In the studio, you have total control over the lighting conditions and the arrangement of your subjects. The light sources you have are a basic tool and can be modified to give you the lighting effects you want.

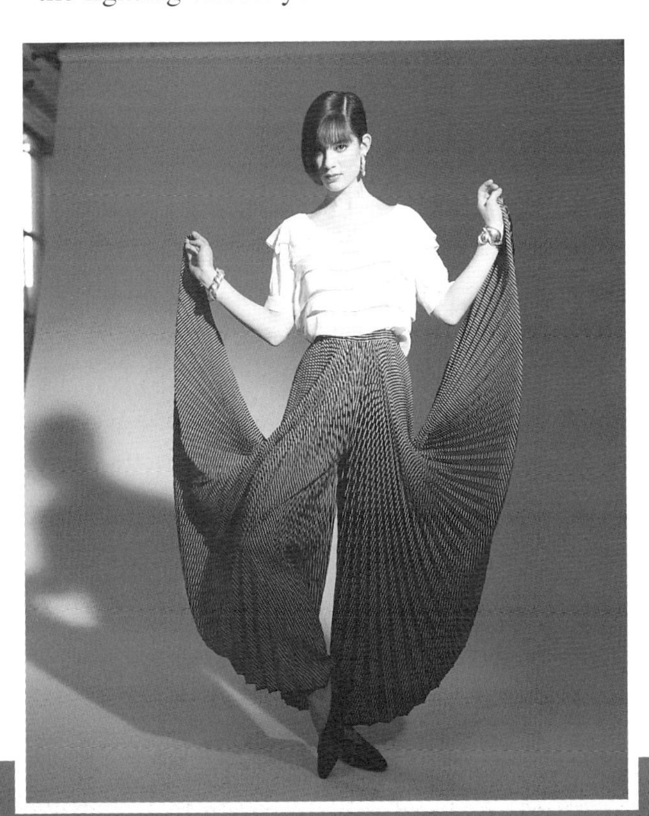

There are three useful ways of doing this.

1. Spots – in some shots you will need a concentrated beam of light to get strong shadows, so use a black card cylinder and wrap it around the light to simulate a spotlight.
2. Reflectors – to soften shadows and make the light more even, make the light source broader. A simple way to do this is to make the light bounce off a big white surface, so the subject is then lit by the reflector, not the direct source. A reflecting umbrella can also be used.
3. Diffusers – reflectors have the disadvantage that they absorb a lot of light or can't be fixed in the needed place, which is when a diffuser comes into its own. It can be made of thin white fabric, tracing paper or a similar material. Hang this in front of the light, but be careful not to hang it so close that it burns.

The sorts of equipment needed for these lighting effects are shown in the top photograph. A photograph produced using this kind of equipment is shown on the left.

Using a digital camera

The digital point-and-shoot (still video) camera makes it easy to add digital pictures to reports, presentations and other documents. These cameras provide a creative alternative to using scanners (see page 68). The more advanced digital cameras will also record sound in short bursts.

A number of pictures can be taken before downloading to the computer and, of course, you do not need any film and there are no developing costs or waiting. These cameras have automatic adjustable exposure and a lens-change facility as well as a built-in flash.

Using a software package such as Photo Enhancer with the camera allows you to view your images as thumbnails, make simple colour corrections, retouch images or export them to other applications.

Digital cameras and the image they produce on screen

The Kodak 40 – a typical digital camera

You might also use the images in other ways, for example:

- portrait shots can be printed out and made into badges (using a badgemaker) or applied to T-shirts (using a photocopy transfer medium)
- technical detail can be photographed instantly and the image used instead of a technical illustration
- you might record the stages of your work on a project and 'wrap' script around the images to give a professional look to your portfolio
- news pictures can be instantly transferred into your school DTP system to use in the school newspaper or newsletter to parents.

Multimedia information

The next few pages will guide you as to how to produce information as a multimedia presentation. The example used is the production of information useful to tourists visiting an area for the first time. The idea is that instead of buying a guidebook, which might become out of date, the visitor would simply 'interrogate a screen' at the local travel agent before travelling or on arrival at the airport or at a Tourist Information Centre. As the information is in electronic form, it can be updated easily.

Analysing the information

The first step in providing this sort of information is to sort it into useful groupings. In the case of information for tourists, the analysis might lead to the information being sorted as follows.

First, it might be sorted according to area, which could be central, north and south.

Second, the information might be sorted according to places and activities, as follows:

- places to eat out
- places to stay
- places for sports
- places for entertaining
- places for sightseeing.

For each of the three regions, there could be information about each of the above categories.

Interrogation possibilities

The next step is to think about the way a person might want to ask questions – the so-called interrogation possibilities. A tourist might want to find out about a particular region and simply investigate the activities and information particular to that region. Alternatively, a tourist might want to look at a particular category across all the different regions. So it is important for the tourist to be able to access the information by asking about either regions or categories. It is also important for the tourist to be able to move from finding out about the same category across different regions to finding out more about the different categories within a region and vice versa.

Screen design

Your screens will be made of the following elements:

- headings
- subheadings
- main body text
- main image
- navigation controls.

When you design the arrangement of these elements into a screen, you will need to use some guiding principles. Here are some possibilities.

All screens have the same structure – that is, the different elements always appear in the same arrangement. This has the advantage that once users are familiar with the layout they can use any screen with confidence. It has the disadvantage that it can seem dull and boring.

The layout of the screen is dependent on the region it represents. Thus, different regions will have different layouts and all the screens describing categories within a region will be based on the regional layout. So, for our tourist guide, there will be three different sorts of screen layout; one for each region.

The layout of the screen is dependent on the categories it is describing, so different categories will have different layouts. Therefore, all the screens describing a particular category will be based on that category's layout. So, for our tourist guide, there will be five different sorts of screen layout, one for each category.

It is possible to combine the two previous forms of screen design. Each screen describing a category could also carry information indicating in which region the category was located, for example.

Finally, it is possible to create a series of screens that vary widely in their appearance without any underlying unity. These screens are likely to appeal to younger users (15 to 25 year olds) who have experience of using multimedia and are happy to explore information in an uncertain environment.

Of course, in addition to regional and category screens, you will need a screen to attract potential users' interest and a main menu screen. You will need to use writing software such as Macromedia Director to control the different forms of information that appear on screen.

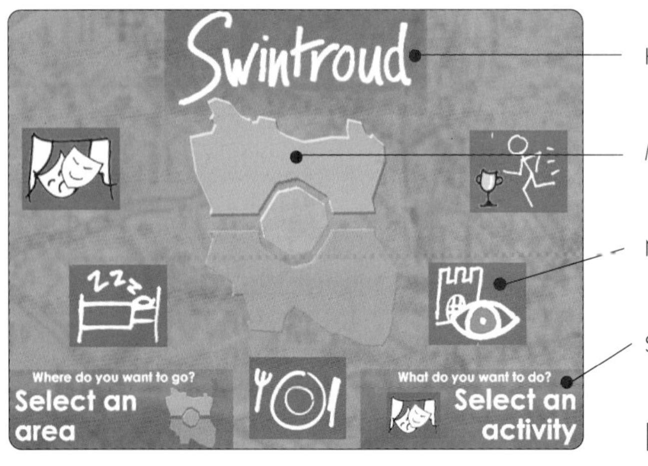

A typical main menu screen in a multimedia presentation

Navigation controls

The tourists who will use the information must have ways to move around the information you have provided. To do this they will need what are called navigation controls. These are simple areas on the screen that may be touched by hand or with a mouse-driven pointer to obtain information. These are usually called buttons. Exactly what happens when a button is 'pressed' will depend on the programming of the multimedia presentation.

The appearance of the buttons themselves is very important. If they cannot be recognized easily by the user, then the multimedia presentation is useless. There are three forms of buttons:

- Basic button – this looks just like a button on a telephone or music centre and it may have a word on it indicating its function. It is very formal and usually used in presentations for those not used to dealing with multimedia.

Restaurants

- Icons – these are simple symbols that represent visually the word or words used on a basic button.

- Animated icons – these are simple symbols that, when pressed, move or cause the contents of the screen to move. This can result in extremely sophisticated visual effects. These can sometimes act as distracters to those not used to multimedia presentations, so they should be used with caution.

The pressing of each sort of button can be accompanied by a variety of sound effects, from simple musical notes to short pieces of music or spoken commentary.

Forms of information

The information can come in the following forms.

- ***Text (words and numbers)***

  Here is an example.

  This region is famous for the wine it produces. The vineyards are among the finest in the world and this is largely due to the nature of the soil and the climate. The region produces around 50 000 bottles of wine for export and a further 10 000 bottles for local consumption.

- ***Moving pictures (animated graphics, live video)***

- ***Sound***

  This can be in the form of a spoken commentary, background music or startling sound effects.

- ***Still pictures (graphics & photos)***

  Here is an example.

Capturing and handling the information

The forms of information you want to be available to the user have to be captured onto the computer's hard disk. This requires suitable applications software and appropriate hardware. The table below summarizes these.

Ways to capture information for multimedia presentation

Text	Cut and paste from existing documents using a word processing package, e.g. Word, Wordperfect, Write	no special extra hardware required
Still pictures *Graphics*	Drawing on screen using a graphics package, e.g. Macromedia, XRes, MS Paintbrush	an interface board can be used
Photographs	Scanning in and retouching using image package, e.g. Adobe Photoshop, Paint Shop Pro (**graphics can also be edited this way**) Directly from digital camera using related capture software, e.g Kodak DC40	scanner digital camera
Moving pictures *Animated graphics*	Moving objects on screen or creating flickbook type animation using software such as Micromedia Director	no special extra hardware required
Live video	Capture from videotape or camcorder using video editing software, e.g. Adobe Premiere	standard camcorder equipment; related hardware such as interface board
Sound	Microphone capture from tape or disk using existing sounds; use of editing software afterwards, e.g. SoundEdit 16 or SoundForge	some computers have necessary hardware built in, others will need a sound card/related cables

ATTRACTOR SCREEN

Screen constantly changing so as to attract the attention of passers-by. The whole screen nets as a start button

Main title and image of Swintroud stays on screen in same place

Images change (apparently at random) by fading from one to another

Words move across the screen. Text moves at different speeds and appears in varying sizes

Scrolling text encouraging passer-by to touch the screen and use the system

MAIN MENU

User can select whether to look at certain types of activity in all areas or all activities in a certain area

Standard title in text and back-ground colour. (Text handwritten and scanned in)

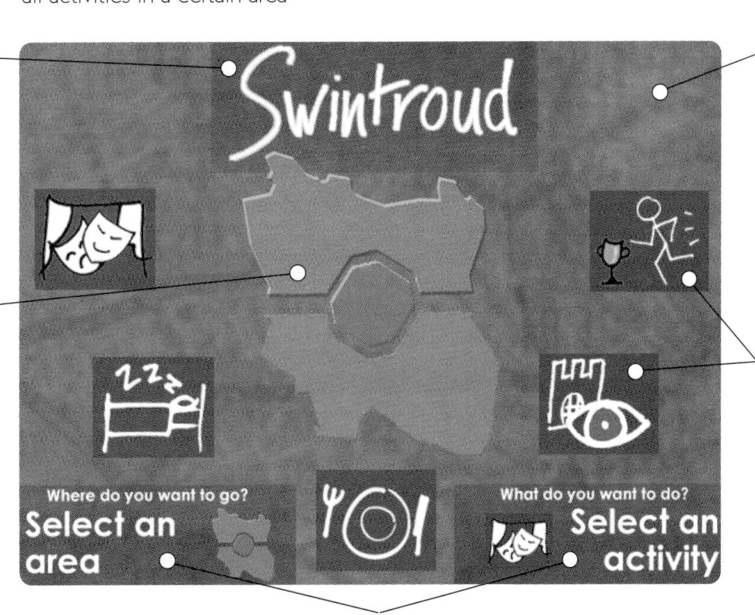

Constant backdrop of faded / blurry map. (Page of street map scanned in and blurred in graphics package)

Map is divided up into 3 areas each of which acts as a button. (Map scanned in and graphically changed so just the outline remained)

Buttons selecting an activity (images for buttons drawn on paper and scanned in. Colour added in graphics package)

Instructions explaining what to do next based on what user wants to find out – hence the questions

REGION 1

User wants to look at details by region and has selected 'South'

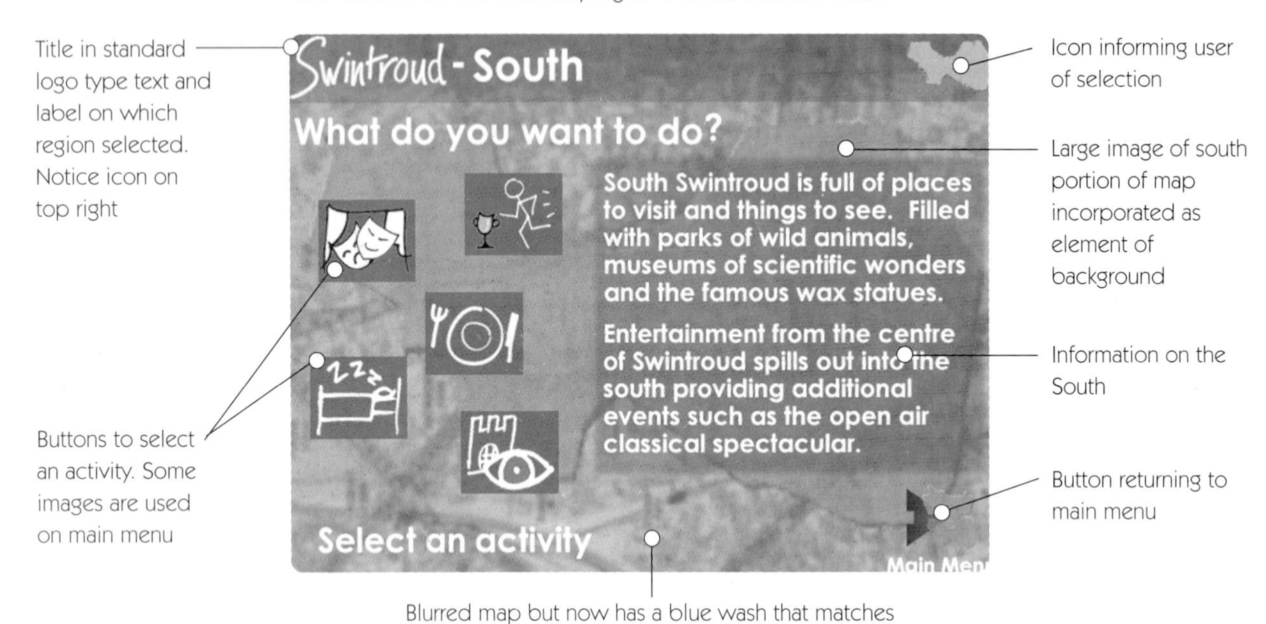

REGION 2

User has selected to look at details by region and selected 'Central'. Layout stays exactly the same in terms of title, buttons and text

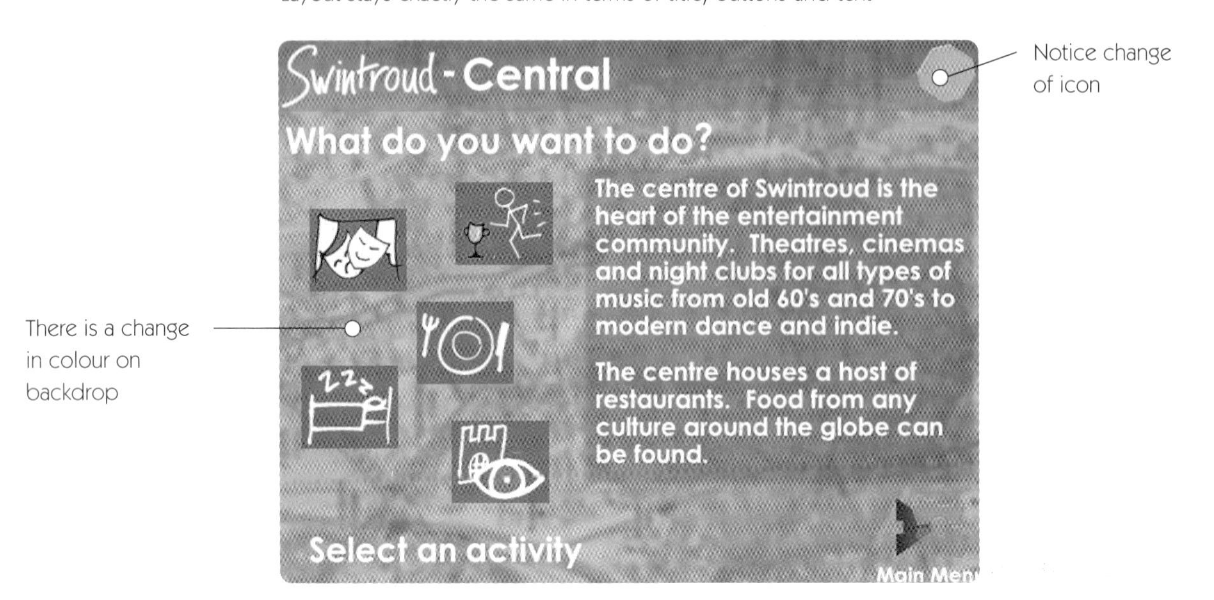

ACTIVITY 1

From South region screen the user has selected the Entertainment section

Standard logo title and background

Standard blurred map with blue coloured wash for 'South' region

List of activities to look at. The darker band indicated the present selection

Buttons as used on previous screens

Info on price and where to buy ticket (if applicable)

Displays subtitles for video if required by user

Icon showing activity selected in addition to words

Small dot shows location of activity

Still displays icon of south map segment. Words 'South' added for extra clarification as 'South' in main title has been removed

Video containing info on activity: where it is, maps on how to get there, buses etc.

ACTIVITY 2

Exactly the same layout with different contents

Distributing multimedia presentations

Once you have produced a multimedia presentation on the hard disk of your computer, it can be transferred to either a CD-ROM or a floppy disk.

Industrial production of pop-up books

The designer produces an accurate prototype to ensure that the mechanisms work with the weights of paper and card that will be used. Then the card is printed and the parts cut out. As labour costs for assembly are much less abroad, it is cheaper to assemble the card overseas, even with the cost of transportation to and from the country. Pop-up cards are often assembled in Colombia and Romania.

The cards are usually cut out by a stamping machine fitted with a special cutting die made to give the exact shape required. These machines can also crease the card so that it folds in the right places. Each card is stamped out individually at a rate of 60 cards per minute.

More recently, computer-controlled lasers have been introduced to cut pieces from sheets of card. The problem with this method is that the laser tends to leave burn marks on the edges of the card, but this is being overcome by firing the laser in short bursts to give a series of perforations (like on a postage stamp only much smaller). The cut-out shapes can be easily pressed out from the sheets of card. Such machines can cut shapes from individual card.

Producing an accurate prototype

Printing the cards

The pieces are transported to the assembly country and made up into the finished card. Some of this is done by machine, but a lot of the intricate assembly is carried out by hand. One nimble-fingered worker can assemble over 100 cards in an hour.

Laser cutters will cut out from individual sheets of paper between 1000–2000 sheets per hour depending on the complexity of the cut.

Cutting and creasing

Assembly is an intricate and skilled process

The finished item

Industrial production of a hand-held remote control unit

The design of the hand-held remote control unit for televisions and videotape recorders has changed in the past ten years. Several trends can be identified – they are:

- getting smaller;
- becoming simpler to use with fewer buttons;
- becoming simpler to read with fewer hieroglyphics;
- becoming more ergonomic in terms of the arrangement and style of the buttons;
- utilizing new technologies – membrane panel switches and more advanced electronics.

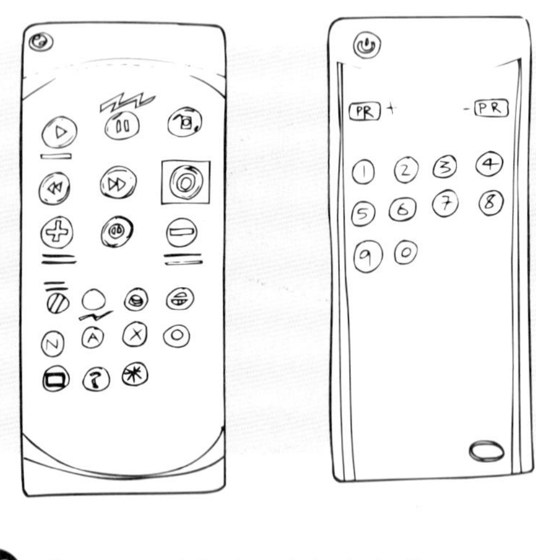

Can you spot the trends in design?

In the future, we can expect to see these trends continue as the dedicated microchips become smaller and require less power, leading to the use of smaller batteries.

The electronic workings of the controller are produced on a printed circuit board with the components surface mounted for rapid assembly by pick-and-place robots.

The conducting membrane panel that is used to make connections within the printed circuit board is placed above a non-conducting spacer so that it only makes connections when depressed by a switch.

The casing and switch assembly is produced by injection moulding to give the split shell, which will house the printed circuit board, membrane panel switch elements, battery and connectors.

The controller is assembled by hand. Hieroglyphics are printed on to the shell by machine.

At each stage in its production, quality is assured by the following quality control procedures to ensure that no defective parts or assemblies are passed along the assembly line.

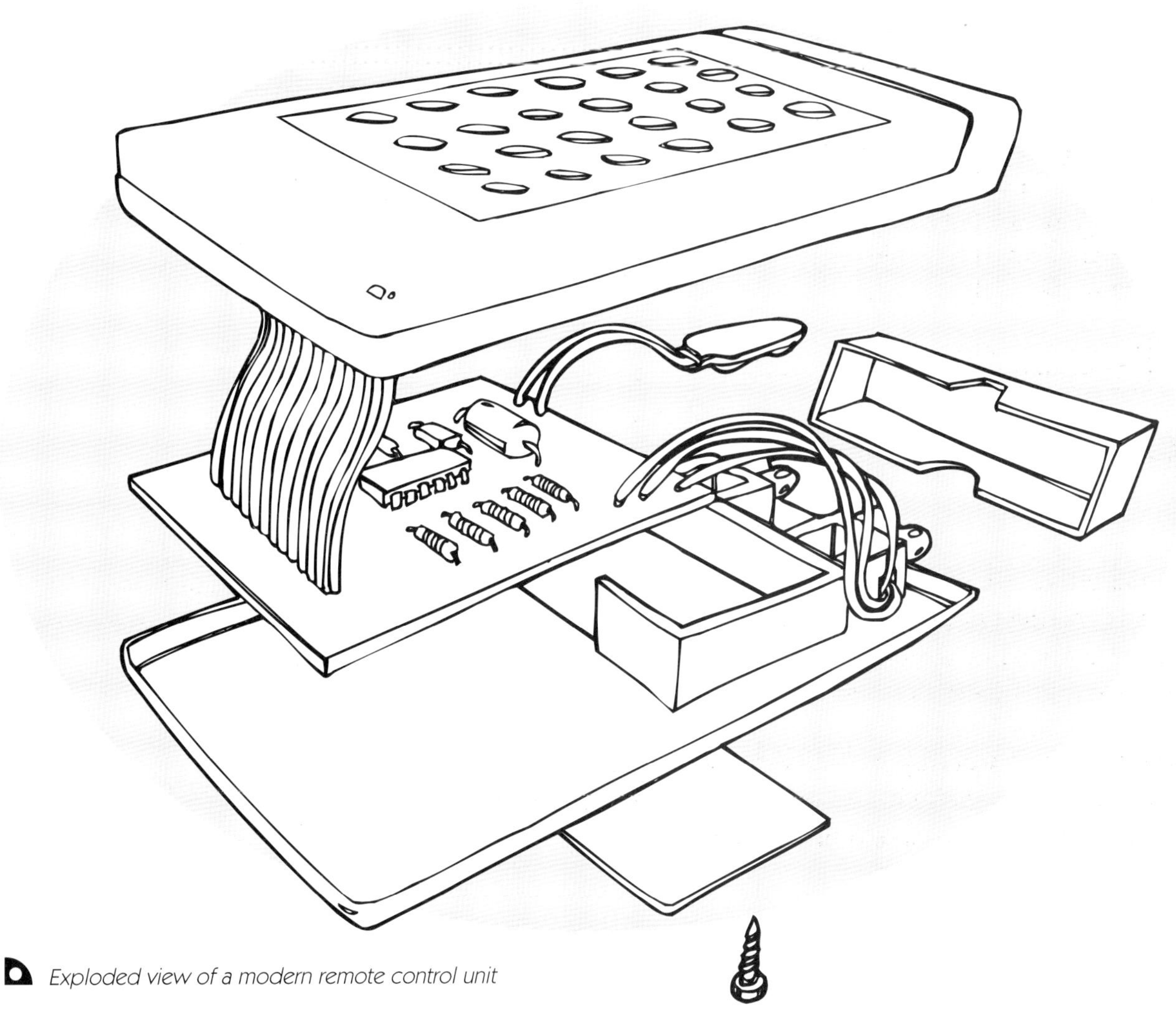

Exploded view of a modern remote control unit

15 Health and safety

Important ideas

If you are to avoid accidents and harm, you need to know how to look at situations to take into account health and safety matters. You need to know about hazard, risk, risk assessment and risk control. A hazard is anything that might cause harm or damage. The chances of a hazard causing harm or damage is called the risk. You can work out how big the risk is by thinking about how likely it is that the harm or damage will happen. This process is called risk assessment. Risk control is the action taken to ensure that the harm or damage is less likely to happen.

Safety in the workplace

No workplace is risk-free and the Health and Safety at Work Act ensures that employers identify the risks, assess them and then actively seek ways to control those risks. This involves identifying safe practices and providing both training and supervision to ensure they are carried out. The workers do, of course, have to follow the procedures laid down properly if risks are to be minimal.

A useful way of looking at this problem is shown in the diagram.

The diagram lists the following elements:

- the workplace environment
- light and ventilation (the window in the diagram)
- the means of access (getting in)
- the means of egress (getting out)
- the machinery (plant)
- the handling, storage and transport of articles and substances
- the people working in the workplace.

The diagram shows that risk assessment has to take into account the interactions of all the elements.

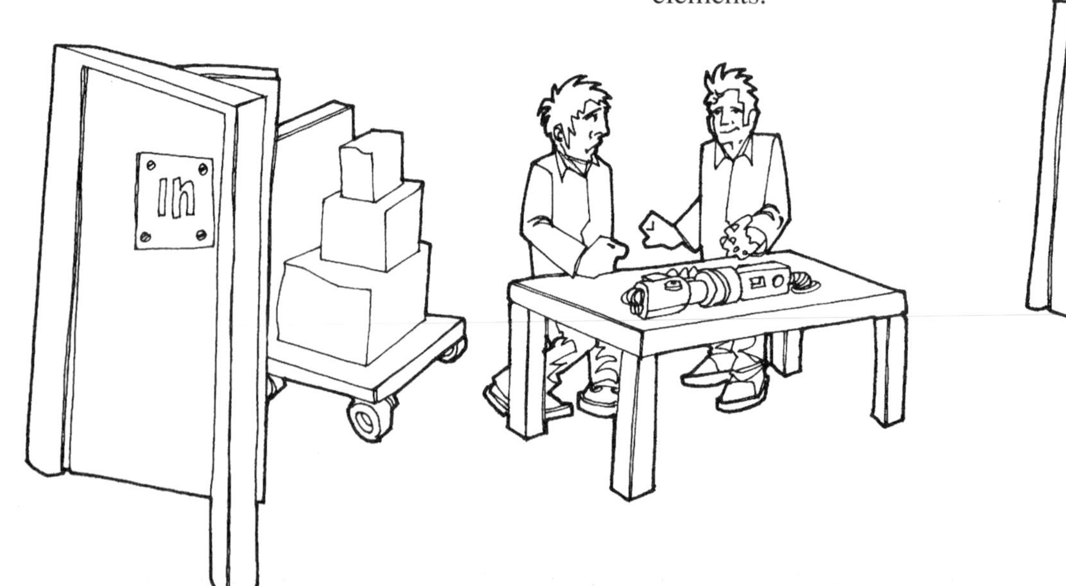

It is often the interactions that get forgotten. People and things move around. It is these interactions that affect health and safety. For example, a small pile of bricks stays still, but someone might trip over it, so it represents a hazard. Once the bricks start to be moved, they can become an even greater hazard – strain injuries can be sustained as a result of lifting them, head and feet injuries if they are dropped and so on. So, if bricks are around people, and hence have the possibility of 'interacting' with people, then the people must wear hard hats and steel-toe boots.

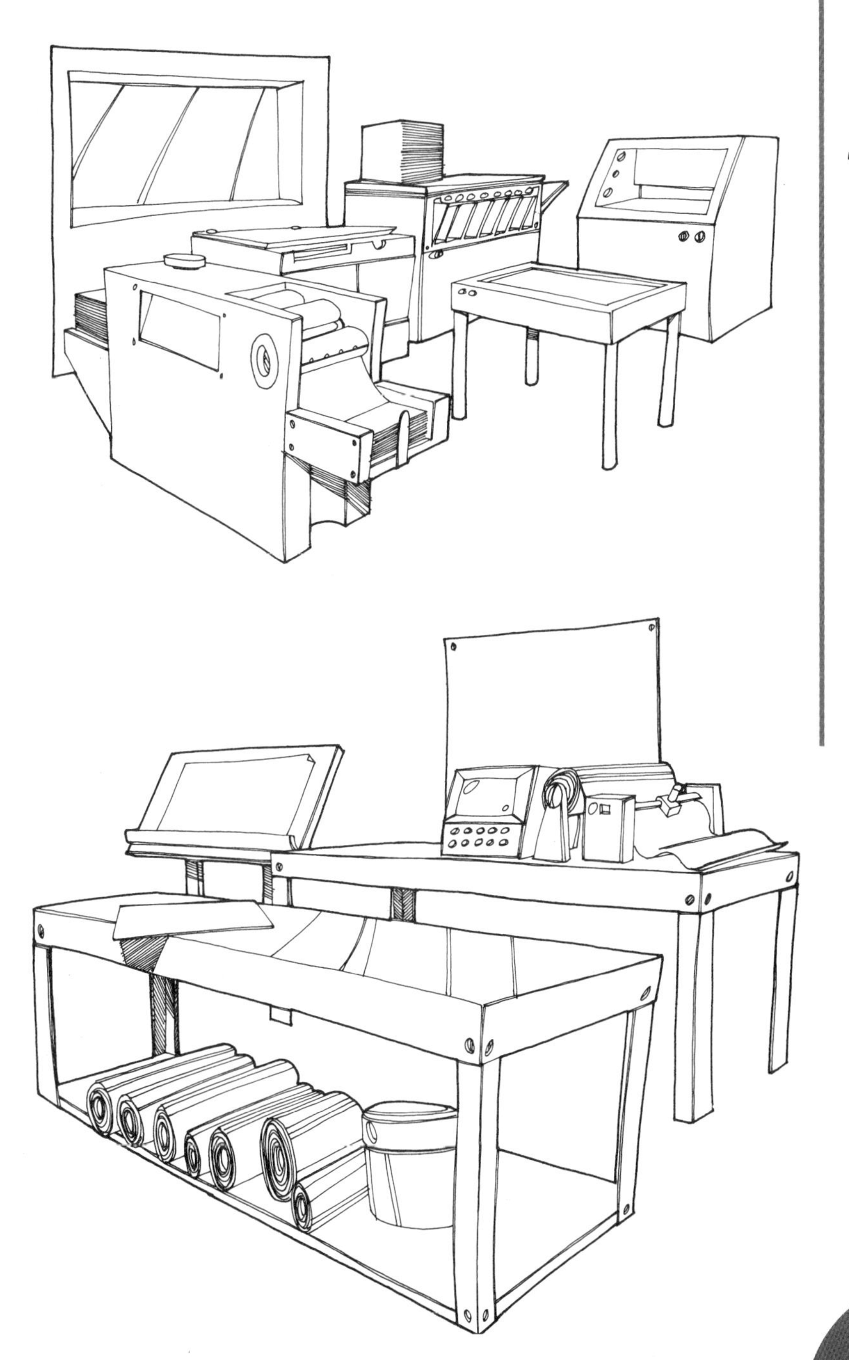

In graphic product manufacture, there are many potential hazards. Many of these you will recognise because they apply just as much to working with graphics in school or at home as in an office. How would you assess and control these risks? As a worker, what could you do to help ensure safe and healthy working?

Here are two situations for you to consider. Both are well-ordered industrial environments where the risks are controlled. Look carefully at them to see if you can spot potential hazards and how the risk from those hazards has been controlled.

Glossary

anthropometrics : design considerations that take people's sizes and shapes into account

block printing: a printing process using a block in which ink spread over a pattern in the form of a raised surface is transferred to another surface by pressing the inked pattern onto the second surface

body text: the main text of a written piece of information

brainstorming : a process for generating design ideas

capability tasks: designing, making and testing a product that works

clients: those people in business and industry who commission the development of new or improved products

closed design brief: a sufficiently detailed summary of the aims of a design (indicating the kind of product required) that limits the possible design solutions

closed-loop system: a system in which information is passed back along the system so controlling the behaviour of the system

computer-aided design (CAD): designing using computers to produce 2D or 3D drawings, surface envelopes or simulations of electrical and mechanical systems

computer-assisted manufacturing (CAM): a manufacturing process which is controlled by computers

concurrent engineering: a manufacturing process where many of the different activities required to make the final product are going on at the same time (sometimes called parallel processing)

coverline: an area of a magazine cover, usually at the bottom, which highlights a number of things in store in that issue

cross headings: headings used to divide body text into readable amounts

cutting die: a cutting tool used in manufacturing to produce a particular shape in the object (e.g. card) being cut

diffuser: in photography, a thin sheet of white fabric or tracing paper used in front of the camera to diffuse light

dummy: an accurate, correctly-sized drawing or 3D model of a design which looks exactly like the final product

The Dual System: A system in Germany where shops have a responsibility to receive back packaging for recycling

ergonomics: design considerations that take people's movement into account

feedback: information sensed by closed-loop control systems so that they can respond to change

flash: a 45 degree line across the corner of a magazine highlighting something of particular interest covered in that issue

flatplan: a plan showing all the pages of a magazine laid out, indicating such things as which pages will be colour and which will contain advertisements

floor plan: a drawing showing a slice through a room at a height above floor level. Used to show the positions of furniture and windows in a room

footer: the place at the bottom of a printed page where additional information may be presented outside the body text

hazard: any feature of a situation which may cause harm or damage

header: the place at the top of a printed page where additional information may be presented outside the body text

image board: a collection of pictures or things that a person or group of people might like, places they might go or activities they might do

interviewing: finding out about people's preferences by asking them questions and listening to their answers

isometric view: a 3D representational drawing in which horizontal lines are drawn at 30 degrees

lineboard: a stiff board onto which graphic designers paste up text and illustrations when producing artwork for printing by hand

line of interest: a term used to define a group of similar products, e.g. packaging or interiors

locus: the path of movement of a point in a mechanism

masthead: the top part of a magazine's title page; the part of the page on which the magazine's title appears

mdf: medium density fibreboard

mock-up: a rough, full size 3D model of a 3D product which shows the graphics that will be used on the final product

net: the flat sheet from which a three-dimensional form such as a box can be created. Sometimes called a surface development

oblique view: a drawing based on a front or side view that uses 45 degree angles to create a third dimension

offset lithography: a printing process requiring a printing plate. Used for long print runs

open design brief: a summary of the aims of a design offering the possibility of a wide range of alternative design solutions

open-loop system: a system in which there is no feedback from any part of the system to any other part and which therefore cannot be controlled

operator interface: the parts of a system used by an operator

orthographic projection: an accurate scale drawing that shows elevations (square-on views; usually plan, front and side) of a product

origination: the stage in publishing where the pages of a magazine or book are being set up for printing

parallel processing: a manufacturing process where many of the different activities required to make the final product are going on at the same time (sometimes called concurrent engineering)

performance specification: a description of what a product you will design should do, look like, and any other descriptions it should meet

pictogram: a graphic device that conveys meaning by using an illustration of a specific action

planometric view: a three-dimensional view generated from a plan view. Often used in maps and guides

plans: drawings of a product that give the information needed to make it (sometimes called working drawings)

presentation models: accurate 3D models giving a clear idea of space and proportion that are made to scale and are used to help clients imagine how a design will be used

proof: a pre-publication draft of a magazine or book used to check that there are no errors

reflector: in photography, a device (often a big white surface) used to soften shadows and make light more even by reflection

registration marks: the marks on colour-separated proofs that allow the proofs to be accurately aligned

resource tasks: short, practical activities to develop knowledge and skills

reviewing: checking your design ideas as they develop against the specification

risk: the chance of a hazard causing harm or damage

risk assessment: calculating how big a risk is by thinking about whether the harm or damage is likely to happen

risk control: action taken to ensure that the harm or damage is less likely to happen

router: a machine tool in which a spinning blade is used to cut out a profile

scale drawing: an accurate plan showing elevations (side views) and sections (cut-through views)

scamps: rough sketches that nevertheless contain some detail which help explain an idea to a client

screen printing: a process for printing images onto a variety of surfaces using stencils, a fine-mesh screen and thick printing ink

single-point perspective: a system of drawing in which all horizontal lines converge at a single vanishing point. Useful for interiors

site model: a 3D model used to demonstrate the lie of the land around a site

sketch models: three-dimensional versions of a rough sketch/scamp

SLR (single lens reflex) camera: a camera in which the image you see in the viewfinder has reached your eyes via the lens

stereo lithography: a modelling process in manufacturing whereby a 3D computer image of a proposed product is made into a solid model by a laser causing a liquid resin to harden into the solid form of the product

strapline: the sub-heading part of a magazine's title, explaining what the magazine is about, how much it costs, the issue number and the price

surface development: the flat sheet from which a three-dimensional form such as a box can be created. Sometimes called a net

systems thinking: a way of thinking that helps you understand complex processes or products without dealing with the detail

three-point perspective: a system of drawing using three-vanishing points. Gives an aerial view

transfer printing: a printing process in which an image in the form of a wax crayon design or a picture from a magazine is transferred onto another surface

typeface: any one of the many different styles of lettering available

user interfaces: the parts of a system used by people

wall elevation: a drawing showing flat views of walls in a room. Often includes the furniture/fittings that will be positioned on or in front of the walls

working drawings: drawings of a product that give you the information needed to make it (sometimes called plans)

Index

A

B

C

D

E

F

G

H

I

I (cont)

K

L

M

N

O

P

T

U

V